# ANCIENT NUMEROLOGY
WITH
# MODERN INSIGHT

**( COMPLETE GUIDE FOR BEGINNERS )**

**SOWMYA ANIL**



BlueRose ONE.com
Stories Matter
NewDelhi • London

**BLUEROSE PUBLISHERS**
India | U.K.



BlueRose ONE
Stories Matter
NewDelhi • London

For permissions requests or inquiries regarding this publication, please contact:

BLUEROSE PUBLISHERS
www.BlueRoseONE.com
info@bluerosepublishers.com
+91 8882 898 898
+4407342408967

ISBN: **978-93-7542-384-3**

Cover Design: Shivam Gaur
Typesetting: Sagar

First Edition: February 2026

# Acknowledgment

This book would not have been possible without the encouragement and support of countless individuals, known and unknown. I begin by expressing my deepest gratitude to those who played pivotal roles in its creation. First and foremost, I thank the Almighty Lord Shree Guru Heragodeeshwara and Ketaki Sangamnatha for guiding me onto the path of numerology with their boundless blessings, strength, and courage, propelling my professional journey forward.

With profound respect and honor, I offer my sincere gratitude to my Guruji, Shri Channa Basava Sharanaru Malgathi Swamiji, for his unwavering guidance, support, and encouragement throughout this endeavor. I am equally thankful to our Gadag Guruji, Shri Putta Raj Hiremath, for his continuous support and guidance on the path of numerology. I extend heartfelt thanks to my best friend, Mrs. Shwetha Baliga, who has played the role of an elder sister, encouraging me and holding a lamp of hope during the darkest days of my life.

I thank from the core of my heart to my family: My husband, Dr. Anil Kumar Khaple, who always believed in me and stood as Everest even in the hardest times; and most importantly, my dearest son, Master Harsh Khaple, whose cute smile and words inspired me to stay committed to my path.

Special thanks go to Ms. Gayatri Jettur for her invaluable contribution towards the completion of this endeavored journey.

Finally, I thank all my well-wishers for their motivation and moral support in bringing this work to fruition.

# About The Author and Book

ಮುನ್ನುಡಿ

ಪ್ರಪಂಚದ ಇತಿಹಾಸದಲ್ಲಿ ಅಗಮ್ಯ ಚೇತನಗಳು ಗೋಚರಿಸುವೆ ಈ ಜೀವ ಜಗತ್ತಿನಲ್ಲಿ ಸಾಮಾಜಿಕ ಪರಿಸ್ಥಿತಿ ಅಸ್ತವ್ಯಸ್ತಗೊಂಡಾಗ ಧಾರ್ಮಿಕ ನೀತಿ ತಲ್ಲಣಿಸಿದಾಗ ಸಾಂಸ್ಕೃತಿಕ ಪ್ರಜ್ಞೆ ಅವನತಿಯ ದಾರಿ ಹಿಡಿದಾಗ ಮನುಷ್ಯನ ಬದುಕು ಸ್ಥಿತಪ್ರಜ್ಞ ಕಳೆದುಕೊಂಡಾಗ ಜೀವನದಲ್ಲಿ ಬರುವ ತೊಂದರೆಗಳಿಗೆ ನಿವಾರಣೆಗಾಗಿ ಸದಾ ಕಾಲ ದೇವರೇ ಬರಬೇಕೆಂದಿಲ್ಲ ಅವನ ಕುರುಹುಗಳಾಗಿ ವೇದಗಳು ಶಾಸ್ತ್ರಗಳು ಉಪನಿಷತ್ತುಗಳು ಆಯುರ್ವೇದದ ಗ್ರಂಥಗಳು ಕಾಮಧೇನು ಕಲ್ಪವೃಕ್ಷಗಳಾಗಿ ಲೋಕ ಕಲ್ಪಿತ ವರಗಳಾಗಿವೆ. ಅದರಂತೆ ಪ್ರತಿಯೊಬ್ಬ ಮನುಷ್ಯನ ಜೀವನ ದಲ್ಲಿ ಜನನ ಸಮಯದಿಂದ ಆತನ ಬದುಕು ಯಶಸ್ಸು ಕೀರ್ತಿ ಜೀವನದಲ್ಲಿ ಬರುವ ತೊಂದರೆಗಳಿಗೆ ಮಾರ್ಗೋಪಾಯಗಳಾಗಿ ಜ್ಯೋತಿಷ್ಯ ಶಾಸ್ತ್ರ ಸಂಖ್ಯಾಶಾಸ್ತ್ರ ಅಂಗರೇಖಾ ಶಾಸ್ತ್ರ ಗ್ರಹ ಗೋಚಾರ ಫಲಗಳು ಪ್ರಶ್ನ ಶಾಸ್ತ್ರ ಮನುಷ್ಯನ ತೊಂದರೆಯುಕ್ತ ಬದುಕಿಗೆ ಉತ್ತರಿಸುವ ಸಂಜೀವಿನಿಯಾಗಿವೇ ಅದರಲ್ಲಿ ಸಂಖ್ಯಾಶಾಸ್ತ್ರ ಪ್ರತಿಯೊಂದು ಸಮಸ್ಯೆಗಳಿಗೆ ತನ್ನದೇ ಆದ ಸಂಖ್ಯೆಗಳ ಆಧಾರದ ಮೇಲೆ ಪರಿಹಾರೋಪಾಯಗಳನ್ನ ನೀಡುವ ದೇವವಾಣಿಯ ಕುರುಹಾಗಿದೆ ಇಂತಹ ಶಾಸ್ತ್ರ ಸಂಗ್ರಹ ಮಾಲಿಕೆಯ ಅಕ್ಷರ ಲೋಕಕ್ಕೆ ಸೇರ್ಪಡೆಯಾದ ಮತ್ತೊಂದು ಮಹಾನ್ ಗ್ರಂಥವೇ.

“ ಏನ್ಕನ್ಸ ”

ಸಂಖ್ಯಾಶಾಸ್ತ್ರದ ಚಮತ್ಕಾರಗಳನ್ನು ತಿಳಿಯ ಬಯಸುವವರಿಗೆ ತುಂಬಾ ಸರಳ ರೀತಿಯಲ್ಲಿ ಕಲಿಯುವ ಕಲಿಕಾರ್ಥಿಗಳಿಗೆ ಹಾಗೂ ಪ್ರತಿಯೊಬ್ಬ ವ್ಯಕ್ತಿ ತನ್ನ ಜೀವನದ ಮುಖ್ಯ ಹಂತಗಳನ್ನ ತಿಳಿದುಕೊಳ್ಳಲು ಸಮಸ್ಯೆಗಳನ್ನು ಪರಿಹಾರ ಕಂಡುಕೊಳ್ಳಲು ಈ

ಗ್ರಂಥ ಅತ್ಯಂತ ಚಮತ್ಕಾರಿಯಾಗಿದೆ ಈ ನಾಡು ಕಂಡ ಪ್ರಖ್ಯಾತ ಲೇಖಕರು ಶ್ರೀಮತಿ ಸೌಮ್ಯ ಅನಿಲ್ ರವರು ಸುಮಾರು 15 ವರ್ಷಗಳ ಅನುಭವಗಳ ಸಾರವನ್ನು ಈ ಗ್ರಂಥದಲ್ಲಿ ತಿಳಿಯಪಡಿಸಿದ್ದಾರೆ ಸುಮಾರು 10000 ಸಮಸ್ಯೆಗಳಿಗೆ ಪರಿಹಾರಗಳನ್ನು ನೀಡಿದ ಅನುಭವದ ಆಧಾರಗಳ ಮೇಲೆ ಅಳವಾದ ಅಧ್ಯಯನದೊಂದಿಗೆ ಓದುಗರಿಗೆ ಈ ಗ್ರಂಥವನ್ನು ವರವಾಗಿ ನೀಡಿದ್ದಾರೆ ಅವರ ಮೊದಲನೆಯ ಆವೃತ್ತಿಯ ಈ ಪುಸ್ತಕದಲ್ಲಿ ಸಂಖ್ಯಾಶಾಸ್ತ್ರದ ನಿಯಮಗಳು ಸಂಖ್ಯಾಶಾಸ್ತ್ರದ ಸೂತ್ರಗಳು ಪ್ರತಿಯೊಂದು ಸಂಖ್ಯೆಗಳು ನವಗ್ರಹಗಳ ಆಧಾರದ ಮೇಲೆ ಯಾವ ಸಂಖ್ಯೆಗೆ ಯಾವ ಗ್ರಹಗಳ ಗೋಚಾರ ಫಲಗಳು ಸಿಗುವುದು ಎಂಬುವ ರಹಸ್ಯವನ್ನು ಬಿಚ್ಚಿಟ್ಟಿ

# About The Author and Book

In the history of the world, unseen spirits appear in this living world. When the social situation are chaotic, when religious ethics are shaken, cultural consciousness is on the path of decline, when human life loses its sense of consciousness, God answers to the problems in life are represented through the Vedas, Shastras, Upanishads, Ayurvedic texts, Kamadhenu, and Kalpa (Kalpavruksha) trees are his symbols, and the world is endowed with imagined blessings. Accordingly, in the life of every human being, from the time of birth, follows his success and fame. As a way out of the problems that come in life, Astrology, Numerology, Palm-reading Science, Planetary transits, Results, and Questions, science are the medicine that answers the problems of a human being. In this regard, Numerology is a symbol of the divine voice that gives remedies to every problem based on its own numbers. This is another book that contributes or adds literary to the world of numerological collection of books.

**"ANCIENT NUMEROLOGY<br>WITH<br>MODERN INSIGHTS"**

This book will be enthusiastic for readers who wish to explore the wonders of numerology, as well as for those who want to learn the subject in a simple and practical manner. It outlines the major stages of an individual's life and offers effective solutions to various life challenges. The book is a well-researched and compelling publication that provides an insightful and engaging reading experience.

Authored by "Smt. Sowmya Anil", the book reflects nearly a decade of her professional experience in the field of numerology. It is a thoughtful work, grounded in rigorous study and enriched by her extensive practice in providing practical solutions to complex problems. The author presents this book as a valuable offering to readers, drawing upon her long-standing experience in addressing diverse life situations.

In this first edition, the author presents comprehensive knowledge of numerology, including its fundamental rules and formulas. The book explains the significance of each number in relation to the nine planets and describes how planetary transits influence outcomes through specific numbers.

# How To Use This Book:

This work represents a step in the unfolding of inner understanding, where the universe responds in harmony with intuitive awareness. When engaging with numerology, choose a quiet and undisturbed space that allows you to turn inward. Approach the practice with intention and openness, drawing upon your own inner wisdom alongside the guidance offered in this book. Select a time when you feel calm, receptive, and prepared to undertake the work. Each concept is introduced with explanations and examples, followed by a step-by-step process designed to support personal exploration and understanding.

- First, try to understand the meaning of the numbers and letters.
- Then take five people's details (family members or friends) whose names and dates of birth you know.
- Make separate charts for each person.
- Read the explanation chapter carefully, but do not try to remember or fully understand all the information at once.
- The doing chapters will take you step by step through the process.
- You can use the explanation chapters later as a reference.
- Keep your pen and notes ready and refer to the names with their date of birth.
- Start calculating with the Life Path Number.
- Be gentle with yourself if you get lost or confused; for most of us, it does not come quickly and requires time and effort. Relax, take your time, and enjoy the process.

# CONTENT:

**6. MASTER NUMBERS.**

(Understanding the power and responsibility of Master Numbers).

**7. KARMIC DEBT NUMBERS.**

(Explanation of karmic lessons linked to past-life actions).

**8. POWER OF WORDS IN NUMEROLOGY.**

(How Names, Words, And Vibrations Influence Destiny).

**9. LETTER DETAILS.**

(Complete letter chart based on the Pythagorean system).

**10. NUMEROLOGY CHART ANALYSIS.**

(Chart interpretation is divided into two major parts).

**PART – 1: CORE NUMEROLOGY NUMBERS.**

- **LIFE PATH NUMBER.**
  (Represents life purpose, destiny, and the main journey of an individual).
- **BIRTH DATE NUMBER.**
  (Represents special talents and unique personal qualities).
- **EXPRESSION NUMBER (DESTINY NUMBER).**
  (Shows natural talents, abilities, and life goals).
- **HEART'S DESIRE NUMBER (SOUL URGE).**
  (Reveals inner motivations, emotional needs, and true desires of the soul).
- **PERSONALITY NUMBER.**
  (Reveals how the Sociality and others see you).
- **GROWTH NUMBER.**
  (Highlights areas of personal development and future expansion).
- **MATURITY NUMBER.**

(Describes the energy that becomes prominent in the second half of life).

- **MISSING NUMBERS.**
  (Identifies qualities that need conscious development due to their absence in the chart).
- **COMBINATION OF NUMBERS.**
  (Interpretation of number combinations such as: Life Path + Expression + Heart's Desire.)

## PART – 2: ADVANCED & PREDICTIVE NUMEROLOGY.

- **PERSONAL YEAR NUMBER.**
  (Shows yearly themes, opportunities, and challenges).
- **PERSONAL MONTH NUMBER.**
  (Guides monthly planning and decision-making).
- **PERSONAL DATE NUMBER.**
  (Provides daily vibration insights for important actions).
- **PINNACLE NUMBERS.**
  (Describes major life cycles and long-term achievements).
- **CHALLENGE NUMBERS.**
  (Highlights obstacles, lessons, and karmic tests during life phases).

## 11. REMEDIES.

- **COMPLETE CHART INTERPRETATION.**
  (Step-by-step method to read and analyze a full Numerology chart. Techniques to balance absent vibrations through Mantras, Numbers, colors, Rudraksha Stones/Crystals, Direction, Days).
- **COMPATIBILITY ANALYSIS.**
  (Numerology-based compatibility for: Marriage and relationships).
- **NAME ANALYSIS.**
  (Name correction points explained).

# Introduction To Numerology

The Study of numbers and their mystical significance in life is known as Numerology.

It's about decoding the universe's language to understand yourself and your path, which is written in Numbers. Before taking birth, the Soul Signs an agreement with God or the universe about what will be the purpose of taking life on earth in this lifetime, and what challenges and obstacles a soul has to experience and learn in this life journey.

If you consider the complete name and date of birth, once we add the full date of birth (date + month + year), we arrive at a single-digit number called the Life Path Number. The Life Path Number reveals the purpose of life in that lifetime. Next, adding the complete name (using Pythagoras's chart to assign numbers to alphabets) gives the Expression Number, which speaks to a person's talents, skills, and learning abilities. The vowels in the name yield the Heart's Desire Number, revealing core inner desires. The consonants in the complete name produce the Personality Number, which defines the soul's perspective of the universe and how it reacts to this life's journey. Finally, the Birth Date Number describes connections and relationships in this lifetime. These are the five major numbers on the chart."

contract can be decoded by using numerology chart

Occultism is the study of the hidden side of Nature: it observes nature as a whole rather than examining it in parts, as science does.

"As William Eisen, a scientist by profession and author said in one of his workshops: 'Science has many questions to which it is searching for answers, while the occult has all the answers and is waiting for the questions. When the day comes that the two meet, there will be greater strides in science than have ever been made before.'"

# Planetary Influence in Numerology.

The universe, crafted by divine intelligence and encoded in sacred numbers, reveals profound interconnections where planets resonate with numerical vibrations, linking cosmic forces to human essence. Humans, as integral elements of this divine tapestry, align with specific planetary energies through numerology, unveiling hidden harmonies that guide destiny and self-realization.

Creation springs from Shunya, the primordial void governed by Brahma, an unseen force orchestrating the cosmos methodically, known by many names yet singular in essence. Humanity's first awakening revealed only the Sun and Moon aglow in the heavens, their rhythmic dance the sole luminaries guiding existence with unwavering precision.

## Sun's Foundational Vibration (1).

Daily dawns crown the Sun with primacy, embodying the number 1—intimately tied to universal and personal souls, as well as the spiritual vitality pulsing through individuals and all creation.

The Sun, as the first cosmic object humanity ever beheld, stands eternal as the primordial force of energy. In the vast theater of the cosmos, it was the Sun that first pierced the veil of darkness, rising like a golden sovereign over ancient horizons and commanding the gaze of our earliest ancestors. They named it "Sun"—not merely a word, but an invocation of its raw, unyielding power: the life-giver, the destroyer, the eternal pulse of vitality. This primal witness imprints the Sun with the pure essence of Number 1, the archetype of beginnings, leadership, and singular force.

## The Sun's Embrace of Number 1.

Numerology reveals the Sun as the living embodiment of 1, channeling its energies through light, heat, and rhythm. Consider how this cosmic pioneer mirrors the number's core traits:

- Initiative and Creation: Just as 1 sparks all manifestation, it ignites life itself, photosynthesis birthing forests, oceans stirring under its gaze. Without its dawn, no journey begins.
- Vital Force and Will: The Sun's energy courses like an inner fire, fueling human ambition and resilience. Those ruled by 1 (born on the 1st, 10th, 19th, or 28th) radiate this solar charisma, bold leaders who blaze trails, unapologetic in their pursuit.
- Independence and Unity: Alone in its solar system throne, the Sun embodies self-sovereignty, yet unites all under its warmth. It teaches that true power flows from oneness, not division.

Ancient seers, from Vedic rishis to Pythagorean mystics, knew this bond. The Sun rules Sunday (1st day in many calendars), its golden hue vibrating at frequency 1, aligning chakras for clarity and purpose.

## Solar Energies in Daily Life.

Harness the Sun's 1-energy practically: Greet dawn with intention, wear gold or orange to amplify will, or meditate on its orb for breakthroughs. Yet, imbalance warns excess 1 breeds ego's scorch; harmony tempers it into enlightened rule.

This fresh lens reveals the Sun not as a distant star, but as humanity's first mirror: See its rise, and awaken your own Number 1 fire.

## Moon's Reflective Duality (2).

The Moon, architect of night, claims number 2, linked to sensory joys and the gift of thought. Deemed masculine, the Sun holds first rank; the feminine Moon, second, manifesting as a girl child or wife, each with a distinct essence. Its waxing-waning form traverses' constellations in 27 days, mirroring a woman's menstrual rhythm, priming her for life's renewal.

The Moon, as humanity's second cosmic beacon, emerges as the gentle counterpart to the Sun's blaze, veiled in silver mystery, whispering secrets of emotion and intuition. While the Sun commands the day with Number 1's fierce independence, the Moon rules the night, embodying Number 2's feminine essence: nurturing, receptive, and harmoniously dual. Our ancestors, awed by its phases waxing and waning like a mother's breath, revered it as the cradle of feeling, tides, and the subconscious soul.

## The Moon's Dance with Number 2.

In numerology's cosmic symphony, the Moon vibrates as 2, the number of partnerships, sensitivity, and subtle flow, infusing life with its yin grace. Picture its glow reflecting the Sun's light, a perfect metaphor for 2's cooperative magic:

- Nurturing and Empathy: Like a lunar tide pulling oceans, 2-energy soothes and connects. Moon-ruled souls (born 2nd, 11th, 20th, or 29th) excel as healers, diplomats, drawn to care and deep bonds.
- Duality and Cycles: The Moon's phases teach rhythm new to full, dark to light, mirroring 2's balance of opposites: yin-yang, emotion-reason. It governs Monday, the second day, stirring inner worlds.
- Intuition and Receptivity: Feminine by nature, the Moon heightens psychic senses, dreams, and maternal instincts. It

softens 1's fire into fluid wisdom, reminding us that strength lies in yielding.

From Chaldean mystics to modern astrologers, the Moon links to soma (divine nectar), its cool rays balancing solar heat for holistic growth.

## Lunar Energies in Practice.

Invoke the Moon's 2-power: Bathe in moonlight for emotional clarity, use pearl or silver talismans, or journal under its phases to unlock hidden insights. Beware, excess 2's shadow brings indecision; equilibrium fosters profound unity.

Thus, the Moon as cosmic 2 invites us to embrace our feminine depths,

## Jupiter's Boundless Expansion (3).

Gazing upon endless skies, lands, and oceans, early humans glimpsed divine infinity, birthing number 3 for growth and vastness. Jupiter assumes its lordship, nurturing soul-wisdom and revealing the universe's and self's ever-unfolding dimensions.

Jupiter, the third wandering giant in our solar tapestry, reigns as the cosmic Guru, expansive teacher, benevolent guide, and boundless wellspring of wisdom. Following the Sun's singular fire (1) and Moon's dual embrace (2), Jupiter bursts forth as Number 3: the vibratory force of creativity, joy, and abundant growth. Ancient sky-watchers named it Brihaspati or Guru, honoring its role as the philosopher-king, swelling horizons with optimism and divine knowledge.

## Jupiter's Symphony with Number 3.

Numerology crowns Jupiter as 3's celestial ambassador, channeling its energies into expression, multiplicity, and higher learning like a sage multiplying seed into orchards. Envision its massive orb, scattering light across the zodiac, embodying 3's playful triad:

- Expansion and Abundance: Jupiter multiplies blessings, fueling prosperity and adventure. 3-influenced individuals (born 3rd,

12th, 21st, or 30th) brim with charisma, artists, and optimists who inspire multitudes.

- Creativity and Expression: As a Guru, it ignites imagination, poetry, music, storytelling flow like Jupiter's gaseous storms. Thursday, its sacred day, pulses with 3's joyful rhythm.
- Wisdom and Guidance: The planet of dharma teaches ethics, philosophy, and big-picture vision, balancing 1's will and 2's feeling into harmonious growth.
- Vedic texts hail Jupiter as the deva of knowledge, its yellow hue vibrating 3's frequency, aligning throat and solar plexus for eloquent truth.

## Jupiterian Energies Unveiled.

Tap Jupiter's 3-magic: Chant mantras on Thursdays, don a yellow sapphire or citrine, or travel mindfully to expand horizons. Shadow side? Overindulgence; mastery brings disciplined abundance.

Jupiter as cosmic 3 beckons: Step into your inner Guru, letting wisdom's river overflow into a life of vibrant purpose.

## Rahu's Chaotic Illusions (4)

As primordial awareness expanded, the first human beheld four cardinal directions, birthing number 4 from this elemental frame, mirroring the four Vedas, four Upvedas, and four Varnas structuring society. Linked to Rahu (or Harshal), it evokes transformation, intensity, and worldly vitality; calamities assail from all sides, while life's four awareness stages, Dharmas, and sacred sites align here. The body dons four sheaths: Annamaya (physical), Pranamaya (vital), Manomaya (mental), and Anandamaya (blissful).

Rahu, the enigmatic fourth celestial shadow, emerges as the cosmic disciplinarian master of iron will, shadowy resolve, and unyielding structure in the numerological ascent. Trailing Jupiter's expansive joy (3), Rahu embodies Number 4's grounded essence: the builder, the architect of endurance, forging order from chaos through relentless focus. Ancient stargazers knew it not as a planet but a nodal force, the dragon's head devouring distractions to instill the rigor of purpose, demanding humanity earn its stability through trial.

## Rahu's Forge of Number 4.

In numerology's planetary choir, Rahu vibrates as 4, the square of stability, labor, and meticulous discipline, like a cosmic hammer shaping raw ambition into lasting foundations. Its smoky veil mirrors 4's no-nonsense discipline:

- Practicality and Restriction: As the taskmaster, it curbs excess, ruling Saturday's disciplined rhythm and earthy tones that ground flighty energies into productive soil.
- Transformation via Trials: Rahu's shadowy discipline strips illusions, teaching that true freedom blooms from mastered limits, balancing Jupiter's abundance with focused karma.

Vedic lore casts Rahu as the north node, its serpentine gaze piercing veils, aligning the root chakra for unshakeable resolve.

## Rahu's Discipline in Action.

Channel Rahu's 4-power: Practice austerity on Saturdays, wear a blue sapphire or hessonite, or build daily rituals to harness its forge. Shadow alert rigidity breeds stagnation; mastery yields unbreakable strength.

Rahu as cosmic 4 summons: Embrace the discipline of shadows, crafting your empire one unyielding step at a time.

## Mercury's Swift Intellect (5)

Pentad of Elements (5) Humanity discerned five foundational elements: sky, water, air, fire, earth, manifesting as sound, touch, form, taste, smell, inspiring five deities for intellect, eloquence, and learning. Mercury, the planetary prince, claims lordship over 5, fueling mental acuity, wisdom, and sensory delights; it governs five senses, gems, Cupid's arrows (mesmerism), libido forms, arts, Makaras, Vedic Richas, and life forces.

Mercury, the fifth swift messenger in the cosmic parade, shines as Budha Graha, the planet of intellect, adaptability, and eloquent exchange. Building on Rahu's stern discipline (4), Mercury embodies Number 5's vibrant pulse: curiosity, versatility, and the thrill of transformation. Ancient sky-gazers revered it as Budha, the awakened one, darting between Sun and stars like thought itself, quick, clever, bridging worlds with mercurial grace.

## Mercury's Spark with Number 5

Numerology aligns Mercury as 5's celestial voice, channeling restless energy into communication, learning, and fluid change like a cosmic scribe translating divine whispers into human action. Its green gleam captures 5's dynamic essence:

- Intellect and Adaptability: Mercury sharpens minds, fueling wit, trade, and innovation. 5-natives (born 5th, 14th, or 23rd) dazzle as communicators, travelers, multitaskers who thrive on variety and mental agility.
- Communication and Versatility: Ruling Wednesday, the fifth day, it governs speech, writing, and commerce, turning Rahu's rigid structures into lively networks of ideas and connections.
- Curiosity and Freedom: Budha Graha stirs exploration, dissolving boundaries for growth, yet warns against scattered focus; balanced, it births genius from flux.

Vedic wisdom hails Mercury as the lord of analysis, its emerald vibration quickening throat and heart chakras for truthful expression.

## Mercurial Energies Awakened

Invoke Mercury's 5-magic: Study or network on Wednesdays, wear emerald or green aventurine, or practice breath work for mental clarity. Excess scatters; mastery channels it into purposeful speed.

Mercury as cosmic 5 invites: Let your inner messenger fly, weaving change into the wisdom of fluid mastery.

## Venus's Harmonious Bliss (6)

Hexad of Sensual Harmony (6) Next, six tastes emerged: sweet (Madhura), sour (Amla), salty (Lavana), pungent (Katu), bitter (Tikta), astringent (Kashaya), alongside six Darshanas (Vedanta, Sankhya, Mimamsa, Vaisheshika, Nyaya, Tark), six seasons, Gunas, Koshas, Dakinis, penances, Shatkon Yantras, and bases. Venus, named for sage Shukracharya, master of revival sciences, occultism, and 64 arts, rules 6, kindling emotional depths, sensitivities, and pleasures. Sixfold Bhag (fortune) blends prosperity, allure, wisdom, fame, might, and joy; bodily phases span hunger, thirst, sorrow, attachment, decay, and death; formed from paternal semen (nerve, bone, marrow) and maternal blood (skin, flesh, blood).

Venus, the sixth jewel in the cosmic sequence, captivates as the planet of beauty, luxury, and sensual delight, is associated with Shukra Graha, the enchanting force of harmony and pleasure. Following Mercury's quicksilver mind (5), Venus blooms as Number 6's radiant essence: love, artistry, and nurturing allure, drawing humanity into realms of aesthetic bliss and relational grace. Our ancestors gazed upon its shimmering evening star, naming it for its irresistible charm, a celestial siren weaving desire into the fabric of creation.

## Venus's Allure with Number 6

Numerology casts Venus as the 6's divine seductress, infusing life with elegance, compassion, and a voluptuous flow, much like a cosmic artist painting passion across the soul's canvas. Its rosy glow embodies 6's harmonious triad:

- Love and Harmony: Ruling Friday, the sixth day, it fosters bonds, diplomacy, and luxury transforming Mercury's ideas into tangible delights of home, romance, and refined pleasure.
- Nurturing Luxury: Shukra Graha balances sensuality with responsibility, teaching that true luxury flows from giving

hearts; its shadow tempts excess, but mastery elevates to selfless grace.

Vedic seers revered Venus as the guru of demons, its diamond-white vibration opening heart chakras for unconditional affection.

## Venusian Energies Embraced

Awaken Venus's 6-power: Indulge mindfully on Fridays, wear diamond or rose quartz, or create beauty rituals to amplify charm. Beware indulgence's trap; equilibrium births enduring allure.

Venus as cosmic 6 whispers: Surrender to beauty's embrace, letting love's luxury sculpt your world into perfection.

## Ketu's Mystic Detachment (7)

Skyward vigilance unveiled the Saptarishis (Ursa Major), seven sacred rivers with their tributaries, and music's seven notes, thus number 7 emerged, governing seven upper Lokas and seven nether realms. Ketu (or Neptune), its planetary lord and Moksha's harbinger, bestows imaginative faculties and inner ecstasies; 7 encompasses seven mountains, continents, netherworlds, seas, planets, kings, Rishis, firewood, flames, Sun-chariot horses, colors, and metals.

Ketu, the seventh mystic shadow in the celestial lineup, haunts as the dragon's tail intimately tied to Naga, the serpentine guardians of hidden wisdom and primal mysteries. Succeeding Venus's lush harmony (6), Ketu embodies Number 7's ethereal vibration: spirituality, introspection, and detachment from the material veil. Ancient visionaries perceived it as the south node, a coiled Naga force dissolving ego in the fires of enlightenment, urging souls toward the infinite beyond.

## Ketu's Serpent Wisdom with Number 7

Numerology unveils Ketu as 7's otherworldly sage, channeling Naga energies into seclusion, occult knowledge, and karmic release like a cosmic serpent shedding skin for rebirth. Its smoky aura captures 7's sacred solitude:

- Spirituality and Intuition: Ketu awakens psychic depths, drawing 7-natives (born 7th, 16th, or 25th) to mysticism, meditation, and Naga lore as healers detached from worldly snares.
- Detachment and Moksha: Linked to Tuesday's undercurrents and Naga shrines, it severs attachments, transforming Venus's pleasures into pure consciousness Naga's venom purifies illusions.

- Hidden Knowledge: As Naga's ally, Ketu reveals esoteric truths, guarding treasures in silence; its shadow isolates, but mastery grants unshakeable inner sovereignty.

Vedic epics portray Ketu as the headless warrior, its vibration piercing third-eye realms for Naga-guided transcendence.

## Ketu's Naga Energies Unleashed

Invoke Ketu's 7-power: Offer sesame on Tuesdays, wear cat's eye or lehsunia, or meditate in serpent shrines for clarity. Excess breeds alienation; balance unlocks divine seclusion.

Ketu as cosmic 7 hisses: Coil into the Naga's silence, emerging enlightened from the shadows of the soul.

## Saturn's Steadfast Discipline (8)

Saturn's Dual Discipline (8) For safeguarding these sacred sevens, rituals honored eight Bhairavas, Ashtasiddhis, and power seats assigning 8 to Saturn, arbiter of trials or transcendence, commanding bodily consumptions. Eight Vasus, mothers, nerves, organs, fragrances, and nooses hatred, shame, fear, sorrow, disgust, lineage, virtue, caste ensnare souls; transcendence yields Sadashiva's purity.

Saturn, the eighth stern sentinel in the cosmic order, looms as the planet of judgment, Shani Dev, the unerring arbiter of past karma, enforcing accountability with inexorable justice. Capping Ketu's mystical detachment (7), Saturn resonates as Number 8's profound vibration: discipline, endurance, and karmic reckoning, compelling souls to reap what they've sown across lifetimes. Ancient sages trembled before its rings, naming it the taskmaster who weighs deeds on scales of time, transforming suffering into hard-won mastery.

## Saturn's Scales of Number 8

Numerology positions Saturn as 8's cosmic judge, channeling karmic debts into structure, authority, and long-term reward like a divine ledger balancing Venus's indulgences and Ketu's illusions with iron law. Its leaden blue hue embodies 8's dual infinity:

- Judgment and Discipline: Saturn delivers justice for prior karma, forging 8-natives (born 8th, 17th, or 26th) into leaders, managers, and stoics who rise through trials, wielding power responsibly.
- Karmic Responsibility: Ruling Saturday (echoing Rahu's 4), it governs longevity, legacy, and retribution for previous lives' actions manifest as lessons, urging ethical living for elevation.
- Endurance and Ambition: Shani tests limits, building empires from ashes; its shadow breeds fear, but mastery yields profound wisdom and material-spiritual wealth.

Vedic hymns depict Saturn as Yama's ally, its vibration grounding the crown chakra for karmic clarity and timeless resolve.

## Shani's Karmic Energies Mastered

Harness Saturn's 8-power: Fast on Saturdays, donate black sesame or iron, wear blue sapphire mindfully, or reflect on past actions for liberation. Avoid resentment; embrace yields unbreakable strength.

Saturn as cosmic 8 decrees: Face your karma's mirror, forging judgment into the throne of eternal victory.

## Mars's Fiery Drive (9)

Mars' Sovereign Fire (9) Next, visions of nine Goddesses, gems, treasures, Rasas, and Kumaris activated nine Vargas, crowning 9 as independent essence under Mars planetary general, soul's champion, fostering self-reliance. All numbers, extended infinitely, reduce to 9's pinnacle. Numeric Cosmos Unveiled: Each digit pulses with nature's arcane potency, binding worldly mysteries in harmony. Humanity decoded this by sequencing 0 through 9, awakening their latent expressions from Shunya's void to 9's completion.

## Mars's Human Fire with Number 9

Numerology crowns Mars as 9's humanitarian champion, channeling aggressive energy into service, leadership, and completion–like a cosmic general rallying tribes for justice and renewal. Its crimson glow pulses 9's boundless compassion:

- Courage and Protection: Mars fuels heroism, defending the vulnerable. 9-natives (born 9th, 18th, or 27th) embody this as activists, soldiers, healers who charge into battles for humanity's upliftment.
- Selfless Action: Ruling Tuesday, the dynamic ninth day in the cycle, it transforms Saturn's lessons into dynamic change related to humanity through blood ties, family loyalty, and global kinship.
- Completion and Renewal: Mangal Graha burns away stagnation, linking to moksha; its shadow sparks conflict, but mastery forges universal love from warrior's grit.

# Types Of Numerology

Numerology offers a diverse system of decoding life's vibration through Numbers derived from the Name and the Birth date. Fresh perspectives emphasize their unique cultural lenses and modern applications beyond ancient roots.

There are several major Systems, each with a unique method for aligning the meaning to the number from the Date of birth and the complete name. Common types include Pythagorean, Chaldean, Kabbalah, and some Tamil Numerology, often used for personal insights & predictions.

- **Pythagoras Approach**
  Developed by the Greek philosopher Pythagoras, this system maps the alphabet sequentially. It freshly highlights personal evolution via core numbers like Expression for purpose, Soul urge for desire, and Personality for outer traits, Ideal for self-discovery in today's fast-paced world.
- **Chaldea's Method**
  Ancient Babylonians crafted the Vibration-based chart (1-8, skipping 9 as divine), prioritizing sound over position. A modern twist views it as predictive of a career shift or relationship, urging name tweaks to align with current energies.
- **Kabbalah Tradition**
  Jewish mysticism Simplifies to name analysis on a 1-22 scale linking to life's spiritual blueprint without reductions, freshly applied, it guides karmic healing resonations with seekers exploring inner wisdom amid global uncertainties.
- **Other Variant**
  Tamil numerology ties numbers to planets for fortune telling, while Vedic blends astrology, an emerging hybrid like Chinese or New Age numerology, adapted this for the digital era, with tools like apps.

# Pythagoras Numerology Method.

## Pythagoras's Life and Numerology Roots:

Pythagoras links numerology to Kabbalah, Hebrew letters, Bible wisdom, ancient secrets, and his own teachings. An oracle told his parents their baby boy would be wise and help others. Born in Syria, named after Pythia (oracle goddess). Studied at the Melchizedek temple ("Son of God"). Jesus later studied there, too, with the Essenes. Lived 100 years, stayed youthful. Traveled 30 years learning secrets:

- Rabbis taught Moses mysteries
- Egyptian priests: Isis secrets (22 years), "Hidden Light" in everything, "Seek the light."
- Taught that good exists in all people
- Egypt: Goddess Isis (flowers, fruits, flight mysteries)
- Greek thinkers, Babylonian/Chaldean secrets
- Zoroaster: Zoroastrianism (good vs. evil, afterlife)
- Euphrates: Chaldean love magic
- India: Brahman Vedas

Indians called him Acharya ("Ionian teacher"). Wise men were Sages ("knowers") or Sophists ("wise ones"). Pythagoras made "philosopher" mean lover of wisdom.

## The Pythagorean School (536 B.C.)

At age 46, he started a school in Crotona, southern Italy (Greek colony). First university ever - mixed religion and science. Shared number vibration secrets only in private. So secret, nothing written down. Later writers hid truths with fake details to confuse outsiders.

Secret fact: 600 years later, Jesus started five mystery schools (one in Palestine) with the same secrets. Rosicrucian Max Heindel discovered this.

We know the school from student tales and old writings. Strict rules: No personal contact until passing initiations. Kids with Life Path 7 join easily, "born for mysteries."

Numbers show quantity. Pythagoras taught that numbers are living energy. Egyptians used number science in religion. Nature follows number laws.

## Law of Opposites

Nature proves opposites: light-dark, cold-heat, high-low, solid-liquid, hard-soft, calm-storm, good-bad, life-death. One force acts two ways by vibration speed. The Pythagoreans saw the triangle as the first earthly shape (three lines). Matches God's Creative Trinity.

From triangles, Pythagoras made his famous theorem: In a right triangle,

The hypotenuse square = The sum of the other two sides' squares.

Top mathematicians, they advanced medicine and astronomy.

Pythagoras said the math blueprint creates reality. Nothing exists without numbers. Math truths so powerful that some members were killed for sharing. Now those secrets teach school math.

## Music Revolution

The Greeks used a 7-string lyre. Pythagoras invented the monochord (wood box with one string, a movable bridge). String length changed the tone by vibration. Created an exact music scale. Invented the 7-tone scale we use. 8th note matched 1st (higher octave). Added 8th lyre string for new modes.

## Healing Power

Music, color, and poetry heal. Some melodies cured illness. Soft music calmed wild emotions. Lute/flute sounds balanced mind.

## Astronomy as Astrology

Taught stars link to humans. Used 500 B.C. Babylonian Chaldean knowledge (trusted source). Astrology = astronomy until the 1600s. Far planets move fast. Fast motion = friction = sound. Planets make tones: faster planet, higher note. Speeds matched music math. Planets "sing" - "music of the spheres." Pythagoras heard it.

## Prediction System

Greeks read the future in animal guts. Pythagoras rejected this. Used Orpheus' secrets (music god) for the number system. Made a wheel of letters, numbers, and zodiac around the globe. Birth name/date numbers predicted the future. Numbers applied to all teachings, not just prediction. Pythagoras didn't invent numerology.

## Family and Death

Married student Theano (age 60). Had seven children. Death stories differ, but assassins killed him. The rude man who returned with a gang burned the school. Widow/students continued but faced attacks. School ended, but the teachings survived.(source: the secret science of numerology)

## Pythagoras' Chart of Alphabets:

| Pythagoras Chart | | | | | | | | |
|---|---|---|---|---|---|---|---|---|
| 1 | 2 | 3 | 4 | 5 | 6 | 7 | 8 | 9 |
| A | B | C | D | E | F | G | H | I |
| J | K | L | M | N | O | P | Q | R |
| S | T | U | V | W | X | Y | Z | ~~~~ |

# Meaning Of Numbers.

Every number in numerology carries a unique vibration, spotlighting the core issues or energies at play in your personal journey. Think of it as a cosmic blueprint: these numbers highlight strengths to lean into and weaknesses to develop.

In your name, your lifelong personal signature, each letter translates to a number using systems like Pythagorean numerology (A=1, B=2, ..., I=9, J=1, and so on). Count the frequency of each number from 1 to 9. A cluster of the same number means that energy pulses strongly through your personality, like a dominant note in your inner symphony. Few or no instances of a number? That's your growth edge, a trait where you'll naturally face hurdles until you cultivate it consciously.

**<u>For Example the Number 2 defines the following traits:</u>**

Spotlight on Number 2: The Power of Partnership and Balance

Let's zoom in on number 2, the gentle harmonizer ruled by the Moon. It embodies duality, cooperation, intuition, diplomacy, and emotional sensitivity. Twos thrive on connection, empathy, and finding middle ground.

Abundance of 2s: You're a natural peacemaker, intuitive listener, and team player. Relationships flow easily; you sense others' needs and nurture bonds with grace.

Scarcity of 2s: Challenges arise in relational realms. Friendships might erupt in storms of misunderstanding. Romantic partnerships could fizzle due to unspoken tensions or power struggles. You may grapple with dualities like honoring justice for a betrayal while extending mercy and understanding to the wrongdoer. Picture this: a colleague wrongs you at work. Your instinct screams for fairness (justice), but without 2's balancing mercy, resentment builds, blocking forgiveness and forward movement.

**Real-life example:** Someone with no 2s in their name might excel solo as an entrepreneur but clash in marriages, swinging between fierce independence and clingy dependence. Friendships? Intense but short-lived, like summer squalls.

Number 2 in Your Life Chart: A Call to Heal and Harmonize

Your life chart (derived from birth date reductions) pinpoints timed lessons. When 2 emerges essay, in a personal year (current year + birth day + birth month reduced to a single digit), it's prime time for relational work.

# Numbers in Details.

## 1,"Build it your way, Stand-alone design your destiny, Solo trailblazer."

1 is considered a karmic number that brings a feeling of urgency when appearing in key spots on a numerology chart. Circumstances often compel the person to rely on their own resources. Challenges demand courage and self-starters, which become straightforward once the individual builds assurance through their unique skills and personal identity. It represents initiation, too, as 9 holds the cumulative wisdom of prior numbers and faces trials on that foundation. Upon completing those tests, it achieves wholeness in 10. As both beginning and end, 19 maintains purpose; it prepares to launch fresh endeavors before wrapping up the prior one. Creative concepts stream endlessly to them, with the 1's eager to kick off each, allowing 9 to manage the execution and closure so 1 can dive into the subsequent pursuit.

### 10/1.

The number 1 represents the self, infused with the strength and leadership abilities of the great "1 AM" within each of us; it embodies. intelligence, pioneering spirit, and ambition all in one, zero is the cosmic egg holding the attributes of God across each of the steps of birth within it from the foundational 10/1 stage onward maturity arises via life experiences and trust in the bestowed gift (0) of spiritual discernments; intuitively sensing the light's call amides one's deepest inner urgings their purpose lies in channeling creative power productively and beneficially. Those aligned with positive 10/1 are directed by a sharp inner sense of direction.

A score of 10 reveals your ambitious, innovative, and resolute spirit paired with an enterprising drive, you're fiercely independent and bold, thriving on launching new ventures yet eager to avoid the grind of handling routine details, and you always like to be in position 1 in any kind.

### 28/1.

When the root is preceded by 28, the traits of the 2 take precedence and hold greater strength. The 2 embodies the peacemaker, while the 8 represents the executive with sound judgment. Thus, in 28, the 2 attains leadership via diplomacy. Known as "the breaking number," 28 heralds fresh experiences, surprises, and boundless opportunities, as 2 + 8 = 10, signaling a new beginning. When 28 is behind the root, the qualities of the 2 come first and are therefore stronger. The 2 is the peacemaker, and the 8 is the executive with good judgment. So, in 28, 2 achieves leadership through diplomacy. The 28 is known as "the breaking number." New experiences are in store, surprises and unlimited opportunity, because 2 + 8 = 10, which is a new beginning.

A 28th birthday, much like a 1st birthday, signals strong determination and independence. Those with a 28th birthday often struggle internally with following rules, yet their unyielding drive ensures they never remain down for long. Indeed, your leadership ability as a 28 arises from this sharp clarity.

### 37/10/1.

The 37 reaches perfection (10) via study (7) to cultivate talents (3). The 7 constantly pursues the perfection of 10, as shown mathematically: adding numbers from 1 through 7 (1+2+3+4+5+6+7) totals 28, which reduces to 10. Thus, the ancients declared that perfection lies hidden within 7. "PERFECT" totals 37 and starts with P, the 7th letter. Its full value is 73, placing the perfectionist 7 upfront. The 3 implies that perfection is visually pleasing and a delight to behold. The central letter F, around which the word turns, indicates that true perfection demands care, time, and patience. F bears the double cross and, as the sixth letter, embodies responsibility.

### 46/10/1.

Individuals on the 46/10 life path must address challenges related to creativity and lofty ideals, channeling their dynamism and inner gifts into practical, step-by-step methods to realize their vision of a better world. They can improve the world modestly at home or within a friend group, or on a grand scale; the scope doesn't matter. The 4 and 6 qualities, which precede and shape the 10, give 46/10s unique challenges, strengths, and issues compared to other 10s. They often connect with the vitality and strength of 4, yet may feel creatively blocked by 6's perfectionism. Using the book's method for birth numbers, we avoid adding the final two digits of four-digit numbers. However, if we did (1+0), it would yield 46/10/1, highlighting added creative energy (1) amplified by the inner gifts of sensitivity, strength, expressiveness, and sharp intuition (0). Most 4s struggle with gradual, step-by-step progress, and most 6s grow impatient, demanding flawless results immediately. The 46 blend poses special hurdles in embracing the process toward goals. Though 46/10s sense their creative potential, actualizing it requires overcoming innate difficulties: slowing down, building a solid foundation through meticulous preparation, and honing essential skills.

### 73/10/1.

The wisdom of 7 takes precedence. The beauty of 3 thrives when supported by someone who has studied and applied themselves (7) to attain perfection. We see this in these 73 words: Comprehension. Inspired-artist. Extraordinary. Ultimately, birth names totaling 1 belong to people capable of leading organizations. They are natural inventors and exceptional planners. If the 1 is absent from the name, the person must cultivate self-confidence, ambition, and independence. We need 1s for self-confidence

## Number One (1): The Pioneer

**The number 1 stands for leadership and new beginnings. It's the spark that starts everything. People with strong 1 energy are like trailblazers; they light the way for others.**

### Positive Traits

These are the strengths of 1. They shine when you embrace this number's power.

- Active: Full of energy. You jump into action and get things done.
- Ambition: You dream big and chase goals with fire in your belly.
- Creative ideas: Your mind buzzes with fresh thoughts. You invent solutions no one else sees. Determination: Once you decide, nothing stops you. You push through tough spots.
- Good mind: Sharp thinking. You solve problems fast and learn quickly.
- Individuality: You stand out. You're true to yourself, not copying others.
- Inventive: A natural maker. You build new tools, ideas, or ways of doing things.
- Originality: One-of-a-kind. Your style and thoughts are uniquely yours.
- Self-confidence: You trust yourself. No fear of failing, you know you can win.
- Starts many projects: You love fresh starts. Ideas excite you, so you launch lots of them.
- Willpower: Iron will. You stick to your path, no matter what.

Example: Think of an artist who sketches a wild new painting idea at dawn, full of drive to make it real. That's pure 1 energy, bold and unstoppable.

## Negative Traits

These pop up when 1 energy gets blocked or overdone. Spot them early to balance.

- Aggressive: Pushy or rough. You might steamroll others without noticing.
- Braggart: Boastful. Talking too much about your wins annoys people.
- Impulsive: Acts on whims. You leap before looking, causing messes.
- Lazy: Starts strong but quits easily. Energy fizzles when it's hard.
- Self-conscious: Worries too much about looks or opinions. Doubts creep in.
- Represses feelings: Hides emotions. Bottles up hurt instead of sharing.
- Selfish: Me-first mindset. Forgets others' needs. Sensitive: Takes things personally. Small words sting deep.
- Stubborn: Won't budge. Clings to your way, even if wrong. Tip: If you're feeling stubborn, pause and listen. It turns negatives into growth.

## Destructive Traits

These are the dark side, rare but harmful if unchecked. They hurt you and everyone around.

- A bigot: Narrow-minded. Rejects ideas or people who differ from you. A bully: Pushes others down to feel big. Uses power to control.
- Antagonistic: Always fighting. Picks a battle just to win. Domineering: Bosses everyone. Crushes free will.
- Extremely egotistical: Thinks only you matter. The world revolves around your ego.

- Puts self-first at all times: No room for others, steps on toes without care.
- Tyrannical: Rules like a harsh king. Demands total obedience.

Warning: Destructive 1 act like a lone wolf gone mad, isolated and raging. Heal it with humility and teamwork.

Number 1 teaches independence, but true power comes from lifting others, too. Wear white or silver (the colors of 1's), eat light foods, and surround yourself with open spaces to boost its good vibes.

# 2."Bridge hearts, Build peace, Feel deeply, Heal together, Diplomats light in every bond."

Pythagoras called the 2 "odd and even" because it's an even number formed from two odd 1's. This number represents partnership, companionship, and marriage. Eve arrived second as Adam's helpmate. She embodied 2. The 2 makes an excellent companion, leaning toward the 1 because it seeks to assist. It feels incomplete alone. The 2 connects to pairs, as evident in the Roman numeral II, which is also 11, reducing to 2 on a higher plane. While 2 follows, 11 stands independently on its own two feet, revealing leadership potential. An unbalanced hoarding 2 can turn into a "collectomania" (kleptomaniac). "Kleptomaniac" has a Soul's Urge (vowel count) of 22, double the power of 2, clearly on the negative side of the vibration. Look closely at 2: it's the upper half of a 3, like a plant with roots buried deep underground, revealing only its surface self. This grants 2s profound sensitivity; their feelings run as deep as those roots and sting sharply (Morals and Dogma, 362). The 2 also foster a tendency to conceal things. Negative 2s act seriously, masking their deeds with lies ("LIAR" totals 22). 2s are skilled talkers, but with the bottom half buried, they obscure the truth: the 2 might say one thing (its upper part) while meaning another (its hidden part). As a feminine, receptive number (Eve came second), 2 exerts a gentle, kind, helpful influence without leading. It thrives working behind the scenes, meticulously perfecting detailed tasks, content without full credit, as long as the results earn admiration.

20/2.

Notably, "DEATH" totals 20. If death were final, it would sum to 7 or 9; instead, 20 suggests companionship like an angel at the transition.

People fearing death or holding odd views on it often feature the 20s prominently in their charts. 2s earn fame as peacemakers, seeing both sides of any issue, balancing emotions, and preserving harmony with innate tact that prevents flare-ups. Those with many 2s or a strong 20 in their name make our finest diplomats.

## Number Two (2): The Harmonizer

The energy of 2 is feminine and receptive. It draws in, nurtures, and connects.

### Positive Traits

These qualities make 2 a natural peacemaker and team player.

- Affectionate: Warm and caring. You show love easily.
- A way with words: Speaks smoothly. Your talk charms and persuades.
- Beautiful expression: Shares thoughts and feelings with grace.
- Better at continuing projects than starting them: Excels at building on ideas. You polish and perfect what others begin.
- Considerate: Thinks of others first. Always mindful of feelings.
- Cooperative: Works hand-in-hand. Thrives in partnerships.
- Diplomatic: Smooths conflicts. Finds middle ground with ease.
- Friendly: Easy to like. Builds bonds quickly.
- Good companion/business partner: Reliable sidekick. Makes teams stronger.
- Good with details: Spots the little things. Handles fine points well.
- Helpful: Steps up to assist. Puts others' needs first.
- Loving: Deep heart. Gives love freely.
- Modest: Humble. Doesn't boast or show off.
- Neat: Organized and tidy. Keeps things in order.

- Sensitive to self and others: Feels emotions deeply yours and theirs.
- Sincere: Honest to the core. Means what you say.
- Tactful: Chooses words wisely. Avoids hurt.
- Works well with others: Fits into groups like a puzzle piece.

Example: Picture a friend who listens, comforts, and turns a group argument into laughter that's 2 in action.

## Negative Traits

These arise when 2 energy feels overwhelmed. Balance them with self-care.

- Conflict: Draws drama. Stirs up tension without meaning to.
- Dissatisfied: Never quite happy. Always wants more.
- Easily offended and hurt: Takes slights to heart. Bruises fast.
- Fastidious: Too picky. Obsesses over perfection.
- Glib: Smooth talker who skims the surface. Lacks depth.
- Indecisive due to being able to see both sides of an issue: Knows all angles, so picks none.
- Insecure: Doubts yourself. Fears rejection.
- Meticulous or careless: Either fusses endlessly or skips details.
- Occasional moods of depression: Dips into sadness now and then.
- Over-emotional: Feelings flood in. Hard to stay steady.
- Subservient: Puts yourself last. People-pleasers too much.
- Tactless: Blurts out hurts without thinking.
- Timid: Shy and hesitant. Holds back from shining.

## Destructive Traits

These extremes damage trust and peace. Rare, but they poison relationships.

- Bad temper: Explodes in anger.
- Cruel: Lashes out to wound.
- Deceptive: Hides the truth.
- Demanding: Clings and expects too much.
- Lacks self-control: Emotions run wild.
- Leans too much on others: Depends fully, stands alone poorly.
- Liar: Twists facts.
- Sly: Sneaky and cunning.
- Sneaky: Moves in shadows.
- Wants to control others: Pulls strings from behind.

Number 2 thrives with orange (its color), gentle music, and paired items like twins or duos to amplify harmony.

# 3."Express Boldly, Inspire endlessly. Where Art meets Hearts."

Humans possess a threefold nature: spirit, mind, and body. Similarly, every system includes a beginning, middle, and end, making 3 the first perfect number. Pythagoras named 3 "the One and the Many," signifying a finite blend of 1 and 2, and several talents since 3 embodies the Creative Principle in the Godhead, the essence of self-expression, artistry, and entertainment. The 3 resembles an 8 with its left side open, allowing 8 to set its own limits through organized efforts. In contrast, 3 remains open, dispersing its energies freely. Both excel at generating money, yet 8 focuses on growing wealth, while 3 avoids organization to pursue pleasure over labor; it craves fun, not work. People with a life purpose of 3 are meant to channel their emotional sensitivity into positive, heartfelt self-expression for the world. However, this purpose involves overcoming challenges such as blocked or distorted expression, emotional oversensitivity, and the self-doubt that accompanies them.

### 12/3.

A 12th birthday suggests you're friendly, enthusiastic, and keen to forge your own unique identity. Creativity defines you. You're emotional, sociable, and warm-hearted too. People with life purpose 12 harness their emotional sensitivity to deliver positive, heartfelt self-expression to the world. Yet, fulfilling this purpose requires first addressing challenges such as obstructed or warped expression, emotional hypersensitivity, and the resulting self-doubt. Would you prefer a more formal tone, shorter length, or integration with the rosebud metaphor? and 12/3s must summon courage to beat back insecurity and self-doubt that could block them, and learn to guide their creative and emotional energy productively. If not, when weighed down by doubt or insecurity, they might release that energy harmfully via alcohol, tobacco, or other drugs.

The order of the initial digits (1 and 2) while cooperation matters (2) dominate for 12/3s, when 12/3s stifle their emotions, it shows up in the body as tension or assorted other symptoms. Individuals pursuing 12/3 paths stand out as some of the most balanced, adaptable, and creative souls on the planet. Words like "strive," "stress," and "strain" all start with STR, which equals 12/3. When I first delved into this discipline, I grasped the uplifting forces of 3 happiness, joy, talents in expression, and communication.

## 21/3.

A 21st birthday means socializing comes naturally to you. You boast a wide circle of friends and diverse hobbies, and you truly relish others' company. When shining brightest, your creativity motivates those around you.

Balance People on the 21/3 life path exist to draw from creativity, emotional expression, balance, and cooperation to back people or causes. They channel their energy in positive, constructive directions to teach, uplift, and inspire. To meet the unavoidable challenges of their life path, 21/3s. With 2 offering backing and resilience, the 21/3s shine at inventing, pioneering, combining, or crafting standout achievements in any area. They convey creativity via any medium or substance, and the essence of their message always shines through. The swapped order of the initial digits (1 and 2) makes creativity concerns (1) more urgent for 21/3s, thanks to each number's placement and impact. It is said that 21/3s. Their life purpose is to bring confrontations with harmful expressions, like criticizing or griping. Usually, negativity emerges when their emotions feel wounded. Would you like this shortened, made more conversational, or adjusted for length

## 30/3.

People on the 30/3 life path focus on mastering expression and sensitivity. They overcome self-doubt to share their inner gifts, inspiring, uplifting, and encouraging others. While most face a mix of life issues,

30/3s have a clear, concentrated destiny tied to their work. They draw on powerful inner gifts like heightened sensitivity, inner strength, expressiveness, and intuition that all bolster one core theme: emotional expression.

A 30th birthday signals that you're magnetic, artistic, and extroverted. You draw in folks from all backgrounds, with a keen eye for beauty and balance. The 0 in your birthdate lends you exceptional verbal influence and the knack for uplifting others. 30/3 grapples with the core challenges of sensitivity, self-doubt, and emotional expression issues that concentrate intensely in 30/3s.

The most ancient is the cosmic egg (0) and the creative triad (3), dubbed by some "the ancient of ancients." Its full word total is 66, known as the Father-Mother God. Those on the 30/3 path have a strong innate drive to express themselves; this comes out either positively or negatively. Emotional expression doesn't always come easily at first; they may begin inhibited, but once they start, the words flow freely. 30/3s may express in large arenas like performance, teaching, or speaking to crowds, or in smaller circles with family and friends. Regardless, their challenges and joys stem from voicing feelings through speech or creative outlets like painting, music, or other media and from helping others do the same. Their expression thrives with people, often starting one-on-one. With courage, many eventually speak to groups; I often recommend public-speaking courses for 30/3s.

**39/12/3.**

The number 39 embodies affection and compassion. It yearns to offer devoted support and contribute to improving the world. It maintains a relaxed demeanor. The 9 symbolizes humankind along with its sentiments, passions, and zest for existence. This manifests through the 3, which signifies delight, bliss, and harnessing one's abilities to embrace life completely.

### 48/12/3.

The number 48 involves pursuing fulfillment and attaining tangible achievements. It requires equilibrium through inner transformation. The 4 leads off as a steadfast advocate for home, family, and nation note the pair of 4s within 8, denoting robust leadership. It's no surprise that terms like "patriotic" and "diplomatic" resonate with 48, and indeed, the fundamentals hold since 4+8=12/3.

### 84/12/3.

The vibration of 84/3 resonates as highly mental and intelligent, driven by the authoritative power of 8 at the forefront, which channels ambition, material success, and executive strength. Supporting it is the disciplined energy of 4, renowned for its unyielding focus on security, structure, and building solid foundations that foster true independence—think of 4 as the steadfast architect who turns visions into enduring realities. Creative and expressive 3 brings joyful completion to this dynamic trio, infusing optimism, communication, and social magnetism to ensure the mental prowess of 84/3 manifests not just in intellect, but in inspiring, world-impacting achievements.

### 57/12/3.

The 57 diligently strives to improve adverse situations. It comprehends others' challenges and recognizes when to request assistance, as the 5 seeks to grasp people's emotions through its own lived experiences.

### 75/12/3.

The 75 embraces obstacles; it strives for perfection in its efforts and returns to fundamentals 1, 2, 3 to achieve success. The downside of 75 involves potential failure stemming from delay.

## Number Three (3): The Performer

The vibe of 3 is masculine and active. It bursts out with joy and creation.

**Positive Traits**

These sparkles make 3 the star that lights up any room.

- Artistic: Natural artist. Colors, shapes, and beauty flow from you.
- Attractive: Draws eyes. Magnetic pull.
- Charming: Wins hearts. Smooth and delightful.
- Good imagination: Dreams vivid worlds. Ideas pop like fireworks.
- Cheerful: Brightens days. Smiles come easily.
- Creative: Makes magic from nothing. Turns thoughts into art.
- Enthusiastic: Full of zip. Excites everyone around.
- Expressive: Shares feelings boldly. No holding back.
- Gift of gab: Talks endlessly. Captivates crowds.
- Good at writing: Words dance on the page. Stories come alive.
- Good host/hostess: Welcomes all. Parties thrive under you.
- Good sense of humor: Quick laughs. Jokes land perfectly.
- Optimistic: Sees the sunny side. Hope never fades.
- Outgoing: Loves the crowd. Shy? Not you.
- Singing: Voice that soars. Melodies pour out.
- Sociable: Friend magnet. Builds big circles.
- Speaking: Orator's touch. Words inspire.
- Talented: Gifts galore. Skills shine bright.
- The life of the party: Centers the fun. Energy explodes.

Example: Imagine a storyteller at a gathering, cracking jokes, singing tunes, and pulling everyone into the fun that's 3 stealing the show.

**Negative Traits**

These shadows dim 3's light when energy spins out. Tame them with focus.

- Bored: Craves new thrills. Stays restless.
- Critical of others: Judges harshly. Points out flaws.
- Dislikes responsibility: Dodges duties. Prefers play.
- Exaggerates: Stretches truths. Stories grow huge.
- Hates work; wants only fun: Chases pleasure. Skips the grind.
- Impulsive: Acts fast, thinks later. Regrets follow.
- Jealous: Envious of others' shine. Greens with envy.
- Moody: Ups and downs. The weather changes quickly.
- Scattered: Jumps here and there. Finishes little.
- Self-centered: World spins around you.
- Vain: Mirror-gazer. Loves one's own looks too much.
- Wasteful: Spends freely. Resources vanish.
- Wears too much makeup or gaudy clothes: Overdoes flash. Tries too hard.
- Worrywart: Frets over nothing. Anxiety nags.

**Destructive Traits**

These poisons twist 3's joy into harm. They isolate and wound.

- Cowardice: Runs from fights. Hides in fear.
- Deep jealousy: Burns with resentment.
- Dual-personality: Two faces. Shifts like wind.
- Gossip: Spreads tales. Stirring pots.
- Greedy: Grasps for more. Never enough.
- Hatred: Holds grudges. Darkens the heart.
- Hypocrite: Says one thing, does another.
- Intolerant: Rejects differences. No room for others.
- Uses hurtful words: Cuts deep with talk.

Boost 3 with yellow (its color), upbeat music, and creative spaces to keep the good vibes flowing.

# 4."Four walls, Endless strength, Work hard, Stand firm, Discipline forges destiny solid to the core."

The Sacred Trinity sent energy through spoken words into the physical world. People show the Trinity, or Godhead, as a triangle. It sits on a line that signifies the spirit descending into matter. This makes the symbol 4. Some see it as a standing person holding the Godhead Trinity.

Pythagoras named it "Right and Left." This means the lands on your right and left when you stand, or the four corners of the Earth. In shape, 4 is a square, the steadiest form. When someone is honest, we say they are "square" with you. The number 4 stands for uprightness, honesty, and strong morals. People with 4 love their family, community, church, temple, and country.

A 4 birthday shows you value form and order highly. A "Sense of humor" isn't the first trait people typically associate with 4s. (Forgive us, 4s, we know you enjoy good times, rest, relaxation, and fun too!) The dependable, stable 4 recognizes the worth of honest hard work and tackles jobs with diligence.

4's are Sevens face limits. They stick to rules or hard facts. This makes them serious. Four acts on feelings, slow down, and finish projects. Not surprisingly, 4s make devoted, thoughtful, faithful, and kind partners. They love home. They handle money well and don't spend more than they have. You can always count on a 4 to be reliable and predictable. A great extra is that the 4 always cleans up its own messes! People call the 4 both the "salt of the Earth" and the "pillar of the community." It forms the strong base of any group, family, or marriage. You can count on your 4 to be reliable, steady, on time, and good at handling the job. The 4 sees things in a practical, common-sense way. Born to build, the

4 loves making things that last like a marriage, a system, a job, or a company from the start. But note: the 4 does not start new ideas. It needs others, like the 1, 3, and 8, for inspiration and vision. The 4 stays calm and doesn't get swept up in feelings or dreams; we leave that to the 3 and 9. Still, the 4 hold high standards of honesty and courage. It succeeds through hard work, tough lessons, and duty.

## 31/4.

GOSSIP: 761197 = 31/4 This word sounds like what it means: a hissing snake ready to strike. In these numbers, it starts and ends with 7 letters, G and P. The dark side of 7 is fault-finding, deceitful, and sarcastic with words. The Soul's Urge (vowels) of Gossip is O=6 and I=9, totaling 15/6. The good 6 is responsible and kind, but its bad side hurts others and uses words like a sword. The Personality (consonants) is 7117=16/7. This shows the cold, secretive, unfeeling side of 7. It seems to turn its back on the person being talked about. It first adds to the karmic 16, meaning it creates karma. The full expression of Gossip is 31/4, which means bringing things into reality. It can make something from nothing with mean words (3) and cause pain. The full number is 85. The 8 means continuity, and 5 means talking. Here, 5 talks endlessly, like a cycle that never stops, and the gossip keeps spreading. The 8 also means the Law of the Circle: what you send out comes back. No wonder its Personality is the karmic 16. All 4s make good doctors, but 31s and 13s are the best. The 3 makes them easier to reach, willing to talk, and seem more understanding. The 31 is fully reliable and takes responsibility seriously. SCIENCE: 1395535 = 31/4 This is basic knowledge (4). Each science is unique (1) and follows its own creative (3) rules. The first letter S seeks knowledge and has strong ideas. The first vowel is I, which must learn self-control. It is a 9-letter word for serving people. Its full number is 58: always (8) seeking answers (5).

## 40/4.

He active God-power of 0, brings things into reality on Earth. This is the story of 40. It goes through four levels of creation. Each level is a separate Sephirot Tree, totaling 40 Sephiroth. This makes 40 completions. Creation. Terrain. Biology. Fundamentals. The first three words total 85. Constant change (5) is part of the 85's life cycle (8). Fundamentals total 130: the Creative Trinity (3) in the middle of perfection (1 and 0). In the Bible, 40 links to spiritual growth and completion. Jesus fasted for 40 days. The great flood lasted 40 days and 40 nights. Related 40-word phrases are: The very negative 40 can be very dangerous. It has no sense of humor, takes everything too seriously, and can turn violent.

### 49/13/4.

49/13/4 This combination signifies individuals with diverse talents who channel them toward remarkable success, incorporating the energies of 13 and 4. 4: Transforms concepts into reality via disciplined, methodical abilities, a steadfast builder. 9: Compassionate toward others, dedicated to serving the greater good. 1: Natural leadership and unwavering determination to complete endeavors. 3: Innate creativity eager for expression. People with 49 strongly value home and family. This comes from 4's love for safety and 9's deep emotional bonds. Positive words: Appreciate. Patriarch. Pregnancy. Intensify. The 49 needs to balance mind and feelings. 4 thinks with the mind, while 9 feels with emotions. Negative words for this are: Irritable. Criticism. Unemotional. Constricted. Pomposity. If bad emotions control the mind, the results can be very harmful. This is because 4 makes ideas real: Destruction. Demolished. Both words start with D, which is 4. This shows 4's power to destroy, not build. Note that "Destruct" starts with D-4, but "Construct" starts with C-3. And 3 means creativity. "De" always means "take away from." It begins with words like Detract, Debit, Default, Defeat, Deface, Defame, Defer, Deficit, and Defraud. E is 5, and 4 and 5 clash. 4 wants limits, but 5 needs freedom.

### 58/13/4.

58/13/4 The 58 points to deep thinking, smart topics, and gaining insights, a number for knowledge. 5: Curious mind. Seeks facts, imagines well, and analyzes sharply. 8: Strong leadership skills. Great at organizing. Skilled with good judgment. Physically tough. Positive 58-words: Realization. Imagination. Profundity. Forgiveness. Independence. Pythagorean. On the other side: Profiteer. Self-indulgent. Opposition. Elimination. Competition. Licentiousness.

**67/13/4.**

Cares about people, offers loving help, and accepts duties. Thinks deeply about itself, stands out as special, and people look up to it for wisdom. It acts like a professional. It also has all the creative skills of 13/4. We see these qualities in these 67 words: Administration, Distinguished, Practitioner. All 4s do well in brain work, especially when hands and mind team up. This includes top engineers, mechanics, jewelers, electricians, mathematicians, musicians, teachers, managers, and foremen.

## Number 4 Expanded: The Builder of Stability

Number 4 grounds numerology's spectrum as the architect of form, channeling Uranus (innovative structure) and Rahu (material discipline) energies. It manifests dreams into reality, like the four elements (earth, air, fire, water) stabilizing chaos. Those dominated by 4 excel as engineers, farmers, or administrators, envisioning steady empires from raw ideas. Imbalance, however, rigidifies into unyielding fortresses, echoing Rahu's obsessive hold.

### Positive Traits:

- Precise: Measures twice, acts once for flawless results.
- Dutiful: Honors commitments with unwavering resolve.
- Traditional: Values time-tested ways for enduring security.
- Self-disciplined: Master habits to build lasting foundations.
- Dependable laborer: Delivers consistent, high-quality work.
- Truthful: Speaks plainly, fostering trust.

- Cherishes home, family, and nation: Roots deeply in loved ones and homeland.
- Timely: Respects schedules as sacred.
- Genuine: Authentic in word and deed.
- Scholarly: Studies diligently for practical mastery.
- Reliable: The rock others lean on.
- Insists on rule enforcement: Upholds order for the collective good.
- Faithful: Loyal through trials.
- Systematic: Organizes chaos into efficiency.
- Enduring: Patiently perseveres to fruition.
- Patriotic: Serves the country with pride.
- Sensible: Chooses realism over fantasy.
- Cautious: Weighs risks wisely.

**Negative Traits:**

- Quarrelsome: Debates to defend unyielding views.
- Bland: Life feels monotonous from routine rigidity.
- Overlooks leisure: Forgets play amid endless toil.
- Stubborn: Resists change like concrete.
- Lacks levity: Struggles with lightheartedness.
- Rigid: Rejects differing paths.
- Envious: Covets others' freedoms.
- Insists on evidence: Doubts without tangible proof.
- Close-minded: Shuts out new ideas.
- Reserved in showing warmth: Affection hides behind duty.
- Dogmatic: Imposes opinions forcefully.
- Overburdened by labor: Burns out from overwork.

- Biased: Judges through narrow lenses.
- Excessively solemn: Rarely smiles or relaxes.
- Compulsive worker: Equates worth to productivity.

**Destructive Traits:**

- Brutish: Reduces to base instincts.
- Hostile: Clashes aggressively.
- Vulgar: Speaks or acts coarsely.
- Ruthless: Crushes opposition mercilessly.
- Loathing: Nurses' deep hatreds.
- Intense dark passions: Emotions erupt violently.
- Savage: Unleashes primal fury.

The 4 symbolizes realization, succeeding the creative trinity: conception, sowing, nurturing. The 4 yields the harvest. For harmony, 4s benefit from green gemstones (emerald for Uranus balance) or rudraksha (4-mukhi for focus). In life paths, 4 demands building tangible legacies turn discipline into a nurturing home, not a prison.

# 5."Freedom feels the fire. Adapt, Explore, Conquer chaos, Born wild, Live free, Velocity of life."

The 5 loves freedom and wants to move as it likes. Notice how the number opens on both ends? How is the base rock? It adapts easily, craves variety, and sometimes feels confused about direction. The bottom half of 5 looks like the top half of 3, giving it strong speaking skills. Remember, 3 excels with words. This makes 5 a top salesperson. 5's hate routine and feel very restless. They need freedom to set their own schedules. A daily job in one spot, trapped inside four walls, makes them extremely uneasy.

Pythagoras named 5 "Masculine and Feminine" because it combines 2 and 3, the feminine and masculine numbers. So, 5s are popular and mix well with both men and women.

In travel, 5's prefer side roads and exploration. They enjoy seeing how locals live and speaking their language. Many 5's in a chart bring changes and surprises. At heart, 5's are curious. They want to know how things work and what's happening. They investigate everything. It sits right in the middle of the numbers, and humans have five senses. At birth, we first notice our senses. We feel warmth and cold. We see light and recognize parents' faces, other people, and our surroundings. We touch objects and sense different textures. We like some foods' tastes more than others. We smell food aromas and changing air.

Learning about our five senses is the first life lesson. As a child grows, temptations target one or more senses. The child finds sweets taste good, but too many cause a stomachache. The same happens with each sense. So, we must learn to choose wisely; we are all Adam and Eve. Adam stands for active male energy, shown by A. Eve stands for receiving female energy, shown by V, which is flipped, and with the "rib" taken out. V, said as Vee, rearranges to Eve (The English Cabbalah, Vol. 1:172).

Man starts with M: right in the middle of the alphabet, like 5 in the middle of numbers. M has two feet balanced on the ground. Flip M to get W, the first letter of Woman. Negative-Live polarity. Emotional. So, Adam shows active male force, and Eve shows passive female force. For good balance, everyone needs a bit of the opposite force. Man needs some receiving side to soften him. A woman needs some active side to strengthen her.

### 41/5.

41/5 14 and 41 are numbers of nature. Nature shows perfect order (4) through smart thinking (1 and 5). It is a shape (4) built from ideas (1 and 5). When 4 comes first, the freedom-loving 5 gets structure, as in these 41 words: Astronomy. Geology. Universe. 4 is made of two feeling-based 2's, so when first, it shows sensitivity. At the same time, 4 builds strong character and makes 5 more responsible: Character. Emotional. Feelings. Generous. Giving. Prudence. Purify. Respected. Sensitive. Negative words: Antagonism. Blasphemous. Brooder. Condemned. Dangerous. Fright. Pessimism. Prudish. Transgress. Wretched. 5 is a marriage number. It creates its own children (5 x 5 = 25. 5 x 7 = 35. 5 x 9 = 45). In 41/5, the self (1) puts family (4) first and thinks of starting a family and having kids: Married. Admirer. Promise. Pregnant. Existence. MARRIED: 4199954 = 41, starts and ends with 4 letters. This shows it plans to set boundaries. It begins with M, two feet firm on the ground. M is the 13th letter and links to the 13th Tarot card, Death; but here it means change something new in life. It is the end of the old single self and the birth of a loving partnership. The 41/5 is smart and a good speaker. The 5 collects facts, and the 4 comes from two 2's that notice details. The 5 is made of 2 and 3, are smooth talkers. No wonder these words add up to 41.

## 50/5.

Kabbalah says all past and future knowledge fits in the 10 numbers, 22 paths (the letters), and 50 gates of knowledge. These gates sort all existence into five groups of 10 (The Book of Splendors, 134). This makes 50 a smart number. See it in these words that add to 50: Concordance. Efficient. Engineer. Explorer. Fact-finder. Instructors. Investigate. Memorize. Organize. Professor. Prophesy. Physician. Technician. Theosophy. The fun, popular side of 5 grows stronger with the zero: Admiration. Considerate. Delightful. Sincerity. Remember, we said 5 takes risks and fears nothing? INTREPID means fearless, and it adds to 50. We also said 5s adapt well and love change. DIVERSITY means that, and it adds to 50.

## 23/5.

The 23/5's must deal with issues of independence, honest feelings, and teamwork. They learn freedom through self-control and deep life lessons. Life paths bring challenges to beat, so 23/5s face inner struggles with dependence vs. independence, duty, and sharing true emotions. Most 23/5s bloom late. They take longer to gain confidence because of stronger 3 traits, and 2 is likely to be sensitivity and self-doubt. They also have bigger fears but a stronger push to express themselves.23/5s skips teamwork issues, which means the 23/5 people don't struggle more with teamwork. 23/5s have lively energy and a wide worldview. Even if they have not yet lived their adventure or freedom side, in time and in their own way, with full confidence.23/5s find their life's potential, the depth, and endless inner freedom. The 2's habit of over-teamwork, mixed with the 3's and 5's dramatic side, can create a martyr mind. These people want to save others, save the world, and fight for freedom. They love drama on TV and in real life, too. In the end, they need a good balance. They find it by testing each side, like learning independence by facing dependence from an accident, illness, money loss, or self-doubt about self-care. Their test is to use these to rebuild healthy independence and right teamwork, meaning they can accept help from others.

Out of fear, 23/5s hide behind social roles. 23/5s gain by recalling they are more than their roles. Their skill at pretending lets them control others on purpose or not using feelings like anger to win.

**32/5.**

The 32/5s can focus too hard on one thing and miss the big view. Like all 5s, they need self-control, focus, and clear priorities to gain true freedom. Their top goal is inner freedom: to be themselves, free from self-doubt and fear. Only with this inner growth can they find outer success. But facing outer life builds inner freedom. The outside world mirrors our inner self. They learn the spiritual rules behind all life. This gives deeper freedom. Without control, they skim the surface or scatter, trying everything at once. By setting clear goals and sticking to them, they go deeper into true freedom. The risk is a broad but shallow experience with self-control and focus; they dive deep into a few areas.

Like all 5s, they need self-control, focus, and clear priorities to gain true freedom. Their top goal is inner freedom: to be themselves, free from self-doubt and fear. Only with this inner growth can they find outer success. But facing outer life builds inner freedom. The outside world mirrors our inner self, so by meeting outer tests, 32/5s face and beat self-doubt and teamwork issues. Adventures big or small, help as they push limits, take on risks, and test their strengths. Most 32/5s struggle more with teamwork because they can't connect with others so easily. Many 32/5s burn the candle at both ends; they understand things lately.

**59/14/5.**

59/14/5 This number fits the person who does work well: Cooperation. Experience. Professional. 9 means lessons end soon, with change ahead after 9 comes 10, a fresh start. 9 holds all knowledge from earlier numbers and adjusts to change thanks to the 5. So, 59 finishes strong, and 14 is the wise sage. Environment. Hierarchy. Precipitate.

Scintillating. PRECIPITATE, totals 59. In hidden knowledge, it means to create from nothing, as sages and magicians did. It starts with P, the eternal circle up high on the self (1), closed to store deep wisdom. P is a 7-letter word, linked to spirit, science, thought, and grasping secret mysteries.

**68/14/5.**

This number marks the well-educated person. 6 grasps the law and knows right action. 8 brings executive power, sharp judgment, and leadership.

CIVILIZATION totals 68 and relies on education. Without it, people act wild and uncivilized. This word is fun to study in Kabbalah. Remember, civilization means all humanity, whose number is 9. Its full total is 149, which is 14/5 or 9/14/5 the amount of humanity. Letters for those numbers spell NINE. People with the name total 5 make natural salespeople, travelers, and excel in jobs needing flexibility and quick change. This covers actors, writers, inventors, detectives, speakers, and promoters. We need 5s for their adaptability and hunger for knowledge.

## Number Five (5): The Adventurer

### Positive Traits.

These electric qualities make 5 a whirlwind of excitement and connection.

Adaptable: Rolls with changes. Bends like the wind.

- Alert: Sharp eyes and mind. Nothing slips by.
- Analytical: Breaks things down. Sees the gears inside.
- Attractive to the opposite sex: Magnetic charm. Hearts follow.
- Charming: Wins smiles everywhere. Irresistible vibe.
- Clever: Quick thinker. Smart tricks up your sleeve.
- Courageous: Fearless heart. Faces the bold.

- Curious: Nose for the new. Questions everything.
- Dynamic: Full throttle. Energy explodes.
- Gets along with all types of people: Fits any crowd. Universal friend.
- Learns languages easily: Picks up tongues fast. Words flow.
- Love of freedom: Hates chains. Needs open skies.
- Loves to travel: Wanderlust calls. Roads beckon.
- Popular: Crowd favorite. Always in demand.
- Social: Party spark. Thrives in the mix.
- Super salesman: Sells ice to penguins. Persuasion pro.
- Wants adventure: Craves the thrill. Safe is boring.
- Witty: Sharp tongue. Jokes fly fast.

Example: Picture a globe-trotter chatting up strangers in a new city, picking up the local lingo, and diving into wild escapades, that's 5 alive.

**Negative Traits.**

These wild swings hit when the 5's fire burns too hot. Ground it wisely.
Careless: Sloppy moves. Details drop.

- Discontent: Grass is always greener. Never settled.
- Impatient: Taps feet. Waits poorly.
- Impulsive: Jumps blindly. Thinks after.
- Irresponsible: Dodges duties. Plays hooky.
- Procrastinates: Puts off till tomorrow. Always.
- Restless: Can't sit still. Itches to move.
- Takes dangerous chances (daredevil): Risks big. Thrill chaser extreme.

## Destructive Traits

These excesses crash 5's freedom into chaos. They trap more than they free.

- Gambler: Bets it all. Lady Luck's fool.
- Overindulge the senses in sex, drugs, alcohol, or food: Drowns in pleasures. No brakes.
- Perversion: Twists desires dark.
- Rude: Blunt and brash. Manners vanish.

Fuel 5 with turquoise (its color), spicy foods, and maps to channel the wanderlust right.

# 6."Love heals, Nurture thrives, Care deep, Keeps balance, Beauty in every Bond, Love's true anchor."

The 6 always gives solid advice. It is generous, kind, ready to give up its own needs, caring, and a great counselor. Look closely at how 6 is written. It has a round belly full of love, like it is pregnant. The 6 stands for romantic love, hot passion, motherly love, and gentle love. It rules marriage and a happy home life. It shows the heart of things, where love lives and grows. In community work, caring for animals, or teaching kids, the 6 does it all with love. It shows a man (1) next to the family circle (o), like "lo" or 6. So, it means new life and growth. The 6 is the "Cosmic Mother." In family matters, it is the loving parent at the center, like the hub of a wheel. It nurtures, loves, supports, and cares for the family (not always the mom; some dads do this well). Best of all, the 6 loves this job. But sometimes it acts too motherly for the 1, 5, or 7. The number 6 stands for home, family, and service. Everybody has six sides.

Pythagoras named 6 "Rest and Motion" because both are key to good health. People call 6 the "Cosmic Parent" for four reasons: It loves to care for family, pets, or anyone who needs help. Those born on the 6th, 15th, or 24th often have a special voice. The open top of 6 shows this. They speak well, sing, and teach. They make great counselors because they know what to say, stay calm, listen well, and help others relax. They like comfort and hate dressing up. 6 people are artistic. They want their home to show good taste, with nice colors and careful arrangement.

The 6 brings energy that nurtures, loves, and cares. The 6 energy looks after what already exists. It is both humanitarian and focused on service. The cosmic vibe of 6 is warm, soothing, and protective. The 6 energy works best when helping others. It does this through teaching, counseling, nursing, healing, making things beautiful, and creating cozy homes. A 6 needs harmony in everything. This number wants balance most of all. If there is an argument or trouble, a 6-year-old wants to fix it at home right away. Home is like a nest for the 6. When things go wrong there, the 6 hurries to make peace. A 6 uses free time for gardening, fixing up the house, or home tasks, usually with a partner. The 6 brings money. It gets cash by helping others, not by chasing gain for itself. The 6 works well in business such as small home crafts, work from home, or service jobs. 6s give their full heart to a business and care for it like a baby until it grows strong. When something is wrong or unfair, the 6 tells the truth. It speaks plainly and straight, sometimes too sharply. The 6 stands up for the weak. That is why 6s like social work, community fixes, and teaching children.

The gift of the 6 is wisdom and living by heart guidance. The power to fully commit, handle big duties, and do them well with love is the 6's blessing. The 6 builds a cozy home with good food, warm fire, close family ties, and pretty workspaces. The test for the 6 is to avoid being a suffering martyr and stay real about love. If you are a 6, learn not to give so much of yourself that nothing is left to give or love with. In its wish to love and be loved, to care and take duty, the 6 may not seem as strong as it is. People who do not get "heart-based" ways may see the 6 as selfish or weak. In seeking beauty and love, the 6 can dream too much about romance and marriage. It struggles with real daily life (which feels like a heavy load to the 6). The 6 may demand too much from a partner or stay single because of high ideals. In the end, 6s must learn to love themselves. Then they can be loyal, kind, sensitive, and caring to themselves. They will not run dry on love but become a full source of love for all. Relationships: The 6 is called the marriage and divorce number. It brings deep heart matters into life. If the 6 loves, it is deep and committed, not like the 3's flirty pull or the 5's body-based affair. It is true "marrying" love (as real as a dream love can be). This is the top devotion. But if a marriage loses heart, the 6 leads to divorce. It is common for people to.

## 15/6.

The 15/6s must work through issues of idealism and creative energy. They find smart ways to beat perfectionism, neediness, and hidden fears. They do this by first accepting themselves, then sharing their vision with others. Life purpose means facing hard challenges first; the 15/6s can see and share their big dreams of what could be. This higher vision may make 15/6s reject real life now. They may write or dream, lead or follow. They may sing about old times or future hopes. But only by focusing creative energy do 15/6s bring heaven to Earth. High ideals are good, but 15/6s must make them real to change the world. 15/6 people do not seek freedom or ideals; they create them. They are starters, inventors, and big dreamers. Almost all 15/6s feel a strong call to serve, like they are on a mission. Questions like "What is the true ideal?" and "What is real freedom?" echo inside them. They search for deep truth and high wisdom. Without staying grounded, 15/6s build and live in their own perfect dream world like some fantasy or sci-fi writers.

## 51/6.

The 51/6s live in dream castles of their imagination. They rarely touch everyday life on Earth. Those working 6 energy face usual problems like perfectionism, high standards, and low self-worth as they climb their path. The 5 influence gives 15/6s a quick mind that craves freedom and new experiences. This pulls them strongly. They long deep inside for the perfect life; they see a world of true justice.

Because of the 5, 51/6s need a real focus. They must sort many interests and tasks. They need one practice or job to use their high standards. Without a goal or path, they wander lost in dreams. With clear direction, they open future doors and show their best potential. But for all the creative, freedom-loving, high-minded 51/6s, some struggle with blocked energy. These 51/6s feel scattered, lost, trapped, or always let down. They chase escape like reading about perfect worlds or using drugs for fake highs. With 5 issues comes a need for strong discipline.

51/6s also have the 1's creative power. This turns dreams and ideals into real form. Working 51/6 in the Positive, Inspired, and uplifting, 51/6s in the positive show new possibilities and a brighter future. With high minds, focus, and discipline, they use active creativity. They lift people from dull daily life to their true higher selves. They accept self-first, then guide evolution for others and themselves. They channel real creative force.

## 60/6.

In numerology, the number 60 has a powerful family vibe. It mixes 6's caring home energy with 0's endless divine spark. This creates a force that builds strong bonds and protects the family like a warm shield. The Cypher of Deity's Creativity. The "cypher" in 60 works like a hidden code. It shows the creative power of God or higher energy. Picture it as a plan: 6 stands for God's loving care for family and creation, while 0 opens unlimited flow from the source. Together, 60 reveals how divine creativity builds worlds, starting with solid family units as the first place for growth. Exposed to a Body When 60 shows up in your chart like birth date sums or name totals, it means this divine family energy enters your human body and life. Your soul takes physical form to live out God's creative qualities. You become a home builder, relationship healer, and channel for infinite love. But watch out, care for family properly, or it turns into drama. In your book, tell readers: Look for 60 in Life Path or Destiny numbers. It's a call to bring God's family magic to Earth.

## 24/6.

In numerology, 24/6 shows a successful person with lots of patience and discipline. It adds up to 6 (2+4=6), the number for family love, harmony, and care. People with this energy succeed big because they stay calm during waits and stick to steady work plans, not rushing. They turn small daily steps into big wins, like strong careers or happy homes. This number is called "cosmic parents" because they nurture everyone like the perfect universal mom and dad. With unlimited patience, they set gentle rules, fix problems early, and build safe spaces. There, families or teams bond closely and grow strong. Find 24/6 in your birth date total, full name sum, or Life Path. It promises easy success if you stay patient, handle duties first, and put loved ones ahead. No shortcuts needed for long-term victories. Everyday Power Live it by breathing through delays, using simple lists, and listening before acting. Skip these, and harmony slips away. Follow them, and life flows smoothly with respect and joy everywhere.

### 42/6.

In numerology, 42/6 is a great number. It brings deep harmony to family life through steady responsibility and a natural motherly vibe. It adds up to 6 (4+2=6), mixing 4's strong duty and structure with 2's gentle peace-making and 6's loving care for home and loved ones. People with this energy in their birth or name totals become the quiet glue in families. They spot problems early, take charge without fuss, and wrap everyone in warmth like an ideal mom who cooks big meals, listens to worries at night, and keeps the home running even on hard days. This strength comes from a perfect blend: 4 handles bills, chores, and plans with discipline; 2 uses soft words to end fights and build trust; 6 gives endless nurturing so kids, spouse, or neighbors feel safe and valued. Life gives them solid marriages, happy kids who thrive, and homes full of laughter. They pick duty over selfish wants, turning small acts like family dinners or bedtime stories into bonds that last through storms. No ego or rush required, their patient service earns natural respect and smooth flow. Spot 42/6 in your Life Path (birth date sum), Destiny (full name letters), or even phone numbers. It means easy family success, good health for loved ones, and inner peace if you fully embrace the motherly role. Live It Daily: Start days with gratitude lists, say yes to helping, and end with hugs. Skip these habits, and small issues grow; do them, and your family turns into real heaven on earth. This proves 42/6 is a golden ticket for those who care deeply.

## 69/15/6.

In numerology, 69/6 is a tricky number. It balances big duties to family and society at the same time. It reduces to 6 (6+9=15, 1+5=6), blending 6's home love with 9's broad world service into a challenging but strong energy. People with this number act like super healers. They mend pain at home and help groups or communities with care and wisdom. But it feels heavy: Focus too much on family, and society suffers; lean toward public work, and home falls apart. With good balance over time, it brings fame, respect, and big successes like becoming known in healing, teaching, or community work. Spot 69/6 in birth totals or name sums. It promises great rewards if you set clear boundaries, rest often, and share the load with others. Spend time with family each day, plus help outside weekly. This builds steady, quiet fame without burnout.

### Number Six (6): The Nurturer

To grasp these numbers fully, we uncover their true nature.

### Positive Traits

These caring powers make 6 the heart of home and harmony.

- Adorers' family, home, children, pets, garden: Cherishes nest. Loves kin, critters, and green spaces.
- Advice giver: Wise words flow. Guides with care.
- Artistic: Creative soul. Beauty in all hands touch.
- Comforter: Soothes pains. Healing hugs ready.
- Cosmic parent: Universal caregiver. Motherly to the world.
- Gives loving service: Serves from the heart. No selfish gain.
- Good education is important: Values learning. Knowledge builds strength.
- Harmonious: Peace-maker. Balances all.
- High ideals: Aims noble. Dreams pure.
- Honorable: Integrity shines. Word is bond.

- Humanitarian: Helps the many. Lifts the fallen.
- Just: Fair judge. Right over wrong.
- Lawful: Follows rules. Order matters.
- Musical talent: Tunes pour out. Melody in veins.
- Poised: Calm grace. Steady under the storm.
- Protective: Shields loved ones. Fierce guardian.
- Responsible: Steps up always. Duty first.
- Sympathetic: Feels your hurt. Empath deep.
- Teacher: Shares wisdom. Lights paths.
- True friend: Loyal forever. Stands through all.
- Understanding: Sees your side. No quick blame.
- Uses voice in career: teaching, singing, speaking, acting, politics: Voice as a tool. Careers in sound and stage.
- Wants to nurture: Innate drive to feed and foster.

Example: Like a parent tending garden, kids, and home with songs and stories, that's 6 weaving love's web.

**Negative Traits**

These heavy loads weigh heavily on 6 when care tips are used to control. Lighten with trust.

- Anxious: Worries swirl. Fears the worst.
- Bossy: Calls shots. Others follow.
- Cynical: Distrusts motives. Sees dark first.
- Egotistical: Thinks superior. Pride puffs.
- Domineering: Rules the roost. No debate.
- Expects too much of people; easily disappointed in them: Sets bars high. Crashes when unmet.
- False pride: Fake front. Hides true self.
- Interferes: Butts in unasked.

- Jealous: Guards close. Envies intruders.
- Meddlesome: Pokes in business. Can't let go.
- Mopes: Sulks long. Mood sinks low.
- Needs to feel appreciated: Craves thanks. Withers without.
- Outspoken: Blunt force. Words hit hard.
- Self- centered: Orbit around me.
- Self-righteous: Holier than thou.
- Smug: Knows-it-all smirk.
- Suspicious: Doubts hearts. Trusts few.
- Sweet tooth: Craves candy. Indulges sweet.

**Destructive Traits**

These shadows choke 6's love into chains. Break free with boundaries.

- Conceit: Arrogance towers.
- Domestic tyranny: Home dictator. Rules with iron.
- Martyr: Suffers for show. Guilt trips.
- Nosy and interfering: Snoops deep. Meddles endless.
- Slavery: Binds self or others. No freedom.

Number 6 links to the body Adam formed on day six, and bodies have six sides. It ties to voice too God spoke creation over six days.

# 7.“Seek within, Truth awaits. Silence speaks the deepest secrets, Analyzes deeply, Evolves higher, Mind’s silent power, Lone sage Universal light.”

The number 7 stands for spirituality, mysticism, wisdom, and success.

Pythagoras called 7 the "Crooked and the Straight." God created the world in six days and rested on the seventh. The 7 turns away from the coming numbers. It skips the hard work of 8. Instead, it looks back at lessons learned from 1 through 6. It reflects on work well done, just as God saw His creation and called it very good. By resting, we recharge energy for the work of 8. The 8 has strong body power and good health because of proper rest on the seventh.

People with strong 7s in their charts need more rest than others. They dislike loud music, crowds, noise, or chaos. They stay balanced through calm and peace. 7s stand tall and proper. They dress, act, and think conservatively. They talk little, but say important things when they speak. The 7 is an intellectual number. They read much and think deeply. They seem secretive. The 7 means faith. They seek spiritual wisdom unless negative. Then faith turns to fear, and the quiet, strong person becomes a nonstop talker. Negative 7s show either faith or fear, sharpness or laziness. 7s always seek perfection. In any job they choose, they must be the best. If doctors specialize. If musicians, they compose and perform. 7s dig for facts and study everything. They work best alone. They prefer quality over quantity. They want to share life with someone they respect, or stay alone. They guard their privacy and can be hard to know. Only when they trust and like you do they open up. They need understanding, love, and kindness. They may seem cold, but they like helping people. 7s have strong intuition. They best remember dreams and often dream in color.

## 61/7.

61/7 in numerology marks very unique people who show care in their own quiet way to finish projects and tasks. It reduces to 7 (6+1=7), blending 6's loving heart with 1's solo drive and 7's deep inner wisdom. These folks nurture without fuss, they spot others' feelings and emotions right away, understand them fully without judging a bit, and find smart fixes that really work. No lectures, just calm help that builds rock-solid trust super-fast, so friends, teams, or clients stay loyal for life. They complete big goals by caring through actions like deep listening in talks, solving hidden issues others miss, and guiding with gentle truth. People open up easily because they feel totally safe. Over time, this draws strong circles, success in healing, advice jobs, or creative work, plus real inner peace from true bonds. Spot 61/7 in your birth date sum, name total, or Life Path, and it promises easy trust and wins if you stick to your special style. Pause, sense hearts around you, act on your insights, and trust your gut for fixes that last forever.

## 70/7.

In numerology, 70/7 marks a deeply thoughtful person. The cypher boosts the main 7 energy (7+0=7), making inner focus and quiet wisdom sharper. Both "listen" and "secret" fully vibrate to 70, linking this number to hidden truths and silent insight. People with 70/7 go inward like a calm lake. They listen without talking, sense unspoken hurts, and keep secrets safe like treasures. This turns them into trusted advisors or healers who fix deep problems others overlook. Spot 70/7 in birth dates or name sums. It brings a life of quiet strength, strong bonds from real listening, and spiritual growth if you embrace silence each day.

## 25/7.

In numerology, 25/7 marks the birth of talented musicians and painters, gifted people with a bright, curious mind that always explores.

It reduces to 7 (2+5=7), blending 2's gentle sensitivity and harmony, 5's free creative energy that loves change, and 7's deep insight into an artistic force. This turns inner visions into sounds and colors that touch people's hearts deeply. These folks have a natural spark for art. Their mind focuses like a laser, they question everything, dive into feelings and ideas on their own, study details from every side, and make bold choices from personal truth. A 25/7 musician might play strings that bring back lost loves or dreams, creating healing melodies on the spot. Painters spot hidden patterns in light and shadow, layering canvases with stories that change each time you look, all from 7's urge to uncover life's mysteries through art. Life rewards them when they follow this path: packed shows, gallery fans, or worldwide quiet fame from heartfelt work. But a wandering mind can lead to unfinished songs or sketches if not focused. Spot 25/7 in your Life Path (birth date sum), Destiny (full name letters), or phone sums. It promises creative wins, loyal fans who understand your depth, and peace from your own choices. Set quiet time to sketch or play freely, journal your questions to hone analysis, ignore others' doubts, and share one piece weekly to gain speed. Over time, your art creates a lasting legacy beyond trends, making 25/7 the top code for souls who reveal the universe's secrets through music and paint.

## 52/7.

In numerology, 52/7 mixes 5's sharp, curious mind, 2's kind, peacekeeping heart, and 7's deep, honorable thinking. This creates a unique seeker who finds answers with grace. The 5 adds curiosity that questions life from every angle, always seeking truth below the surface. 2 brings a gentle, giving nature that ends fights and shares wisdom without ego. 7 tops it with profound inner analysis, making someone who explores big mysteries calmly and respectfully. People with 52/7 shine as quiet investigators. They spot hidden problems, listen to heal splits, and decide with thoughtful honor that builds trust quickly. Jobs in counseling, research, or creative planning fit their kind insights fix real issues without fuss. Life goes well when they balance 5's restless search with 2's peace and 7's depth. This leads to respected positions and strong bonds. Spot 52/7 in birth date sums or name totals. It promises meaningful success if you stay grounded: question daily but act kindly, think deeply before speaking, and help freely. Skip balance, and your mind spins; embrace it, and you become the respected guide everyone seeks.

### 34/7.

In numerology, 34/7 reveals life's and nature's hidden mysteries, a key trait of all 7 energies. The 3 at the start brings magnetic words or ideas like beauty, charm, or creativity that grab attention right away. Then 4 makes it solid, turning dreamy secrets into real things you can touch, build, or share. This creates people who uncover nature's riddles through appealing stories or structured art. Examples: a poet sharing forest secrets in perfect rhymes, a designer turning mystic symbols into jewelry, or a scientist drawing stars clearly. 3 draws crowds with shine, 4 makes it endure, and 7 digs deep for truths others miss. Spot 34/7 in birth dates or name sums. It brings a life of quiet finds that amaze people, fame from sharing beauty shaped by inner searches. Note beautiful nature spots each day, sketch them neatly, and tell stories that hint at deep secrets without giving them away.

### 43/7.

In numerology, 43/7 brings a strong sense of justice. The honest, reliable 4 leads first, adding real dignity to every action. The 3 brings maturity and wise growth over time, while the core 7 makes you a good listener who spots deep truths. People with this number stand up for what's right. They notice unfairness quickly, act with true honor, and stay calm like a fair judge in family arguments or work problems. 4's strong base keeps promises and builds trust fast, 3's maturity changes hot tempers into wise leaders, and 7's quiet listening catches hidden hurts others ignore. Spot 43/7 in your birth date sum or name total. It points to a life where justice roles like law, teaching, or fixing community issues earn respect and inner peace. Speak truth kindly each day, listen twice as much as you act, and pick fair choices even if they're tough.

## Number Seven (7): The Seeker

### Positive Traits

These inner depths make 7 the quiet sage of hidden truths.

- Analytical: Dissects deeply. Sees layers others miss.
- Book-lover: Devours pages. Knowledge fuels the soul.
- Deep thinker: Ponders big questions. Mind dives far.
- Dignified: Carries grace. Noble bearing.
- Educator: Shares wisdom. Teaches truths.
- Faith: Trusts the unseen. Spiritual anchor.
- Good mind: Sharp intellect. Thinks clear.
- Great inner strength: Rock inside. Unbreakable core.
- Inspired: Sparks from above. Divine nudges.
- Intuitive: Knows without words. Gut guides true.
- Knowledgeable: A vast well of facts. Ever-learning.
- Logical: Reason rules. Facts first.
- Loves history, antiques, and the arts: Treasures old tales, relics, beauty.
- More spiritual than religious: Seeks essence, skips rituals.
- Musical: Harmonies stir the spirit.
- Nature-lover: Finds God in green. Wild calls.
- Peaceful: Calm waters. Quiet power.
- Perfectionist: Strives for flawless. High standards.
- Poised: Steady poise. Unruffled.
- Refined: Elegant taste. Classy soul.

- Scientific: Probes mysteries. Lab of life.
- Silent: Words weigh heavily. Listens more.
- Spiritual: Soul seeker. Beyond the veil.
- Wise: Ancient eyes. Timeless counsel.

Example: Like a lone scholar in a library tower, unraveling cosmic riddles by candlelight that's 7's secret glow.

<u>**Negative Traits**</u>

These shadows cloud 7's light when isolation grows too thick. Emerge gently.

- Aloof: Distant drift. Hard to reach.
- Argumentative: Debates are endless. Proves points.
- Broods: Stews in thoughts. Darkens mood.
- Cold: Icy shell. Warmth hides.
- Confused: Mind tangles. Lost in fog.
- Either says nothing or doesn't stop talking: Silent or flood. No middle.
- Fearful: Shadows loom. Dread whispers.
- Haughty: Looks down. Pride lifts high.
- Hermit/loner: Retreats alone. Walls up.
- Lives too much in the past: Ghosts cling. Forward stalls.
- Melancholy: Sad haze lingers.
- Nervous: Jitters inside. Edges fray.
- Peculiar: Odd ways. Stands apart.
- Represses emotions: Buries feelings. No release.
- Sly: Cunning glint. Hides intent.
- Secret motives: Plans veiled. Shares little.
- Skeptical: Doubts all. Trusts none.

- Stubborn: Digs heels. Won't shift.
- Suspicious: Eyes narrow. Plots everywhere.
- Unapproachable: Barricade high.
- Unpredictable: Winds shift suddenly.

**Destructive Traits**

These dark veins poison 7's wisdom. Purge with honesty.

- A cheat: Bends rules sly.
- A gossi: Whispers tales.
- Dishonest: Twists truth.
- Evil intent: Schemes harm.
- Faithless: Drops belief.
- Resentments: Poisons brew.
- Sarcastic: Cuts with wit.
- Slyness: Fox in shadows.
- Thief: Takes unseen.
- Unreasonable: Logic lost.

Number 7 unveils secrets pair with violet (its color), quiet woods, and ancient books to deepen insight.

# 8. "Power Earned, Empire Built, eight face infinity's wealth, Ambition fire, Legacy's Throne, Master money, Balance karma force of fortune."

The 8 stands for the law "As Above, So Below." This vibration knows both the Earth (lower circle) and the mind plane (upper circle). It can take an idea and make it real in the material world. 8s and 3s have strong personalities, but 3s are more outgoing. 3s are performers. 8s are more careful and good at business. The 3 looks like two half-moons sharing light, with the left side removed. It shows personality, humor, and fun. The 8 holds power inside, closed tight. The 3 spend on whims. The 8 saves money and handles it well. On its side, 8 looks like scales of balance. This means good judgment and common sense. The 8 brings good balance, health, strength, and energy.

Pythagoras called 8 "Light and Darkness." Darkness means the selfish, money-focused person. Light means the spiritual person who helps those in the dark. This mix of spirit and matter gives 8s inspiration, leadership, and even genius. It is 4 plus 4, the planning skills of 4 doubled. 44 means Mastermind, Prosper, Unlimited.

The 8 also means resurrection. Jesus rose on the eighth day. The 8 shape shows "the below that rises above." It stands for the law "As Above, So Below." By studying humans and the world around us, we understand higher worlds, the universe, and spiritual life.

Ancient people found the 8 shape matches planet orbits. Science now proves it is the natural path for people and animals, too. In 1928, a University of Kansas zoology professor named Asa A. Shaeffer watched people in woods or blindfolded. They walked in figure-8 patterns. So did blindfold swimmers, drivers, and pilots lost in fog; they all moved in spirals. Shaeffer tested animals and even amoebas. He proved spiral motion is a basic trait of all living things (Why Do Some Shoes Squeak? 221).

## 17/8.

17/8 in numerology holds a cosmic secret: legend says God vibrated at this frequency while crafting the universe, as the original cause unseen and mysterious, like the hidden 7 beneath. It reduces to 8 (1+7=8), blending 1's pure spark of creation, 7's mystic depths, and 8's infinite power into the blueprint of all existence. The 17 hums with divine mystery 1 start the big bang, 7 veils the unseen laws of nature, and 8 loops eternity, birthing stars, souls, and cycles from nothing.

People with 17/8 carry this god-vibe: natural creators who sense invisible forces, build empires from whispers, and lead with quiet authority that bends reality. Spot it in Life Path or Destiny for a life touching the unseen success in hidden arts, spiritual business, or inventions that change worlds. Live it by trusting gut mysteries daily; the universe unfolds through you.

## 71/8.

71/8 in numerology shows great inner strength when 7 leads first deep inside the self, 7 fuels 1's drive to master 8's power. The 7 lives within, seeking perfection in quiet ways, turning people into skilled experts at their craft over time. This number crafts souls who build from hidden depths: 7's mystic search for truth sharpens focus, 1 spark bold start, and 8 delivers real-world wins like business empires or art legacies. They work alone first, perfect every detail without show, then step out to lead with rock-solid skill that others follow blindly. Spot 71/8 in birth date sums or name totals for a path of quiet rise fame comes late but sure, from crafts honed flawlessly. Live it by daily solo practice, chase "better" not "done," trust inner pull to 8's gold.

## 26/8.

The number 26/8 is mainly about the physical world things you can touch, do, and build. It comes from 2 + 6 = 8 as the root. The 8 gives extra power to the physical side of 6, like adding muscle to a strong body. The sensitive 2 makes it special, almost like a passionflower: beautiful but quick to react. People with 26/8 can rush into love or make choices on impulse. They must learn self-control to stay balanced. The 2 loves pairs and teamwork thrive in partnerships, whether at work with colleagues or in marriage with a life partner. The 6 brings a real-world focus. It wants to nurture like a parent caring for family or a coach training a team. It takes responsibility for others, often putting home, community, or duties first. Combined with 8's drive, this creates someone vital and active. Think of athletes who train hard, leaders who build teams, or parents who handle big family challenges with energy. The 8 makes 26/8 look successful from the outside. It shows as strength, athletic build, and endless energy. These people often excel in sports, business, or hands-on jobs. We see this clear energy in key 26/8 words: Athlete for pure physical power and discipline, Action for always moving and achieving, Backbone as the strong support others rely on, Grand for big ideas and big results, Majestic like a king or queen with confident command, and Sports for team games or solo feats that demand body and will. Someone who takes responsibility like an executive fits the 8 perfectly. They lead projects, make tough calls, and get results, like a sports coach, business boss, or family head who runs things with firm but fair strength. There is huge power in their ideas and spoken words. The 6 rules of the voice are clear, warm, and persuasive. The 2 adds skill with words, communication, and listening. Together, 26/8 people inspire teams, negotiate deals, or motivate crowds. They shine in speeches, sales, teaching, or counseling. For example, a coach rallies players with fiery talks using 6's voice, and 8's command, or a leader pitches big plans that win support with 2's sensitivity and grand vision. 26/8 has highs but pitfalls. Impulse from 2 + 6 can lead to rash love affairs or overwork, and the strong 8 might push too hard, ignoring rest or feelings. The lesson is to build self-control through routines like exercise, meditation, or journaling, and channel energy into healthy outlets such as sports, family duties, or creative projects. In daily life, think of a gym owner who coaches clients showing physical 6 and athletic 8, or a wedding planner who pairs couples perfectly with 2's partnership love. In numerology, 26/8 teaches to use your body, voice, and heart to lead and care, but always with control.

## 62/8.

When the 6 comes first in 62/8, it creates a strong sense of duty to a person, place, or thing like a caregiver committed to family, a manager to a team, or a teacher to knowledge. These people are very smart. They learn more through sharp intellect and logic than through gut feelings or emotions. This shows in words like Administrator for organizing with clear thinking, Commissioner for leading official roles, Contributions for giving wisely, and Exercises for disciplined mental or physical practice. The 6 stands for a body, think of anything with six sides, like a cube, symbolizing form and structure. In Contributions, the gift is your own body or effort. In Procreation, it's about giving a body its first form through birth. Philosophy becomes a body of knowledge, a structured collection of deep ideas. The 6 is the womb of life, shown as a lower circle full of potential, and it's the domestic number for home and family harmony. The 2 crave marriage, partnerships, and building a family nest. At its heart, the 6 acts as the Cosmic parent, wise understanding, always ready to give selflessly like a universal caregiver. The 2 knows good and evil deeply; it sees both sides of every issue, so it truly gets people's beliefs, struggles, and inner needs with empathy. The 8 brings top-notch judgment, raw strength, and natural leadership to guide others forward. People with 62/8 energy often shine as administrators, family leaders, teachers, or philosophers. They build strong homes, mentor with intellect, and give quietly like a principal running a school smoothly or a parent nurturing kids through tough changes. Strengths include mental clarity for big decisions, balanced views that heal conflicts, and staying power for long-term goals. Challenges of 62/8 are overthinking will block feelings, or duty might lead to burnout. Balance it with rest and heart connections. Grow by studying philosophy, volunteering secretly, or starting a family project. Famous vibes Think wise leaders like philosophers or midwives symbolizing the procreation cycle. In numerology, 62/8 reminds us: Use intellect and care to build bodies of family, knowledge, or community while life's door always opens to new beginnings.

## 35/8.

35/8 in numerology counts as a very lucky number, full of creativity from 3 and freedom from 5. These two blend smoothly into 8, the shape that stands for endless good things, like a circle with no start or stop. People born with this number or seeing it in their chart live full of new ideas and brave steps. The 3 brings fun talk, art skills, and happy ways to share thoughts that pull others in quickly. Add 5's love for change, travel, and no rules, and you get someone who jumps into fresh starts without fear, like trying new jobs, places, or hobbies that turn into big wins. Then 8 takes all that energy and makes it last forever: money grows steadily, fame builds over the years, and success loops back again and again without end. Luck sticks to them because they mix play with smart work. A songwriter hits top charts from wild tunes, a seller grows shops worldwide from quick deals, or an inventor fixes old problems with a free mind; each win and plants a seed for more. No hard luck spells; life feels open and full if they keep creating and moving. Spot 35/8 in your birth date total (add day, month, year step by step), full name sum, or Life Path spot. It promises long joy, strong cash flow, and a free spirit wins. Live it simply: draw one fun idea each day, try a small change weekly, trust the 8 loop to bring back bigger. Stay true, and fortune runs non-stop like a river to the sea.

## 53/8.

53/8 in numerology shows a tough road to reach goals when 5 starts the mix, leading to 8, since 5 craves freedom and skips discipline often. The 5 brings wild change, fun risks, and hate for rules, great for new ideas, but bad for finish lines. It jumps jobs, drops plans mid-way, or chases shiny things over steady wins. Then, 3 adds talk and play, making distractions even stronger before 8's power can build money or fame. People with this number start strong with smart moves, but their business ideas fizzle easily, books are half-done, and fitness quits fast. Life tests patience hard till they learn to chain 5's fire to 8's grind. Spot 53/8 in birth totals or name sums—it warns of scattered wins unless fixed. Beat it by small daily rules: one task locked each day, say no to fun pulls, and track steps weekly. Over time, freedom serves power, not blocks it.

## Number Eight (8): The Achiever

### Positive Traits

These powerhouse qualities drive 8 to build empires and lead strongly.

- Ambitious: Hunger for heights. Climbs relentless.
- Capable: Handles any task. Skills run deep.
- Dependable: Rock, you lean on. Always delivers.
- Efficient: Cuts waste. Gets straight to wins.
- Executive ability: Runs the show. Big-picture command.
- Fine leadership abilities: Guides teams to glory. Inspires action.
- Good at starting projects and getting others to finish: Sparks ideas, delegates the grind.
- Good judge of character: Reads people true. Spots fakes.
- Good judgment: Wise calls. Sees clear.
- Handles money wisely: Builds wealth smart. No leaks.
- Likes nice things: Enjoys luxury. Earns the fine.

- Makes a good boss: Firm hand, fair rule.
- Musical and/or athletic ability: Rhythm or strength flows.
- Organized: Systems sharp. Chaos tamed.
- Physical stamina: Endures long. Tireless body.
- Practical: Grounded moves. Dreams with feet.
- Prudent: Plays safe. Thinks steps ahead.
- Realistic: Faces facts. No illusions.
- Sets goals: Targets locked. Hits them hard.
- Successful: Wins big. Results prove it.

Example: Like a CEO launching a venture, picking the team, and watching profits soar that's 8 mastering the game.

### Negative Traits

These rough edges grind when 8's drive overrides heart. Soften with balance.

- Careless with money: Splurges wildly. Wealth slips.
- Hard: Tough shell. Unbending ways.
- Impatient: Pushes fast. Waits none.
- Materialistic: Chases stuff. Loses soul.
- Needs philosophical study: Craves deeper wisdom. Surface won't do.
- Pushy: Shoves ahead. Others trampled.
- Represses feelings: Locks emotions tight.
- Thoughtless: Acts blindly to impact.

### Destructive Traits

These storms wreck 8's power into ruin. Channel with ethics.

- Abusive: Lashes power wrongly.
- Cruel: Hurts cold.

- Demanding: Takes all, gives little.
- Ignorant: Blind to truth.
- Intolerant: Crushes differences.
- No feelings for others: Heart iced over.
- Revengeful: Strikes back fiercely.
- Schemer: Plots dark.
- Temper: Erupts hot.
- Uncultured: Rough manners.
- Unscrupulous: Wins any cost.

Empower 8 with black or dark green (its colors), strong teas, and goal journals for focused rise.

# 9."Humanity's healer, Legacy's light Release past, Embrace all, Old soul, New world, Completions call, Infinite compassion."

The 9 shows the unlimited soul expression of all human things and their laws. Its key phrase is universal service. The 9 is the circle of continuity. The tail is a life force that keeps it moving. Math proves this. Take any numbers. Subtract them reversed from each other. The remainder always reduces to 9.

Pythagoras called 9 "Good and Evil." Being wise, 9 knows the difference. Because 9 understands true love, it sees only good even in faults (Vibration, 63). A 9s means the person is born to give loving service. This comes through jobs or the arts. It can use traits from earlier numbers to understand and play any role. So, 9 is called "the stage where drama unfolds." The 9 is emotional, so it can "remote." This vibration fits actors and some politicians. That is why actors want politics, and politicians speak well. Both serve people and love applause. Turn the 9 upside down, and you get 6: the voice that must speak, the vibration that cares for home and community.

### 18/9.

The 18 is sensitive and friendly. It always works toward a goal that ends in 9. People call it "the goal-setting number." The 1 means the self, its wins, and feels. The 8 means body strength, rhythm, movement, music, and sports. The 9 is very dramatic. Music runs strong in 9s, and the 9 is 3 times 3, so it has many talents.

Many actors, and likely politicians, have a big EGO (18/9). The 9 has a large head and strong self (1) plus power (8). That same circle means a mind full of knowledge, not just ego. The 9 naturally loves LAW (9). It wants law and order.

## 81/9.

81/9 in numerology means people with big goals. The number 8 gives clear sight and power. Number 1 makes them good at leading. Since it adds to 9, they use this to help all people. These people want to win big and help the world. They see goals clearly, start fast, and lead teams. They build big things like jobs for the poor or free help for the sick. No small plans, only world good. See 81/9 in the birth date, add or name total. It brings big wins if you stay clear, lead boldly, and give back. Do one help act each week to grow strong.

## 27/9.

This number shows deep feelings, spiritual wisdom, creative power, and love for beauty and the arts. The 2 adds loving and teamwork qualities. It works quietly as a peacemaker behind the scenes. The 7 adds calm grace, quiet reserve, and a wish for study and perfection. The 9 stands for all humanity, people, and brotherly love. Advanced Agree Breath Educated Gentle Honest Public Quiet School Whole World. See how one letter changes "breath" and "breadth"? BREATH (27/9) is unseen like air. First Cause came into matter (2) and breathed life into man's nose. Man became a living soul. The soul is the hidden center of the body (7). A body with a soul belongs to all people (9).

## 72/9.

72/9 Spiritual, when 7 comes first, deep inner feelings lead to sharp, analytical powers. Improvisation. People who seek help 2 by reaching the subconscious mind 7 sometimes use Hypnotherapy 72/9. The 3 cares and acts with kindness in everything. The 6 takes responsibility, even for heavy loads. The 9 stands for honesty and justice. The 9 loves travel, when 3 follows 9, trips go further; the 3 means long-distance travel.

## 36/9.

The 9 feels people and places deeply. Bad feelings hurt it. It gets restless and unhappy, forgets high goals and ideals, and falls into self-indulgence. There, it wastes energy. The 9 is a true test number. It must forget themself and think of others more.

## 63/9.

The 63/9 wants to work for everyone's good. Here are humanitarians and missionaries. Both 6 and 9 are humanitarian numbers. The 6 cares for family, friends, the old, and the young. The 3 wants to do good and bring smiles. The 9 gives to all humanity. It seeks no reward. It feels inspired. Words that total 63/9 are: Corporation, Experienced, Inspiration, Introduction, Millionaire. When 3 goes negative, it holds itself back. The 9 brings things to an end.

The 9 finds true happiness as a 63/9 and by serving others who work for the well-being of all humanity. The true 9 uses its gifts to help others.

## 45/9.

45/9 merges 4's grounded intuition with 5's psychic intensity, peaking in 9's universal wisdom to grant extraordinary mystical gifts like prophetic dreams or energy healing that set bearers apart, though overload demands daily grounding to shine ethically. Together, these show numerology's dance: early digits spark tendencies, the root seals purpose, and balance turns potential pitfalls into profound strengths for lives of impact.

## 54/9.

54/9 in numerology combines a sharp intellect with solid execution, driving toward 9's ultimate fulfillment in service and wisdom. The 5 brings a probing, curious mind that loves to explore deep questions, uncover hidden truths, and chase knowledge without limits. Think of relentless researchers or inventors who dig until answers emerge. Paired with 4's organized strength, this turns ideas into reality: plans get structured, tasks completed step-by-step, and loose ends tied up efficiently, avoiding the scatter of pure 5 energy. Reduced to 9, it channels this mental power and discipline into humanitarian or spiritual completion. Success feels whole when it helps others, like writing books that guide souls, leading teams to solve world problems, or mastering arts that uplift humanity. People with 54/9 excel in fields blending brains and order, such as science for social good, teaching ancient wisdom, or building systems that heal. Spot it in birth dates or name sums for a path of discovery, action, and meaningful legacy. Nurture it by scheduling daily inquiry time while committing to one finish line weekly.

## Number 9 Expanded: The Humanitarian Compassionate

In numerology, 9 crowns the single digits as the universal number, embodying completion, wisdom, and selfless service. Linked to Mars (fiery drive for justice) and Neptune (spiritual compassion), it channels cosmic energy toward humanity's upliftment. People with strong 9 vibrations act as global healers, artists, and reformers think Gandhi's non-violence or Mother Teresa's devotion. Yet, imbalance leads to dissipation, mirroring unchanneled Mars aggression turned inward.

**Positive Traits:**

- Open-minded: Embraces diverse views without prejudice, fostering unity.
- Universal affection: Feels brotherly love for all, transcending personal ties.
- Caring & Humanitarian heart: Driven to aid strangers as kin.
- Compassionate: Deep empathy moves them to action.
- Creative & Theatrical talent: Expresses soul through art, drama, or performance.

- Generous: Gives freely time, resources, love without expectation.
- Exceptional artist: Channels divine inspiration into masterpieces.
- Elevated ideals: Pursues noble causes like equality and peace.
- Philanthropic: Builds legacies through charity and advocacy.
- Romantic & Ultimate lover: Loves profoundly, seeking soul-deep bonds.
- Selfless: Sacrifices for the greater good.
- Deeply thoughtful: Considers others' needs intuitively.

**Negative Traits:**

- Aimless: Drifts without a clear purpose, scattering energy.
- Overburdened: Takes on too much, leading to exhaustion.
- Ultra-sensitive: Feels others' pain intensely, overwhelming the self.
- Changeable: Shifts moods or loyalties unpredictably.
- Frustrated: Battles inner discontent from unmet ideals.
- Impolite: Blurts truths harshly in emotional surges.
- Overly emotional: Flooded by feelings, hard to regulate.
- Resentful: Harbors grudges when generosity goes unreturned.
- Blunt: Speaks without filters, wounding unintentionally.
- Careless: Neglects details in pursuit of big-picture dreams.
- Unfulfilled: Chases perfection, feeling perpetually shortchanged.

**Destructive Traits:**

- Vices: Falls into escapism like excess or addiction.
- Bitter: Turns compassion into cynicism.
- Wastes away: Dissipates vitality through indulgence.

- Immoral: Bends ethics for emotional whims.
- Deceitful: Hides truths to protect fragile ideals.
- Clingy: Possesses loved ones out of fear of loss.
- Crude: Lashes out vulgarly when ideals shatter.

For balance, 9s thrive with grounding practices like meditation or gemstones (e.g., amethyst for Neptune clarity). In your life path, a 9 calls you to release the past and serve the collective, transforming personal pain into planetary healing.

# Master Number:

In numerology, the foundational numbers 1 through 9 form the core vibrations of existence, with all compound numbers reducing to these by summing their digits—such as 15 becoming 1+5=6. However, master numbers like 11, 22, 33, and beyond stand apart. These powerful configurations carry amplified, high-frequency energies, often signaling "old souls" with a karmic mission to uplift humanity. Unlike standard reductions, master numbers remain intact for those attuned to their intensity, demanding discipline to channel their force without burnout.

People born with master numbers in their life path (calculated from birth date), expression number (from full name), or soul urge (from vowels in name) often feel a restless, electric tension. This nervous energy fuels visionary pursuits but can lead to anxiety, sensitivity, or overwhelm if not directed. Parents of children with these numbers should prioritize structured outlets like arts, meditation, or leadership roles to build resilience early.

## Core Master Numbers and Their Categories

While 11 and 22 are the most recognized, the full spectrum extends to rarer forms: 33, 44, 55, 66, 77, 88, and 99. They divide into two vibrational poles, inspired by the Hermetic principle "As Above, So Below."

## As Above (Spiritual/Intuitive Focus)

These odd-numbered masters attune to higher realms, emphasizing psychic gifts, enlightenment, and collective awakening. They thrive in roles like spiritual teaching, healing, or prophecy.

- 11 (The Intuitive Messenger): Heightens inspiration and spiritual insight. Visionaries like channelers or artists channel divine downloads, but imbalance brings hypersensitivity or illusion.

- 33 (The Master Teacher): Embodies compassionate mastery, uplifting through selfless love. Think healers or philanthropists who nurture souls on a global scale; root reduces to 6 (nurturing harmony).
- 55 (The Spiritual Innovator): Drives radical change with freedom-loving energy. Ideal for pioneers in holistic tech or metaphysics, though restlessness can scatter focus; roots to 1 (leadership).
- 77 (The Mystic Seeker): Dives into profound truths, excelling in research, philosophy, or occult studies. Profound intuition borders on genius, but isolation looms if ungrounded; roots to 5 (adventure).
- 99 (The Universal Humanitarian): Culminates in selfless service, dissolving ego for world love. Activists or spiritual leaders embody this, yet exhaustion hits without boundaries; roots to 9 (completion).

**So Below (Manifestation/Practical Focus)**

Even-numbered masters ground ethereal energy into reality, building lasting structures, abundance, and societal impact.

- 22 (The Master Builder): Transforms dreams into empires, architects, CEOs, or innovators who manifest on massive scales. Discipline turns potential into legacy; roots to 4 (stability).
- 44 (The Systematic Enforcer): Masters discipline and infrastructure, enforcing justice within vast organizations. Unyielding work ethic builds enduring systems; roots to 8 (power).
- 66 (The Nurturer of Communities): Fosters harmony in families, villages, or nations through unconditional love. Healers or community leaders shine here; roots to 3 (creativity).

- 88 (The Abundance Architect): Commands ethical wealth and influence, turning karma into prosperity. Business magnates or philanthropists who redistribute riches, roots to 7 (wisdom).
- 99 (Dual Role): Bridges both categories, universalizing love into tangible change.

**Author's Note:** In my years studying numerology, I've found that while the full spectrum of master numbers, the big four 11, 22, 33, and 44, stand out as the most practical and prevalent in everyday charts.

**11.**

## Master Number 11: "Intuition and Inspiration" - The Master Messenger.

This master number embodies the highest intuitive and inspirational energies, serving as the "As Above, So Below" bridge between spiritual insight and earthly action. Rooted in the number 2, it amplifies sensitivity, diplomacy, and partnership into prophetic vision and enlightened communication.

**Positive and Shadow Expressions.**: Light side words resonate with: Awakening, Channel, Clarity, Dreamer, Faith, Idealism, Insight, Visionary. Symbolism includes the gateway arch (11 as twin pillars), rainbow bridges, and lightning flashes of revelation. Shadow warns through: Alarmist, Delusional, Fanatic, Nervous, Overwhelm, intuition twisted into anxiety or escapism.

**Life Path and Occupations.**: 33/11 individuals shine as spiritual leaders, inventors, artists, psychics, healers, motivational speakers, or mediators, channeling higher wisdom into practical inspiration. They excel where empathy meets innovation.

**The Elevated Voice of 11.**: Root 2's gentle harmony elevates to electrifying oratory that awakens souls, with 11-word phrases like Illuminate and Prophecy evoking messages that pierce the veil.

## 22.

**Master Number 22: "Master Builder" - The Practical Visionary.** The most powerful master number, 22, turns cosmic dreams into tangible empires, rooted in 4's discipline and structure but amplified for global impact. "Let there be light" manifests through 22's blueprint mastery.

**Positive and Shadow Expressions:** Positive: Architect, Foundation, Masterplan, Monumental, Realization, Structure, Transformation. Symbols: pyramids (22 as cosmic architecture), double rainbows. Shadows: Oppression, Rigidity, Tyranny, vision corrupted into control.

**Life Path and Occupations.:** 22s dominate large-scale building: architects, engineers, politicians, CEOs, philanthropists, revolutionizing industries or nations. They build lasting legacies from a higher purpose.

**The Elevated Voice of 22:** Root 4's methodical speech becomes commanding vision-casting, with 22-word phrases like Blueprint and Dominion forging reality through authoritative declaration.

## 33.

### Master Number 33: "Selfless Giving" - The Master Teacher of Compassion

This master number stands as the ultimate vibration of spiritual giving, embodying the "As Above" principle by prioritizing the spiritual needs of others above all. At its foundation lies the root number 6, which pulses with the energies of home, love, family, service, and responsibility. These 6 demands to make its voice heard, whether through nurturing family dynamics or devoted career paths, silence is not an option for its fulfillment. Those attuned to this vibration live it profoundly. Consider Jesus, who was 33 years old when he gave his life for humanity.

## Positive and Shadow Expressions.

The light of 33 reveals itself in resonant words like: Ability, Angelic, Blessing, Inner, Inward, Peaceful, Potence, and Unique. These capture its divine potential. Symbolism abounds: The diamond, vibrating to 33, serves as the ultimate spiritual gift from a man to his betrothed, representing eternal, unbreakable love.

## Life Path and Occupations.

Individuals with 33 prominent in their name or Birth Path number possess acute sensitivity to others' needs. They pour themselves into caring and comforting roles, often at personal cost. Occupations align with root 6: healing professions (nurses, therapists), teaching, counseling, homemaking, hospitality, or community service. 33 elevates these to spiritual missions, turning everyday service into acts of divine love. Family-linked 33-word phase underscores this: think of bonds forged in sacrifice and harmony.

## The Elevated Voice of 33

The root 6 governs the voice, the tool of expression. When amplified to 33, it reaches its zenith in the great orator and teacher, whose words inspire masses toward higher truths. Voice- and sound-related 33-words like Quality and Resound evoke this power: speeches that echo eternally, lessons that transform souls.

# 44.

## Master Number 44: "Master of Manifestation" - The Cosmic Architect.

Beyond 22, 44 anchors divine will into unbreakable earthly systems, rooted in amplified 8's power and abundance for humanity's upliftment.

**Positive and Shadow Expressions.**: Lights: Authority, Discipline, Empire, Endurance, Legacy, Systems, Wealth (for good). Symbols:

eternal flames, unbreakable fortresses. Shadows: Cruelty, Dictatorship, Exploitation, and power abused.

**Life Path and Occupations.**: 44s lead transformative enterprises: industrial magnates, reformers, spiritual empire-builders, ensuring abundance flows ethically at scale.

**The Elevated Voice of 44**: Root 8's executive tone masters decree-like commands that shape civilizations, 44-word phrases like Dominion and Sovereignty enacting heaven's order on earth.

# Kamic Debt.

In occult science, your soul selects a small portion of its past karma—known as Sanchita—before birth to address in this life. This portion is called Prarabdha. It's like agreeing with God or the universe to learn tough lessons through real-life events. The four karmic debt numbers reveal this old karma: 13/4 connects to Rahu dosha; 14/5 to Budha dosha; 16/7 to Ketu dosha; and 19/1 to Surya dosha. These numbers appear unreduced in sums from your birth date, name total, or other chart areas, highlighting issues from your past life.

Before birth, your soul is in a planning stage. It reviews all past actions in Sanchita karma and picks just the right amount of Prarabdha for this lifetime.

- Sanchita Karma: Total "karmic pile" from all past lives—stored like a cosmic bank.
- Prarabdha Karma: A small, selected portion of your soul chooses before birth to face this lifetime.

Each debt number links to the negative side of a planet, or dosha, which intensifies life's challenges. You spot them in your Life Path number (from adding your birth date) or Destiny number (from adding letters in your full name). They serve as warning signs until you master the lesson. Your soul enters a "planning realm." It reviews Sanchita, picks bite-sized Prarabdha for growth. Think of it as contracting with God/Universe for hard lessons via real events, painful but purposeful.

**Where They Appear (Unreduced!):**

- Life Path: Birth date sum (DD+MM+YYYY).
- Destiny/Expression: Full birth name letters (Pythagorean chart).
- Soul Urge: Vowels only.

- Personality: Consonants.
- Other: Phone, address, maturity numbers.

## 13/4 Karmic Debt

The 13/4 karmic debt means Rahu dosha in simple terms. It points to old karma from past lives where you dodged work, chased false dreams, or acted greedily. Your soul picked this Prarabdha to fix in this life through hard, real-world events.

Signs You Have It: Sudden troubles hit, you feel directionless, or you start projects but rarely finish. Jobs flop, plans shift quickly, or bad habits drag you down. It peaks in your 30s or 40s.

Main Lesson: Learn steady daily work. Use lists, follow routines, and build step by step. Change lazy habits into strong ones.

People with 13 karmic debt face lots of frustration and must work extra hard on every task. See it as payback from a past life full of laziness, using others, and bad choices. Obstacles keep coming; you have to beat them over and over. The key to success with 13 is focus. A big temptation is shortcuts, but they often lead to regret and the urge to quit.

## Tips to Reduce Difficulties:

- Give 100% effort to your work.
- Step up and take on more than your share of tasks.
- Wear a brown gemstone on your middle finger.
- Chant "Om Raam Rahave Namah" 108 times on Saturdays.
- Skip food after sunset once a week; donate black seeds to the poor.
- Check your birth numbers yearly. 13 turns into plain 4 when you succeed.

**Ask Yourself:**

- Am I following a step-by-step process toward my goal?
- Do I let self-doubt and insecurity block my goals?
- What have I done to explore my creative potential?

## 14/5 Karmic Debt

The 14/5 karmic debt points to Budha dosha, Mercury's shadow side. It stems from past lives where you abused freedom, lied, or let your mind wander without focus, creating undone karma. Your soul chose this Prarabdha to clear now.

Signs You Have It: Life feels restless, you switch jobs, chase thrills, or talk big but do little. Relationships fail from deceit or lack of boundaries, and plans scatter like the wind. It's strongest until ages 35-40.

Main Lesson: Gain control over your choices. Use freedom wisely, stay honest, and focus on one step at a time. Build trust through real actions.

The 14 karmic debt comes from past lives where you misused human freedom. You may have been a prisoner or slave before. Now, life forces you to adapt to constant changes and surprises; you must stay flexible. You risk becoming trapped by your own freedom through overindulgence in food or sex. The key is commitment. Life feels like a rollercoaster, but it heads the right way if you focus on your goals.

**Tips to Reduce Difficulties:**

- Learn from experiences to avoid repeating mistakes.
- Curb your appetite by avoiding things you might get addicted to.
- Stay focused, keep your eyes on goals, and finish them.
- Use tools to stay on task, like day timers or to-do lists.
- Channel your creativity through step-by-step discipline.
- Find something to commit to and stick with it.

- Wear a green emerald stone on your little finger.
- Chant "Om Budhaya Namah" 108 times on Wednesdays.
- Eat green veggies; give books or green cloth to kids weekly.
- Watch yearly 14 shifts to steady 5 when lessons sink in.

**Ask Yourself:**

- Does anyone outside of me really hold me back?
- Where do I need more discipline and focus in my life?
- What do I need to do for more freedom? Am I willing to do it?

## 16/7 Karmic Debt

The 16/7 karmic debt ties to Ketu dosha, Mercury's shadowy twin from past lives. Back then, pride, isolation, or fake spirituality left unfinished karma. Your soul chose this Prarabdha before birth to heal through real inner work and humble connections.

When 16 appears in core numbers, it brings a cycle of destruction and rebirth. This leads to higher consciousness. The 16 karmic debts can be a road to progress and deep spiritual growth. But it's often painful, coming after ego buildup. Life challenges your big plans, and you make choices that break down what you've built, like a self-destructive career move or a dumb act that ruins a great relationship. The 16/7 always rises and falls. People with 16/7 karmic debt had romantic affairs in a past life.

Signs You Have It: Sudden losses strike hard like broken ties, career crashes, or deep loneliness. Ego blocks happiness, or you hide behind spiritual talk without true change. It peaks early, eases after 35.

Main Lesson: Let go of the lonely throne. Find real wisdom in silence, connect hearts openly, and serve without showing off.

**Tips to Reduce Difficulties:**

- Learn to trust the universe's process.

- Build more faith in yourself.
- Stop second-guessing, listen to your intuition.
- Avoid isolating yourself more than is healthy.
- Wear a cat's eye stone on the middle finger.
- Chant "Om Ketave Namah" 108 times on Tuesdays.
- Feed dogs; spend time alone in nature weekly.
- Yearly checks show 16 fades to calm 7 as you grow free.

**Ask Yourself:**

- How have my tough life lessons been perfect for me?
- Have insecurities or perfectionism held me back?
- Where do I have trust issues in my life?

**19/1 Karmic Debt**

The 19/1 karmic debt links to Surya dosha, the Sun's dark side from past lives. In those lives, selfishness, power grabs, or ignoring others created bad karma. Your soul chose this Prarabdha karma before birth to learn true leadership through life's back-and-forth.

Signs You Have It: Life challenges your ego with failed leadership roles, family arguments, or lonely battles. Careers peak, then drop from selfish decisions, health problems occur (like eyes or heart issues), or delays with kids. It's hardest until ages 35-40, then eases up.

Main Lesson: Move from ruling alone to guiding others without ego. Lead by lifting people, sharing recognition, and building silent inner strength instead of flaunting it.

People with 19 karmic debts must learn independence and the right way to use power. Life pushes you to face and beat challenges through your own efforts. You stubbornly turn down help. Your independence is self-chosen; you just refuse to hear others or accept their help or advice. This debt can feel like a prison you built yourself if you don't embrace how we all depend on each other and need love.

**Tips to Reduce Difficulties:**

- Learn to ask for help.
- Accept help and guidance from others.
- Resist being selfish, especially to get ahead.
- Wear a polished ruby stone on your ring finger.
- Chant "Om Suryaya Namah" 108 times every Sunday at sunrise.
- Offer water to the Sun; donate wheat or copper to those in need each day.
- Check your charts yearly. 19/1 turns into pure 1 as you grow and clear the debt.

**Ask Yourself:**

- How do I use my creative energy?
- What am I doing to care for my body?
- Can I surrender and let go easily? If not, why?
- Have I found the courage to stand out and be different?

# Power of Words in Numerology.

Words in numerology vibrate with specific energies based on letter-to-number conversion. Influencing personal power, relationships, and manifestation as a fresh, original guide

## Core principles

Each letter translates to a number in Systems like Pythagorean (A=1, B=2, and Z=8), Name Vibration in numerology. Words, especially Names, carry potent vibration energy in numerology, shaping destiny through letter-number conversions. Words are alive; people speak them into being, this life on in the fourth dimension, and become your home when you cross over. The vibration of spoken words can be measured by their frequency, forming visible patterns captured on a device known as the Ediphone.

"The words of a wise man's mouth are gracious, but the lips of a fool will ruin him (Ecclesiastes 10.12).

## What Are the Letters?

A photo can bring back many memories. A picture tells a full story without any words. A logo holds deep meaning, and some have become famous symbols. That is what letters were first made to do. Letters are more than just tools to make written words. Each letter's shape was chosen with care to show its true meaning. The shapes come from basic forms like point, line, circle, triangle, and square. These shapes create an energy field with their lines. This shapes their special traits. Think deeply about each shape, and you will feel its unique power. For example, the circle has no edges, so it shows endless energy. The square has edges, so it feels very different. To make the world, God used the only thing that existed: Himself. So, these basic shapes show His qualities. Here is the key idea: The sound of each letter makes a vibration that matches those qualities. The shape helps you remember them. The letter's place in the alphabet shows its vibration speed when you think or say it. This makes everything fit together in a clear way. Hebrew Kabbalists made their letters and numbers work together: **A** means 1, **B** means 2, **C** means 3, **D** means 4, and so on. Each letter is like a picture with a clear meaning. But if you learn its symbols, you see even deeper truths. That alphabet shaped hundreds of others. The sounds stayed the same as they came to us, but the shapes changed to fit our uses. Still, the main qualities remain true. We will see this when we study words. As a group, letters describe every kind of life event. Mystics say that if you think deeply about a symbol, it will show its secrets. Your mind will grow. The letters hold answers to all life's problems. Each one is a path on the Tree of Life.

Here's a rewritten version of your text in basic English. I preserved the original meaning while using simple words, short sentences, and clear structure to make it easy to read. We look at a letter from every side. The top half stands for the mind, thoughts, and spirit world. The bottom half stands for the body, matter, and Earth world. A letter that looks the same upside down, like **H, N, O, S, X,** works on both sides. This can make the letter's power twice as strong. A letter that turns into a different letter when upside down has two sides. For example, **M** has a strong base on the ground, so it means order and steadiness. Upside down, it becomes W, which reaches up for spiritual help during emotional trouble (A Guide to Cosmic Numbers, 125-6). The events in your life show up in the letters of your name. Each letter shows the type of event. The root number of the letter shows how long it lasts: **A, J, S**: one year **D, M, V**: four years **G, P, Y**: seven years **B, K, T**: two years **E, N, W:** five years **H, Q, Z**: eight years **C, L, U**: three years **F, O, X**: six years **I, R:** nine years Each name part works on its own. The full name works as one. Each event comes from the good or bad side of the letters and their numbers. They shape our lives, but we choose our path by how we face each event. The California Institute of Numerical Research, Inc., tested this fully. They started to study number vibrations deeply. Numerologists from everywhere agreed with their results. Happy with the answers, the group ended after 25 years of work. Names can sound the same but be spelled differently, like Sowmya and Soumya. The letters matter as much as the sound. When we say a name, we picture the letters in our mind. Their numbers send a mathematical message of vibration. The first letter of your name shows your true nature, your first reaction to things, and how you face problems. In the same way, the first letter of a word shows its true nature. Sometimes the shape alone tells us this.

When we look at the meaning of each letter, we see this is true for all words. But the most important thing is your name. Those special letters are God's gifts given to you at birth. You can choose to use their full good power. The letters may look different, but each has its own vibration speed. Numbers are a language everyone understands.

# Letter In Detail.

## A.

**A-1,** Old mysteries say God made Aleph (say "awl-ef") as the first letter. Its sound was needed to breathe out all other letters. It is God's breath. It stands for the element of Air. It is a "Mother Letter" because it is one of the main parts of creation. Aleph means "ox head." Its star sign is Taurus, the sign of making new life in the body. You can see this star group in the sky each spring. That is when the Earth gets warm in mild places. Flowers grow to start a new time of life. The ox head shape looks like the uterus. The horns are like the fallopian tubes. All these points to making a new physical life. Aleph is the breath of life in every person. Adam was not alive until God breathed life into his nose (Genesis 2:7). This shows when human life truly starts. It is not at conception, when the body just begins to form, that the new body is formed.

Like Adam, it becomes a living being; this is why astrologers care more about birth time than conception time. Aleph is the key life force in everything. It is the breath of life. It flows even through things that do not move. Nothing can live without Air. So, Aleph is in height, depth, and the path between them. You can see this in the shape of the English letter A and the Hebrew letter Aleph (similar to an **N**). Aleph is not a vowel. It sounds like soft breath from the throat. This breath carries creative words, giving them sound and life. Greek had no sound like Hebrew Aleph's throat sound. So, they used it for their **A** vowel and called it Alpha, meaning "first." The Romans took it from the Greeks and named it **"A."** All Indo-European languages start with **A**. They kept the same shape. It resembles a diaphragm, which pushes air out. **A** has three lines, like Aleph. They stand for the Creative Principle: Will, Wisdom, and Activity. A teaches self-control. The middle line splits the top spirit world from the bottom body world. This gives A balance of energies to learn this lesson.

**A** look like a man standing steady on two feet. It shows starting things and leading. **A** means ambition. In a name, it adds strong character. In a year, you feel in charge. You want to lead, not follow. You may feel too proud. I want to lead. **A** means Aggressive. When things go bad, **A** gets upset. It does best when making fast choices. Stays calm with feet on the ground. Upset (upside down), it balances on a point. If it waits too long, it loses balance. **A** stand for one, like "a house" or "a person." The bad side of A is self-centered, stubborn, and selfish. It is 1, so it sees itself as number one. Aleph is a soft breath and an Air element. So, people get colds and lung problems easily. If A is the first letter or vowel in your name, never smoke. In a year, smoking is extra risky. **A** must learn good breathing. Let lungs fill with each breath. Fresh air helps most. Aleph is life and breath. Breath and life are the same. This oneness is ruach in Hebrew, prana in Sanskrit, pneuma in Greek, and spiritus in Latin. Breath, life, and spirit are one. One is Aleph, and Aleph is One.

This letter resonates with the powerful vibration of leadership, making it the most assertive and self-initiating presence in the entire alphabet. **'A'** pulses with an adventurous, trailblazing energy that drives individuals to explore uncharted territories, embracing independence as their core strength. Highly self-reliant, they prefer to forge their own paths, often diving headfirst into new ventures without waiting for others. Those attuned to **'A'** excel at sparking action; they act as natural catalysts, igniting motivation and momentum in people and situations around them. Yet, this fiery drive comes with lessons: they must navigate tendencies toward self-absorption, strong opinions, and stubbornness, channeling these traits into focused, constructive outlets rather than conflicts. Experience becomes their greatest teacher, refining raw initiative into masterful direction.

**'A'** thrives on constant change, novelty, and high-stakes adventure, rejecting routine in favor of dynamic growth. In numerology, this aligns with the Number 1's essence of pure beginnings, originality, and the divine spark of creation, urging **'A'** influences to pioneer while balancing ego with empathy.

# B.

**B-2,** God made **B** as the second letter. It is called Beth (say "bayth"). Its three main meanings are house, mouth, and womb. Beth means "house." In holy terms, it is "birthplace." Earth is our house. Old Hebrew ways say B created Earth. In the Bible, "Beth" means house: Bethlehem (house of bread), Balbeth (house of sun), Bethel (house of God). Bethel means the body as God's holy place. El means God, the light ray inside us all. It opens to wisdom and good. Beth is the womb. It holds the baby while it grows for birth. Beth is the mouth. It holds words ready to come out. **B** is a burst sound from the lips. It is like the big bang that made planets. Beth is the first of seven "double letters" in Hebrew. Each shows two sides: Beth is Life/Death. At first, Beth was a square for a house. Then they took away the left side. It left the roof, one wall, and the floor. The Greeks took it and made a double square. Romans kept the straight side and rounded the loops.

This vibration channels the essence of a deeply sensitive helper, finding its true motivation and purpose through meaningful connections with others. Rather than charging ahead solo, **'B'** draws energy from relationships, excelling in fostering unity and emotional equilibrium. It naturally gravitates toward fields demanding diplomacy, mediation, and subtle improvements, think peacemakers, counselors, or behind-the-scenes enhancers who smooth edges and build bridges.

**'B'** responds beautifully to genuine appreciation, blooming into a beacon of kindness, gentleness, and endearing lovability. However, when confidence wanes or self-worth falters, this warmth can dim, leading to hesitation or withdrawal. The key lesson here is cultivating inner validation to unlock its full potential.

As a quintessential team player, **'B'** thrives in partnership, contributing wisdom, intuition, and unwavering support once it feels securely linked to the group. In numerology, this mirrors the Number 2's duality, cooperation, empathy, and receptive harmony, reminding '**B**' influences to nurture bonds while honoring their own gentle strength.

# C.

**C-3,** The third Hebrew letter is Gimel (ghee-mel). It means camel. It links to the English letter **G**. Hebrew has no **C**. Gimel's main force is wealth. Camels often carry loads of rich goods. In the same way, **C's** like to wear fine clothes and jewels. **C** or **G**, this letter excels with words. It is a 3. A camel's hump stores a lot of water. This lets it travel days in the desert without thirst. A dry throat makes talking hard. Enough water keeps the throat wet and ready. The throat shapes sound. All 3's speak with smooth flow. So "camel" fits the 3-letter well. The Greeks took the shape and named it Gamma. They used it for the G sound. Romans copied the shape. At first, they used it for both **G** and **K** sounds. They wrote "Gaius" for "Caius." Later, they made a new shape, **C**, for the **K** sound. This set them apart. **C** became the third letter in the Roman alphabet. The letter still means "camel." Camel starts with **C**. In Hebrew, the word is Gimel (Guimel). It starts with **G**.

**C** sounds like "see." It does see, for it has psychic gifts. But it may not know this. The shape of **C** is a half-moon. It gives light to Earth. 3's love to let their light shine. They feel best when they make others smile or laugh. **C** looks like an open mouth. It loves to talk. Negative **C's** gossip. They use words in bad ways. **C** opens to take in talents. It shows creativity in many ways. But it can spread energy too thin. Some are show-offs. They want fun and joy in life. They do not take things too hard. They use words, spoken or written, to lift people. They do this well. They have strong creative imagination. **C** finds it hard to save money. Money is energy. It is easy to spread it out. This brings money problems. People born on the 30th with a **C** in their name often leave covers off things. Like toothpaste tubes or camera lenses. Anything with extra parts. They do not keep like items in one box. Parts get lost one by one. That is scattering energy too. **C's** are artistic. They like skilled work. They hate dull jobs and hard labor unless it creates. They want joy in all they do, even work. They need help with business tasks. This lets them focus on art. They see big ideas. They catch them in words, art, or thoughts. **C** looks like a U turned on its side. U holds things like a cup. **C** lets it all flow out. So, emotions spill freely. Negative **C's** may have weak morals. Or be too strict or quick to judge. They lack patience.

Nestled within **'C'** beats the heart of a spontaneous creator, brimming with inspiration and a flair for originality that lets creative work and fresh ideas pour forth naturally. This vibration cannot resist self-expression, turning everyday moments into bursts of innovation and artistry. Outgoing, sociable, and effortlessly friendly, **'C'** draws its deepest motivation from joy, celebrating life's pleasures as fuel for its vibrant spirit.

The graceful, open curve of **'C'** acts like a cosmic boomerang, magnetizing back the positivity, creativity, and goodwill it radiates into the world. Beneath this lively surface lies profound sensitivity and intuition, making **'C'** a natural conduit for emotional depth and subtle insights. It wholeheartedly embraces the arts, whether painting, music, writing, dance, or any form that channels beauty and imagination.

Yet, in moments of imbalance, **'C's'** boundless energy can scatter like confetti, leading to distraction, unfinished projects, or challenges in grounding dreams into tangible results. The path to mastery involves focusing that playful force with gentle discipline. In numerology, this echoes the Number 3's triad of creativity, communication, and expansion urging **'C'** to express boldly while staying centered.

# D.

**D-4,** The fourth Hebrew letter is Dalet (**DAH-let**). It is one of the seven double letters of creation. These hold pairs of opposites. Dalet pairs knowledge with a lack of knowledge. Dalet means womb or door. The womb acts as a door. It is the door of birth. The picture sign for Dalet is a 7. It stands wide open. To the Hebrews, door means a freeway in and out. Greeks took the sign. They named it Delta. It also means door. But they shut it into a triangle: A. To them, the door keeps things in or out. Pythagoras saw a deep secret: 4 adds to 10 (1+2+3+4=10). 10 means a fresh start. When one door shuts, old ones viewed the cube (4) as an un-grown man. He locks himself in. Shutting the door blinds him. The 7 is awake, man. Unfold the cube: it turns into a cross of pain. This marks a man born new **D** matches the Fourth Commandment. "Remember the Sabbath day. Keep it holy." Romans copied the letter from the Greeks. They moved the straight line to the left. They curved the other side to a half-moon. It looks like a cube or square with four sides. **D** closes in. People with names starting with **D** often feel trapped by limits. This grows with more **D's** in the name. They must rise above bad situations.

**D** rests steady on the line. So, it balances well. It grasps the real world. It holds firm views. It can stay very old-way bound by self-set walls. **D** stays shut, unlike **C**. It does not "see" like **C**. It trusts what eyes show. It needs proof to believe. **D** should skip deals with 3. 3 makes art, **4** builds work. They rarely match. They clash with 1, 5, or 7. But 3 needs 4 to run its path. **D** works too much. They can turn plain. But they love family, back their land, earn trust, stay sure. **D** toils hard for gains. Do not wait for big shows of heart. **D** nears a square. So, it seeks "square deal." It stays "fair and square." Honest through. Wants the same back. A strong, safe base matters deeply. Negative **D's** gloom dark, too tight-bound, fixed-view, fight-prone, rock-hard set. In numerology, the letter D vibrates with the steadfast energy of Number 4, symbolizing structure, discipline, and enduring foundations. Shaped like a grounded square with an open door, 'D' represents the builder who constructs lasting realities from raw effort, practical, methodical, and rooted in the material world. Its vibration teaches through responsibility, turning labor into legacy.

## Key Strengths and Traits

- Steady Builder: 'D' excels at long-term projects, approaching work with unwavering patience and realism.
- Practical Anchor: Brings orthodox values, honesty, and constancy, making it a rock for others.
- Tactile Learner: Often prefers hands-on, physical outlets to express and channel his intense energy, especially when words feel elusive.
- Nature's Ally: Immersion in natural environments revitalizes 'D', enhancing its grounded qualities and inner peace.

## Challenges and Growth Lessons

- May grapple with emotional expression or self-acknowledgement, risking rigidity or over-control.
- The journey involves balancing discipline with flexibility, learning to honor personal needs amid duty.

Famous **'D'** influences (eg, names starting with **D**) often manifest as diligent leaders or craftsmen, like David or Diana, embodying reliability. For personalization in your numerology work, **'D'** encourages rituals like gardening or woodworking to harmonize its vibration.

# E.

**E-5,** Hebrew had no symbol for **E** because its alphabet lacked vowels. The Phoenicians took the consonant He (like English **H**) and reshaped it for their own consonant. After 900 B.C., Greeks borrowed it, flipped it to form **E**, named it Epsilon, and used it for the short **E** vowel to set it apart from the long **E** in Eta. Like 5, **E** stays open. It opens up for talking, singing, and speaking, making it a means of communication and words. When negative, it criticizes others harshly with words. **E-5** opens on all sides, so it craves freedom. It often feels nervous and quick to anger. As the 5 of the five senses, it stays "open" to try, test, and taste everything. This openness can lead to excess. The 5 rocks like a cradle, so it shifts easily and often changes its mind. It may lean toward dishonesty. Negative 5's risk trouble with the law. **E** bursts with energy and restlessness, needing meaningful tasks to stay busy. It can show open affection and warmth or the opposite, icy coldness. Overall, it points outward as an extrovert.

This vibration embodies remarkable versatility and inspiration, fiercely guarding its love for freedom while eagerly embracing the thrill of travel, constant movement, and boundless flexibility. It cuts straight to the heart of matters with its straightforward, no-nonsense directness, leaving little room for ambiguity or pretense. Spiritually inclined by nature, it naturally gravitates towards profound metaphysical explorations, seeking wisdom in the unseen realms of existence. A perpetual student at heart, he revels in the art of learning, absorbing knowledge like a sponge and sharing it freely. Words are its playground: whether crafting eloquent written prose that flows like a river or delivering spoken truths with magnetic charisma, it wields language as a tool for enlightenment and connection.

At its core pulses a tremendous reservoir of energy and vitality, fueling adventures and ideas with relentless dynamism. Remarkably, despite the high-octane surge flowing through every "**E,**" it maintains an aura of calm composure, channeling that power with grace rather than chaos. However, when "**E**"s multiply excessively in a name or chart, this vibrant force can tip into impulsiveness, sudden decisions without pause or restlessness, a nagging itch for change that disrupts inner peace.

In numerology, the "**E**" vibration (resonating with the number 5 in Pythagorean systems) mirrors the soul's quest for expansion, reminding us that true liberation comes from balancing freedom's call with mindful direction.

# F.

**F-6, F** comes from the Hebrew letter Vau (V). All 6 letters **F, O, and X** are good teachers. 6's care about their communities and want to help. They know the law and want to follow it. They care for their surroundings and the people they know. Some go into politics, some into counseling, and many into teaching. The 6 also stands for the voice that needs to be heard. This matters in 6's careers. They take on duties as their job. You can see this love for duty in the letter's shape. **F** has a double cross. People bring their problems to **F's. F's** "carry the load" for others. They help actively or just worry a lot. **F** is not as balanced as **E.** It needs calm and no confusion. As a 6, it wants to finish tasks in peace. The two flat lines on **F** look like arms stretched out to help those nearby. 6 is the number vibration of service. **F's** feel best when they do something good for others, like family, friends, or the community**. F** is the sixth letter, and 6 loves artistic places. This number shows up a lot in the arts. 6's may work in music, decorating, acting, or performing. These jobs serve others in a way. A good show brings joy to many.

**F** has an open mind and a sixth sense. It is like letter P, but **F** stays open to new ideas. P is set in its views with a closed mind. (See the closed circle at **P's** top.) **P** is the 16th letter, which is 7. 7 turns away from other numbers and follows its own advice. **Fs** are idealists. They usually want to show beauty. Their calm faces give a kind, parent-like look. The negative **F** takes duty too far. It becomes a busybody know-it-all. This **F** thinks no one else is right. It acts smug and self-righteous. This is the voice that must be heard. When negative, it gets stubborn. It uses silence as a weapon and stops talking for days. People who live on the negative side of 6 want to control family and friends. They act like tyrants without knowing it. They feel so sure they are right. Their stubbornness makes others unhappy and uneasy around them. Otherwise, **F** is a happy family vibration. It stands for Family, Fatherliness, and Fidelity. **F** can be very passionate. It shows the full 6 vibrations, the number of Venus, the planet of love.

The '**F**' vibration pulses with an innate compulsion to serve humanity, coupled with a refined appreciation for all that is aesthetic beauty in art, nature, music, and the graceful symmetries of life. This energy does not exist in isolation; it harbors a beautiful complexity, weaving together layers of emotion, intuition, and purpose that unfold over time.

Fundamentally social and relational, it thrives in the company of others, convinced that its highest destiny manifests through the sacred bonds of home and heartfelt relationships. Family, community, and partnerships form its anchor, providing the emotional soil where it can truly flourish. It holds its values and principles as sacred treasures, guiding every decision with unwavering integrity and a moral compass attuned to the greater good. Yet, this same depth makes it vulnerable; Criticism pierces deeply, often triggering self-doubt or defensiveness, as if questioning its very essence.

# G.

**G-7,** ROMAN **G** PRESENT-DAY Gimel matches letters **C** and **G**. It is the third Hebrew letter. It doubles in hard and soft sounds, and in strong health or its opposite, sickness. Its star link is Mars. It rules riches. This comes from camels carrying costly goods. Gimel means camel. **G's** shape looks like a camel's head and neck outline. Phoenicians and other Semites used Gimel for their **G** sound. Mars, the red planet, rules blood as life's force in the body. Blood and water are key to life. Camels store water, like arteries carry blood. The Talmud says Gimel equals loving kindness to the poor. Science shows that kind acts build good health. Bad feelings and acts make "bad blood." **C** (3) and **G** (7) link to health, since Gimel means health and disease. As Hebrew's third letter, it is our base. The Trinity Father, Mother, Son creates us.

That Trinity matches the three Mother Letters: Alef (Air), Mem (Water), and Shin (Fire). They build our body and good health. Perfect harmony in this Trinity shows in our body's seven parts, giving full health. The Greeks took the letter and named it Gamma. They kept it as a **G** sound. Romans used **C** for both **C** and **G** sounds until the third century BC. To stop confusion, they added a bar to make **G,** and left **C** for the **K** sound. **G** leans toward religion. It is our seventh letter, and 7 loves spiritual things. G turns inward. It searches itself more, thinks deeper, and analyzes more than **C**. **G** suits arts well. It practices until perfect. It fits writing, science, and religion, too. Its sharp thinking and love for perfection make **G** careful. It picks quality over amount. **G** speaks well but talks less than **C. C** is an open mouth. **G** thinks on words, says little, but means much. This shows 7's vibe: spiritual, scientific, or quiet. **G** is not as outgoing as **C**. It is a **C** turning to itself. This gives **G** these traits: It likes being alone more than **C.** It keeps thoughts secret. It works best alone, not in partnerships. It cares more for itself than others. It is quiet, strong-willed, and set in views. It seeks hidden meanings. It wants to know why people act. **G** needs peace, alone time to think, rest, and balance energy. When negative, the balance breaks. **G** seems cold and unloving. People misunderstand it, and it feels lonely. Negative **G** can judge harshly, mock, stay distant, or feel dark, and it uses sharp words. It may get nervous or shy, but it hurts easily. Too, mature spiritual **G's** earn respect for willpower and wisdom.

This vibration embodies the reserved thinker, a quiet observer whose inner world brims with profound reflection. Often misunderstood by those around them for not speaking up assertively, the '**G**' individual prefers the silent depths of introspection, where ideas percolate and truths emerge unhurriedly. Their mind is a constant hive of engaged thought, analyzing, pondering, and seeking hidden patterns in the tapestry of existence. Endowed with exceptional patience, they navigate life's complexities without rush, allowing time to reveal its lessons. This same quality fuels their extraordinary ability to assimilate knowledge, absorbing vast amounts of information like a sponge and synthesizing it into personal wisdom. They excel in fields requiring depth, such as philosophy, research, spirituality, or any pursuit where contemplation reigns over action.

Yet, a key life lesson for the '**G**' lies in building self-confidence; their natural reticence can hold them back from sharing their insights, leading to overlooked brilliance. Through sheer will, determination, and persistent effort, often manifesting as disciplined study or solitary practice, they forge unshakeable assurance. Over a lifetime, this inner alchemy yields profound wisdom, positioning them as trusted guides or silent sages whose words, when spoken, carry the weight of eternity. Having a strong '**G**' influence often draws them towards mystical or intellectual havens, where they thrive in solitude or small, meaningful circles, ever evolving towards self-mastery.

# H.

**H-8,** Number 8 pictures sky orbits and life's cycles. They never end and keep moving like a planted seed grows and returns as ripe fruit to the planter. On the other side, 8 (-) **"H",** it looks like a nourishing breast. It gives food for growth. It is also a justice's scale. Our words and acts get weighed fairly. Cycles return an exact measure to us. Taking what is not yours creates karma debt. It slows progress. We pay it back now or later. Saying Hé or H lets breath out. Hé is the second and last part of God's name. Yod is the male force, Hé is the female. Their joint makes life. Vau links them as both. From this life force, Hé is called the child-bearing letter. Hé's life force links in Kabbalah to Hebrew words for "bear fruit" or "blossom." Hé means window. It points to the eyes as the soul's windows. The Hebrew Hé glyph looks like an open window. A window lets in light and air. It gives a happy or sad feeling. This matches our outlook: positive or negative. Seeing beauty fills eyes with light. Face softens. Negative views make eyes hard, cold, and unkind. We see out through our eyes. Others see in. View goes both ways, based on how we choose to see and be. **H** does more than help speech. It is breath that gives and refreshes life. Spoken words can be **H's**. God's loving, creating breath. It brings back life and heals. So good words create balance and harmony in all we do.

# I.

**I-9, I** is our ninth letter. 9 vibrates with feelings and sensitivity, felt by personal 1. Views are strong, emotions deep. It must master self and trust the big **I** inside. This guides the small I ego or "me." 9 also means humanity. So **"I"** must think of others, learn kindness and understanding. Negative **I's** focus too much on self. They judge hard and act proudly. Like Yod, **I** hold creative power. It is an artist, actor, performer, musician, and doer. **I** seek perfect work. 9 finishes, becomes 10. Tail leaves circle, stands beside as 10. **I** act like 1: starts things. As the ninth letter, it finishes too.

**I** shape like a pen or a needle. People with **I** in their name suit writing, sewing, and designing. **I** also look like a knife. The bearer must handle knives with care to avoid self-harm. **I** lacks strong ground line. It is emotional, up or down. It says **"I am,"** so sensitive to one's own needs. This helps sense others' needs. **I** help and serve **"I am"** in people. It is **"I am"** awareness. Mysteries teach the greatest truth: God lives in man. In each soul burns a divine ray like Yod's light in every Hebrew letter. Our God traits, love, kindness, and understanding flow from this light.

# J.

**J-10** Yod (say "yod") is the 10th Hebrew letter. It matches English **J, I,** and **Y. J** is the 10th English letter. Yod is the sixth of the 12 simple letters. Its main power is in work. Yod means "hand." The symbol looks like "a finger pointing to heaven." With their hands, people work and make things. Yod means God's hands create everything God is 0. God makes man and the world. Man comes from the center of 6. Man stands at 10 as his own creator. He uses God's tools. With his hands, a man makes his own things through hard work. All Hebrew letters are built from Yods. Every letter is a creative force. Like 1 is in all numbers, Yod is part of God's Creative Light in all creation. Greeks took Yod and named it Iota. They used it for vowel **I.** Hebrew had no vowel letters. So Yod matches English consonants **J** and **Y.** Once, **I, J,** and **Y** were the same. **J** sounded like **Y,** as in Jesu (Yesu). Yod was sometimes "Jod." In the 1800s, they set the letters apart. **Y** became the ee-ah sound, except as a vowel. I became 9th, **J** 10th, **Y** 25th. **J** is the 10th. J is the 10th English letter. It starts a new level of awareness, 10 steps above 1. The number 10 means it has been here before and now has fresh paths to try. J people are often religious. J looks like a cross and a crown. The 10 is self (1) plus God power (0). So, J people seek a high place in life.

The shape of **J** is like a fishhook. The hook points are left. **J** people hate being told what to do. They do not follow well. They lead. They have a strong drive and smart ways to reach goals. **J** people rarely ask for help. The 10 makes them fully self-reliant. They draw on inner God power. This explains why many religious leaders had **J** names: Jesus, John the Baptist, John the Apostle, Jacob (father of the Jewish people), James the Apostle, Jeremiah (big Old Testament prophet), and Joshua (who followed Moses). **J** also starts words like judgment, justice, and judges. If **J** is the only 1-letter in the name, the person may lose confidence. **J** sits on a rocker, not steady. **J** people sometimes delay. They must watch for accidents. The 1 is bold, and the rocker is shaky. A bad J is not honest. But most **J** people are funny, smart, careful, and quick. They can shine at work. Yod matches the Tenth Commandment: "Do not covet..." Yod is the hand that works to create. It stands for honest work. We deserve what we earn. Wanting what others worked for harms you. Good actions bring good back. Evil destroys itself.

# K.

**K-11** Kaf (say "kaf") is the 11th Hebrew letter. It is one of seven double letters. It has two sounds: **K** or **Ch**. It stands for two sides: divine love and human love. Hebrew gave it 20, since there was no 11. It is a higher form of Beth (2). **K** (11) relates to **B** (2) the same way. This gives Kaph Beth's traits on a higher level. It shows control over low human love. Kaph means "hollow" or "palm of hand." It stands for holding. It means grab the chances that come or keep what you get. For wisdom seekers, it is the sign of an Initiate. They welcome deeper spirit truths. They passed lessons 1-9, reached a perfect 10, then shared love in 11. At 10, they know and follow the Ten Commandments. At 11, they share light with people. They reach out to bless. 11 means light, like Jesus, who lit the world. Good 11s bring light (29/11) and joy (38/11). They match that vibration. Every letter and number has a bad side. The bad 11 doubles the flaws of 2. This means very sensitive. Tense nerves. Dishonest. Hidden plans. No pity. Narrow mind. Intolerant. Moody. Stealing urge. Thief. Sneaky. Smooth talker. Liar. So beat the low side. Like **K's** top, reach up for light. Open to higher mind, gut feelings, spirit help, and creative thoughts. **K** has strong intuition and trusts hunches. **K's** bottom is an upside-down **V** with firm feet on the ground. It shows body-world pull. **K's** side is a wide V like a crescent moon. It gives light to all. Like **C**, it spreads energy. Success depends on using talents well. **K** needs music to calm and inspire. When **K** lets light shine, it inspires others greatly.

# L.

**L-12** In Hebrew, the 12th letter is Lamed (law-med). It shows God's arm stretched out to act. "I am the Lord. I will save you with an outstretched arm" (Exodus 6:6). Lamed means ox-goad. That is a sharp stick to push oxen forward. **L's** can urge others to do their best. They inspire people to take the right step, like God's arm in Exodus. Lamed is sexual desire. It drives all growth. It is the life force that makes things real. This desire needs a balance between body and spirit. Then it serves well: "Be fruitful, multiply, fill the earth, and rule it" (Genesis 1:28). The Greeks took the letter from the Phoenicians. They named it Lambda. It became Roman **L.** It holds the same place in English and Hebrew: 12. Hebrew had no 12. After 10, they used tens: 10, 20, 30, and so on. Lamed is the 30th. The base of 12 or 30 is 3. **L** stands for "loving." It is romantic and true to family. To "rule" its strong feelings, it must balance the high and low sides. **L** has no clear balance line like **A.**

**L's** can be warm, open, and kind. But when life upsets them, they turn cold, distant, and sharp: two sides of one board. **L's** need self-control. Sometimes they skip it. They feel pretty and think others will like them anyway. They believe they can judge harshly and still charm. (They think so.) But they hurt easily. **L** creates well. It is the 12th letter. 12 divided by 3 gives the creative three. **L** has a strong baseline. It stays steady on Earth. It does not tip or spread out. So, it acts less on impulse than **C.** It collects where **C** spreads. It welcomes good things and holds them better than **C.** So, it chooses wiser.

**L** does not act as fast as **C.** Its base is straight. It will not shift quickly. So, it thinks before it moves. Open **L's** gain friends and success through creative ways. They show themselves and feel happy and friendly. They must guide their skills to learning and self-growth. **L** has art skills and a sharp legal mind. It knows the law's base rules. L is 12/3: A, B, C basics. Law and legal both start with **L. L** pictures God's arm stretched out (Law). **L** grasps the law well. Its gut sense reads people's reasons. It knows why they act. Its first views often hit true. **L's** feel deeply inside. They open fully to the mind and spirit planes. Their shape shows this. Turn **L** upside down: it is 7, a gut-feel number. This gives **L** a psychic sense. It often seeks hidden knowledge and faith training. The 7 lets **L** think deeply. 7 breaks things down and reasons well. It fits that **L's** speak, sing, teach, and preach well. Or, when negative, they speak sharp words, sarcasm, and blame. The talk numbers 2, 3, 6 make **L**: 12/3 = 6. **L** loves to sing. It has a fine voice, best if born on the 12th or 30th. Lamed counts as 30. Negative **L** has no patience. It spots faults everywhere. It sees both sides of issues. So, it wavers on choices. Some feel trapped by their surroundings. That brings anger. They must feel free to share themselves. **L's** are upside-down 7's. So, when life goes wrong, they take 7's dark side: fear, sadness, anger, and chill. People with two or more **L's** in their name face risks and slips. They have much on their mind. So, they rush and miss care.

# M.

**M-13** Mem (mem) is the 13th Hebrew letter. As 13, it counts as 40. It is the second Mother Letter. It stands for the Water element. Water aids all creation. The 4 Letter **D, M, V** Water words like marine and marsh link to it. Mother and water match this letter. Life before birth starts in a water sac inside the mother's womb. **M** is 13th in all Indo-European alphabets. It sits center, like a womb in a woman. And **M** centers the word "woman." All letters and numbers hold hidden senses in tongues. But **M** ranks most holy. Water feeds all life. It joins female and male, or blends both. It ties to W, first of "water." **M** is **W** flipped. Womb starts with **W**, sits in mother with **M**. First Phoenician sign for Mem: W with tail down right: **W**. Greeks took it, cut tail, turned it, named Mu. Romans took it for **M**. Romans saw **M** as a face. Added dot eyes on each side. Big dots grew circles, made "Omo." This turned homo, Latin for man. **M** shows a strong self. Stands firm on two feet. **V** stands clear up middle. This opens it to high ideas. Gives **M** lead skills. Fits rule roles with a neat mind and sharp recall. 4 means trade work. **M** base is 4. Inner V is the 22nd letter, base 4 too. 4 + 4 = 8, lead number. So, managing power runs deep in **M**. Women with the **M** name start shining home keepers. Men with it like to run a house. M sounds with lips shut. This marks still deep-sea. Its lowest waves stay silent. Yet all life flows from it. This silent letter links Tarot's 13th card, Death. But it means shift, not stop. Bright sun low in back recalls: sun sets daily, rises next morn. Each mark on the card shows that the life force goes on.

Silence holds great power, just like the quiet letter **M**. We recharge our energy when we rest. Noise upsets us, but silence calms us. A negative **M** seems dull, cold, tough, and uncaring. People with **M** feel trapped, like all 4's do. They work hard and stay too careful, often forgetting to relax and enjoy their rewards.

The shape of **M** has ups and downs, which show it can be unstable. **M's** might act carelessly. They need to focus their thoughts on higher things, not just earthly ones. That middle **V** with arms raised looks like a call for spiritual help, and intuition provides it. **M** also stands for greatness in size or strong visual effect, like in words such as Mountain, Majestic, Millionaire, Magical, Momentous, all starting with a tall letter. Or the opposite: Minimal. It shows greatness in character, too, like in Master.

# N.

**N-14** Noun (noon) is the 14th letter in the Hebrew alphabet. It is the eighth of the 12 simple letters. It rules the sense of smell. Noun means "fish" and stands for the Initiate. Noun also means growth, or spiritual growth. Fish symbols show deeper teachings for a few reasons. Christianity started in the Piscean Age. The first letters of "Jesus Christ, Son of God, Savior" in Greek spell "fish" (ΙΧΘΥΣ). Jesus lived without sin around sin, as fish live deep in clean water. In other religions, people drew fish with gods and goddesses to show divinity. The number 5 is the middle number. It links to humans and their five senses. 14 is like 5 but higher (14/5). It is the number of the Sage. The Sage beats the lower pull of the five senses. He follows the spiritual path by controlling his thoughts and actions.

When the Greeks took the Noun symbol from the Phoenicians, they called it Nu. They flipped it and later made it even on both sides, as our English, **N**. Etruscans, and Romans used it next. It stayed the 14th letter in our alphabet. **N** stays balanced on Earth, even if turned upside down. It can be very physical or very spiritual. There is no line splitting the two worlds, unlike in **A, B, or H**. Its upside-down V on the left opens to the material world. People who ignore their higher side stay stuck in physical, sensory pleasures. They never move to the right **V**, which opens to higher things. The right **V** looks up to greater ideas and spiritual knowledge. It welcomes spiritual growth. So, Noun means either Scorpio or the Eagle.

Turned on its side, N becomes a Z. This gives it quite psychic awareness. People often ignore it, but it shows in the two intuitive 7's that form the Z. This quiet 7's explains why N people have strong imaginations. Ancient people used this symbol for a scribe. Writers need good imagination (Numerology and the Divine Triangle, page 73). N can grab ideas from the air, like an antenna catches radio and TV waves. N even looks like an antenna. The word is "N-tenna." Of its seven letters, four are 5's: N, E, N, N. So, the main trait of the word matches the.

## O.

**O-15** Letter **O** matches the 16th Hebrew letter, Ayin (ah-yin). It is the 10th of the 12 simple letters. Its main force is anger. Ayin means "eye." It points to the inner spiritual eye that understands and explains what we see. We see in two ways: with the bodily eye, and through the mind by grasping meaning. The second way is when light dawns, and we say, "Oh, I see." This is the spiritual eye, Ayin: the soul's window. Body sight is letter Vau (**V**). Vau means peg or nail: it joins one thing to another. **O**, looks like an eye. The early church used it for God's all-seeing eye. The word "church" comes from the Anglican root Circ or Cyrc, meaning circle. First churches were round to show God's eye. Phoenicians and Semites used Ayin for a strong throat sound; **C**. English and other Indo-European languages lack it. Greeks did not need that sound, so they used the shape for vowel **O**. They named it Omicron, "short **O**," to set it apart from Omega, "long O." Greeks made Omega and put it last in their alphabet.

# P.

**P-16**, Pé or Phé is Hebrew's 17th letter and English's 16th. Its doubles are power and servitude. Pé means "mouth." Power means skill in writing or speaking, or both. The mouth speaks thoughts. It can express good or bad, build up or tear down. Words can create beauty or destroy. Thoughts we hold are mind full, like food sustains the body. We choose thoughts as the food. Wise choices bring health and wisdom. If food tastes bad, the mouth spits it out. It accepts or rejects. Same for thoughts. We control thinking and pick good ones. In the body, Pé is the pituitary gland. It gives intuition, mind-to-mind thought, and inner knowing when awake. Aim thoughts at goals for success, that is, power. Wrong use leads to servitude.

Greeks took Pé, named it Pi, and flipped the shape. Romans closed the top circle to make P. It became English's 16th letter. In shape, P is a circle on a line: head on self. It is smart, curious, and good at focus. But it can be stubborn and fixed in its views. P may be very spiritual or closed-minded, doubting God. People with many P's feel and show strong power. P-heavy names need to be balanced with philosophy study.

# Q.

**Q-17,** Qof (cof) serves as the 19th letter in the Hebrew alphabet and the final one among the 12 simple letters. It embodies the influence of mirth. The term Qof refers to the back of the head, and its glyph, shaped like a **P,** with a semicircle on the right and a sharp vertical Yod descending on the left, evokes a profile of the face and neck, highlighting this region. Located at the brain's base, this area acts as the body's central hub for balance and coordination. We need to harmonize the feminine and masculine energies inside ourselves: the masculine representing active physical power, and the feminine symbolizing spiritual inspiration. The ancients termed this harmony "the mystical marriage," which transcends physical or sensual union. Instead, it fuses our consciousness with divine consciousness, igniting the soul's profound joy of true knowing. Positive and negative forces surround us constantly, demanding we view them in proper proportion. On the physical plane, equilibrium requires a firm, steadfast moral foundation paired with discerning judgment. The number 19 signifies initiation, bringing challenges and ordeals. Its hidden key is balance, transforming 1 + 9 into 10, the emblem of perfection and success in passing initiation's trials. Across history, 19 has linked to the sun in myths and legends. As the life-giving source of vitality and light, the sun leads to perfection, mirroring how 1 + 9 = 10, the amount of completeness. Would you like me to adjust the tone (e.g., more formal or concise), emphasize certain sections, or rephrase specific parts further?

We all have a bit of the sun's life-giving force. It sits in the spleen, home of emotions. A big web of nerves behind the stomach is the solar plexus. It centers our body like the sun centers our solar system. The sun's power is linked to the solar plexus power in us. Here, we balance positive and negative forces. Our best tool for balance is mirth. Mirth means joy or fun. It is a happy attitude, a positive response. It releases pressure like a valve. Seeing humor in bad times lets go of stress. Humor heals body and mind. Ancient Hebrews used Qof for a voiceless velar sound (back tongue touches the soft roof of the mouth). Greeks took it, named it Qof or Koppa, and added a line through a full circle. But their Kappa already had the **K** sound, so they dropped it. The Etruscans gave it to the Romans. Romans used it for **K** before **U.** They kept the circle, moved the line outside. Then curved line right: Ɔ, into English capital **Q.** The circle is the spiritual sun. The line is a balance rod. For mirth, it shows its head with its tongue out. Qof balances the body and mind forces. **Q's** work on both. **O** means all or nothing. **Q's** give 100%. They stay loyal, caring, and understanding. **Q's** draw money well. They aim to be their best. Balanced, they win big success. **Q** feels unique or odd few names have it. It is original. The all-or-nothing circle needs the balance rod. **Q** can swing too far: over-spiritual or over-material, too negative or too positive, even risky. Forces must balance like 8: split evenly between worlds.

The body's power center is the solar plexus. **Q** must know its psychic energies and keep them balanced with spiritual light. Without that light, psychic force pulls from the low astral world. It brings fear, even madness. Used well, the same force gives **Q** a vivid imagination for inspired writing. As the 17th letter, **Q** has 1's unique self and 7's royal ways; 1+7=8, balance **Q** must hold. **Q** often needs aid. That is why **U** usually follow. But U is a cup on a shaky base, not fully steady. Another vowel almost always comes after **U**. Even with this help, like the balance rod sticking out, **Q** likes being alone. This comes from 7. Thoughts, dreams, and make-believe feel real to **Q**. It can get lost there. But in balance, **Q** pulls ideas from the mind/spirit world (8's bottom). Then success is sure.

# R.

**R-18**, Reish is Hebrew's 20th letter. It makes the R sound. Its pairs are peace and strife. Its meaning is "head." This letter focuses on man's spiritual growth. A man chasing only material things never wakes his spirit centers. He never knows true peace. Ignorance makes him seek wins through war. Add death letters by alphabet spots: **T** is 20, not 2. "Death" totals 38/11, not 20. 11 means light to spiritual people; death is light, not dark. It is man meeting Master one-to-one: resurrection, new birth. Greeks took the Reish sign, named it Rho, and kept the **R** sound.

They flipped shape. Romans added the right leg. **R** starts with a left straight line: upright man, the top loop is the head. It means think, gain knowledge, create ideas. Here, it looks like **P,** fatherly creative force. The right leg shows a man stepping forward. It pictures action in life. Leg joins head directly: move ahead with thought. In secret, raise thinking above material. Seek spiritual truth. **R's** are thinkers. They are teachers, writers, and leaders. A closed circle means they hold knowledge and think deeply. R understands others best of all letters. It must build a brotherly spirit. **R** is English's 18th letter. 1+8=9, vibe of humanity and love for others. 9 ends cycles. It is initiation: finish old, pass tests, ready for new. As a 9-letter, **R** feels deeply. Without honesty and unselfishness, **R** fails. Initiation needs honor, patience, kindness, true search for truth. R holds big power to build or destroy. Man must think to use it right. People joke that **R** is a "dog letter" or "snarling letter." "Rrrr" sounds like a dog growl. Very negative **R's** grumble much. Uncontrolled feelings rule them. They must tame basic urges: anger, envy, body wants. Learn patience, drop **R's** right leg to stand still like **P.** Positive **R** is the most beautiful letter, it builds trust as none other gives freely for joy, no payback thought. Then **R** shines: Radiant, Refined, Reliable, Remarkable, Respected. Pass tests, finish initiation.

# S.

**S-19**, **S** is the 19th English letter. It links to Hebrew Shin. Shin is the third Mother Letter of creation. It stands for Fire. **Sh** sounds like fire. Shin has two sounds: **S** and **Sh**. As the 21st Hebrew letter, it shows the creative three (2+1=3). The three elements are Aleph (**A**) = Air, Mem (**M**) = Water, Shin (**S, Sh**) = Fire. In Kabbalah, Shin means "tooth." This ties to Fire. Chewing readies food for the body, like Fire gives heat for life and creation. Shin stands for the Christ idea: "I Am the Way, the Truth, and the Life." This is key to Christian mysteries (The Bible and the Tarot, 103). Shin's shape shows a choice: Take the high path to Christ-awareness or stay in body senses. Pick the high path, and love turns to divine Fire. This grows your mind. It is the Way, Truth, and Life of the Christ idea. Phoenician Shin looked like the first shape, close to modern W. Greeks turned it upright and made Sigma (Σ). They used it for the **S** sound. Romans rounded it to our **S**. As the 19th letter (1+9), start and end, S finishes one job and starts another. **S** starts things and gets them done. **S** creates a lot and aims high. It is 1 and 9 reaching for a perfect 10. This makes **S** a sign of success. The 1 makes **S** people like working alone. They do best without help. They hate orders. They know by feel what to do and can do it. They like showing their own way and do not care what others think. The 9 makes **S** dramatic and emotional. People with these traits make great actors. They use their feelings to play roles.

**S** has two **C's**. One opens to the spirit/mind world. The other opens to the body/physical world. **S** sees both worlds and has psychic gifts. It can guide both worlds, too. Its snake shape shows serpent wisdom. Each C is like an open moon that lights its side. The top half looks to the future. It is open to spirit insights, talents, gut feelings, and creative ideas. It loves the spirit world and dreams there. Once it finds the mind world, it wants to learn all it can. The bottom half looks to the past from the body world. So, **S** remembers farther back than most. Actors with **S** at the start or in their name use good memory from past times. **S** may switch paths halfway to find the best way for a problem. The letter's back curve means sudden shifts: shifts in thoughts, places, or directions. This makes it hard for **S** to plan. **S** must choose someday between the low **C** of body pleasures and the high **C** of spirit. Bad **S** people think only of themselves. They push independence too far and hurt themselves. Some pick the low path over light. But **S** seeks wisdom, as its snake shape shows.

# T.

**T-20**, In English, **T** is the 20th letter. This links it closely to Teith (9) and Tav (22) because: 9 must learn to serve others without selfish gain. 2 wants partners in work and marriage. It must learn to give and take. The 0 after the 2 boosts the power of 2's traits. And 22 doubles 2's lesson. But it adds master skill to give far more of itself. That is why it is "the sign of the cross." The **T** shows self-sacrifice. Its crossbar is a load on its shoulders. It sits on a thin one-line base. All 2's struggle to decide. They see both sides of any issue. The shape of **T** explains this. **T** can go three ways. It makes equal triangles on both sides. Which way should it choose? The cross also shows interest in religion. **T** can be spiritual. It is 20, and the God power of 0 is always there. **T** needs spiritual growth. Or it feels weighed down. **T** gets hurt easily. It often feels used. This is because 2 is very emotional. It feels things deeply. The cross-means self-sacrifice, martyr, or self-pity and "poor me." The negative T has a temper to control. It is stubborn. It must learn patience and tolerance. Positive 2's cooperate and reach out. The negative side pulls back and stays cold. If positive, the traits of 2 grow stronger in 20: co-operative, notices details, neat, diplomatic, peacemaker. All get bigger from the 0 next to it. That top bar is a protective wing. **T** loves family and guards it. The top bar also means "high strung." **T's** often feel tense. When negative feelings take over, they use sarcasm and mean words. Remember, 2 has skill with words, good or bad. If those bad feelings win, they cause trouble in partners and marriage. **T** has more of these traits than other "2 letters" like **B** and **K**. Those do not carry a load on their shoulders.

The flat line stands for matter. The upright line stands for spirit coming down into matter. When they cross (**T**), they form a plus sign: creation. "In the sign of the tally hides the making of all creation" (Book of Tokens, 91). And, "By this letter I reveal all comes from number" (92). **T** Tav is the seventh double letter (**Th**). It links to grace and the beauty of holiness (wholeness). Its opposite is the ugliness of sin and flaw (The Key of Destiny: 319). No Hebrew letter looks just like a cross. But

Phoenicians copied from the Hebrews. They took "sign of the cross" as a real shape and drew their letter as a cross. Greeks copied from the Phoenicians. They moved the flat bar to the top. They named it Tav. The Tav cross also means ten. Its holy sense was perfection, Heaven, the Tetractys, and what it means, plus God's name that can't be spoken. They marked it on the forehead of each person allowed into Mithras mysteries.

# U.

**U-21** Among 3's, **C** spreads out, **L** collects, and **U** takes in most. **U** opens wide for skills and luck (horseshoe shape). But it can tip and spill like a rolling cup if **U** fills up with greed and self-need. This cup **U** holds creative dreams, fresh ideas, charm, and tense nerves to stay steady. Its base shifts from past to future, left to right. This shows doubt and slow choices. **U** holds much inside. But if too nervous or emotional, it tips over and spills. So, **U** should skip bets. This is key with **O**, which means loss. Turn **U** upside down: it is an umbrella. This shows it needs a shield. It builds its own guard. **U** plans. It fills its cup. It may grip too much, too long. **U** loves to gather with zeal. **U** vibrates as 3. But it takes strong 7 traits too. 21 holds three 7's. 7's are warm and faith-filled or cold and thing-focused. **U** opens full. No line splits spirit from body. So, it swings all one way or the other. Its wide spirit door, plus 7 pulls, can make it too wild in faith. All 3's use words well. Like 7's, **U** talks fine or stay quiet and closed. **U** holds high goals. Like 7's, it stays true to old ways. Other 3 letters**, C** and **L,** chase trends and free views. They lack strong 7's. **C** is 3. **L** is 12 (2 times 6). This true-to-old-ways side shows in **U's** high walls. It sets its own lines. Straight sides mean two feeling paths too. Sometimes two clear sides show. A split nature. **U's** sing well and speak clearly. **L** starts things as the leader. It's 1 comes first (12/3). All **Y's** feel deep. But U holds so much inside. It gets too touchy. It can't always share those feelings. Negative **U's** grow jealous, moody, argumentative, and sharp-tongued. They wield words to win or fight (dark 7 traits). They must guard a balance with self-rule. Or they lose all they gain fast. Hebrew has no match for **U. U** comes from **V.** Greeks took letters from Phoenicians. From "waw," they made two shapes. They used it as half-sound W, like in "know." One shape turned to F. This one became the vowel **U.**

# V.

**V-22,** Vav, also called Vav (pronounced vaw), is the sixth letter in the Hebrew alphabet and the second among the 12 simple letters. Light and love form the connection between humans and the Divine. These qualities come from our Creator and appear in the third letter of the sacred name IHVH. When the Phoenicians adopted Vau, they named it Waw and used it for the semi-consonant **W**, as in "know." The Greeks took Waw from the Phoenicians and split it into two letters: Upsilon (**U**) and Digamma for their W sound. Digamma later vanished from Greek. The Romans got Digamma from the Etruscans and turned it into **F**. They shaped Upsilon like **V** to represent **U, V,** and **W** sounds. Ancient Roman writing still uses **V** instead of **U** on government buildings today. The letters **U** and **V** stayed the same in writing until the 18th century. The letter **V** opens fully at the top, so it is highly intellectual with a strong business sense. As the 22nd letter, its 2 energy helps **V** people work well with others. 22 is the Master Builder number, so **V**, especially as the first letter in a name, has leadership potential. It can lead to good or evil, depending on whether the person uses the positive or negative side. **V** people must study metaphysics. With no line dividing spiritual and material worlds, they can fully embrace one or the other. Those focused only on material things become ruthless in business. Those without spiritual light turn into harsh criminals. They need strong moral guides to fulfill their purpose and contribute meaningfully, as they are meant to.

Turned upside down, **V** looks like a mountain peak. **V** people have so much nervous energy that they often feel driven to climb mountains to reach their goals. Normally, **V** balances on a shaky point that touches the earth line. They spend all their money chasing desires, then crave financial safety. But the **V's** point is unsteady, and desires are endless, so **V's** must learn about money management. **V's** need spiritual awareness to calm their restless energy and find inner peace. **V** looks like arms raised, seeking spiritual guidance. It stays wide open to catch ideas for building. It brings vision, strength, and hard work, tied to 22/4, the tireless worker's number. **V** people turn ideas into success better than most, thanks to their talent for directing energy into projects. **V** truly means Victory; they set new goals and win them over and over. **V's** cherished family and love marriage. They work hard to support loved ones. In Latin, life is "Vita," starting with **V** (Vau), the sixth Hebrew letter. Six links to sex. Vau connects man and woman, not just physically, but through the holy spiritual love-force that binds us to the divine. Yod He Vau He names the part of God that gives life to creation. Yod is the male force, He is the female, and Vau is the "nail" or link joining them for birth and all creation from the final He's womb. All life is a sacred gift, and **V** matches the Sixth Commandment: "Thou shalt not kill."

# W.

**W-23,** W comes from the letter V. The Phoenician symbol looked more like a **Y.** They used it for the **W** sound (Oo). They named it Vau or Waw. It stood for man's eye that sees light, and the ear that hears the sound of Ain and the wind. In later Roman times, they wrote the **W** sound as **V.** But one letter covered **U, V, and W** sounds. This caused mix-ups. So, they made a new symbol, **W**, by joining two **V's.** It was for the light "oo" sound. **U** stayed a vowel, and **V** became just a consonant. As a consonant, **W** pictured Water. It stood for taste and hunger. People saw **W** as the image of deepest mystery. The letter rests on two deep valleys. The mystery is the point that divides being from non-being. **W** is the 23rd letter in the English alphabet. This gives it a deep feeling. Both 2 and 3 are emotional numbers. They add to 5, which links to the five physical senses and a need for freedom to handle the changing sides of 5. Too much pleasure in senses, or other bad traits of 5, means living in the low valleys or pits of the W. The high peaks of W rise tall. 5 is the middle number. Ancients called it "the limited master." Wise old men called themselves sages. They controlled themselves by beating the temptations of the five senses. They touched the spiritual. People with a **W** in their name have a shift in awareness at some point in life. They know the consonant side of overindulgence. Some feel it less than others. Those who waste themselves stay in deep valleys, a hard pit to climb. Only a change in awareness lets them escape and reach the peaks. The peaks look like arms raised to seek light. Once done, it is like a man's eye seeing light and ear hearing Air and wind. Only a tuned ear catches these soft sounds and the inner voice. That is living at the peaks of W.

# X.

**X-24,** The Hebrew letter for our **X** is Samekh (saw-mek). It matches **S** and **X**. It pictures a serpent eating its own tail. The Greek name Sigma (**S**) got mixed up with Samekh (**X**). Samekh links to the cross, or Christ principle. So, **S** and **X** swapped places. Schin stands for Fire as the force that cleans and finishes creation. Samekh is the fire that burnt in the world of senses. Some Kabbalists still link **X** to Samekh. Samekh, the 15th Hebrew letter, is the ninth of the 12 simple letters. It means prop or bow. It refers to the bow that shoots an arrow. Its sound is like a serpent's hiss, or the bow string when the arrow flies from the prop. The arrows from the bow are our words. In secret meaning, words either hiss and hurt, or kiss and heal. Samekh rules sleep. If we seek truth and study or meditate for growth, spiritual teachers meet and guide us while our body rests. We often wake with answers to problems or new insights. Those not aware spiritually have mixed-up dreams and nightmares. They wander without guides in strange astral worlds they do not know. The serpent always means wisdom. A serpent eating its tail forms a circle, like a full cycle. A cycle means finish. Like a snake sheds old skin for new life, this sign shows dropping old ways and ending old tasks to start fresh. This follows the "law of the circle": "What you give out comes back. As you sow, so you reap." We must face what we create. What we sow shapes our fate. So good, and **X** is the cross of rising again. So bad, and it is the cross we carry. Greeks took Samekh from the Phoenicians. They changed the shape and called it **Xi**. It became Roman **X.** As Hebrew's 15th letter, it is saint or sinner. It means beat the animal side, or "ex it out." Control emotions fully to become saint-like. As English's 24th letter, it shows magnetic charm. **X** in + shape draws love and family. 6 is the love and family number. Note that both Hebrew 15th (6) and English 24th (6) add to 6 (1+5=6, 2+4=6). On the bad side, it wipes itself out. If crossed, it turns bitter and wants payback. The X shape means self-denial. It opens on all sides, so it is open to harm. Hasty acts can make it **X** itself out. Like President Richard **M.** Nixon, who quit or faced removal. Or actor John Eric Hexum, who played Russian roulette with a gun to his head and died. **X** stands firm on Earth, open to material things. But its arms reach up for spiritual aid. It can be all spiritual or all material, noble or low.

# Y.

**Y-25**, From Yod, Hebrew's 10th letter, come **I, J,** and **Y.** (See **I** and **J** for more on Yod.) **Y's** shape comes from Phoenician Vau, or Waw. Waw was **Y**-shaped. It grew into four letters: **U, W, Y,** and **F.** Romans took letters from the Greeks in the first century BC. They first used **Y** as a vowel. Later, it switched with **I** as a vowel, so **Y** is a consonant. Using an "**i**" sound, it links to Yod. **W** has valleys and peaks for change. **Y** is a fork in the road for choices. Pythagoras said **Y's** as stem is youth. In adulthood, a person hits the fork and must decide. **Y** is a deep thinker. Idle talk feels very uncomfortable. The **V** sits at mind level. It forms a deep cup open to ideas and deep thoughts. **Y** craves quiet, more rest, and calm places. A material-focused **Y** feel pulls to study deeper things. But it may ignore them and choose the wide material road. If very negative, **Y** turns into a loner in this cycle. It falls into excess of sense pleasures. The sudden split into two paths means fast choices. They can be hard. If the person listens to the quiet inner voice and follows it, choices get easier. **Y** shows the path to God. It starts with God's true name, Yod, which is God's light inside everyone.

# Z.

**Z-26,** Zain, or Zayin (zah-yin), is Hebrew's seventh letter. It makes **Z** sound. It rules movement; its meaning is weapon, sword, or arrow, and scepter. This points to conquest. An arrow or sword hits the mark with the right aim and movement. It brings a win. The first seven letters come from Aleph (Air). In Zayin, reach perfect use of Air: master spoken word. Zayin's key weapon is the tongue. Its arrows are words. Words cut like a sharp sword or give love to heal any trouble. Zayin's conquest is tongue mastery. The scepter shows the way from spiritual light.

# Numerology Chart Analysis.

## Part -1: Core Numerology Numbers.

Part 1 of your numerology book serves as the essential gateway for beginners, methodically unveiling the basic calculations for the most pivotal core numbers Life Path, Expression Number, and Heart's Desire Number while empowering readers to decode and analyze their unique personal character traits with confidence and clarity.

### What Your Life Path Number Reveals About You?

In the ancient science of numerology, your Life Path Number stands as one of the most powerful tool for charting the course of your life. Derived from your full birth date, it uncovers the steadfast blueprint you can rely on to unlock true success and fulfillment in the world. This is your singular, God-given path a cosmic roadmap tailored to your soul's purpose.

While many people may share the same Life Path Number, no two journeys are identical. The magic lies in the interplay of all your core numbers: your Destiny Number (from your full name), Soul Urge, Personality Number, and others. Together, they illuminate the best way to navigate your path, revealing shortcuts, pitfalls to avoid, and hidden gems along the way.

Picture your Life Path as a winding adventure: it could be a trail of thorns and blooming roses, testing your resilience while rewarding your courage; or perhaps the enchanted Yellow Brick Road, sparkling with wonder yet demanding heart, brains, and bravery to reach Oz. Every bend and turn brings fresh lessons, synchronicities, and opportunities to express your innate talents, those God-given gifts like creativity, leadership, healing, or wisdom that feel effortless when aligned with your path.

At its essence, your single-digit Life Path Number (reduced from 1 to 9, or master numbers 11, 22, 33) embodies the spiritual imperative placed upon you. It whispers the core lessons your soul came here to master: independence for the 1, harmony for the 2, expression for the 3, and so on. As you place one foot in front of the other, embracing the highs and navigating the lows, this number ensures your journey evolves you into your highest self, step by enlightened step.

## How to Calculate The Lifepath Number?

To calculate your Life Path Number, this foundational number charts the journey of your soul and major life lessons ahead.

- As we discussed earlier, take 5 readings of the closed one's
- Write the 5 different reading sheets. Initially, try to do it manually to get better clarity.
- Now write each Name and Date of Birth in 5 different sheets.
- As its Lifepath, here I'm taking Anvita Hiremat's, taking Date of Birth, and simplifying.
- Date + Month + Year.
- Now Anvita Hiremat's Date of birth is 10/02/1986.
- Date:1 + Month:2 + Year:6= Lifepath:9

Author's Note: Simplify the Date + Month + Year by reducing each to a single digit, then add them completely for your numerology number.

# Lifepath Number Example Chart Date of Birth:10/02/1986.

| Life path Number | | |
|---|---|---|
| Birth Date | Birth Month | Birth Year |
| 10 | 02 | 1986 |
| (1+0=1) | (0+2=2) | (1+9+8+6=24/6) |
| Life path:1+2+6=9 | | |

**Lifepath Number 1:**

Lifepath Number 1 individuals must master their negative self-expressions to achieve their greatest success, most evident in the tactless 1 who alienates others with blunt, overbearing opinions.

A 1's aggression often masks deep loneliness and shaky self-confidence. Their key lesson is to find environments where their strengths flourish; pairing them with steady 4s or authoritative 8s works better than with sensitive 2s or visionary 9s. Impatient by nature, 1s benefit from surrounding themselves with more patient types like 6s, who can gently but firmly challenge them when needed.

Original, inventive, and fiercely independent, 1s spot everything and insist on being first, even if it means shoving others aside. Grasping these traits, whether you're a 1 yourself or dealing with one you love (or tolerate), helps you navigate their intensity with understanding.

**Lifepath Number 2:**

Every number carries strengths and challenges, and the Lifepath Number 2 embodies this duality. Cooperation teeters on the edge of excessive appeasement, while attention to detail can veer into fussiness.

At its core, the 2 shines brightest in partnerships and teamwork. Cooperation defines it, making the 2 the natural diplomat, mediator, and community builder, like the neighbor volunteering with Habitat for Humanity, the committed PTA parent, or the compassionate doctor with Doctors Without Borders.

## Lifepath Number 3:

The Lifepath Number 3: The Sunshine Number. No number embodies self-expression quite like the eternally youthful 3, radiating optimism and bringing more joy than any other. This is the essence of the creative, happy spirit brimming with enthusiasm and imagination. The 3 thrives in the harmonious triad of 3-6-9 (numbers sharing kindred vibrations), ruling the domains of art, inspiration, and spirituality. As the most emotional in this group, it shines through its vivid, dramatic flair. Representing the sacred trinity, the 3 mirrors cycle like birth, life, and death.

## Lifepath Number 4:

The steadfast 4 deeply values honest, diligent work and tackles tasks with unwavering effort to see them through.

While the 3 delights in endless "fun, fun, fun" through its joyful self-expression, the 4 prioritizes discipline, rule-following, seriousness, and caution. Rooted in tradition, practicality, and respectability, the 4 serves as a dependable manager, constructing firm foundations you can always rely on.

Stability defines the 4, leaving it baffled by more carefree approaches. It commits to a full day's labor, stays firmly within boundaries (all four lines), and honors rules and conventions alike. Sober, reliable, persevering, and pragmatic, the 4 embodies endurance. Discipline and dedication fall to the 4, which embraces these qualities with its rock-solid nature.

Efficiency and organization further highlight the 4's disciplined focus and concentration. Trustworthy, honest, and direct, the 4 symbolizes the ideal of an Eagle Scout.

## Lifepath Number 5:

The Lifepath Number 5: The Change-Maker. Change defines all of life, and the 5's existence proves no different. People with 5 in their Life Path or key positions know change intimately it's the steady thread running through their lives, weaving through careers, relationships, and even daily routines. This constant flux opens doors to adventure, risk, excitement, stimulation, and eager exploration, all hallmarks of the number 5. Far from fearing upheaval, 5s embrace it as fuel for growth, turning the unknown into playgrounds of possibility.

Magnetic by nature, 5s stir up the energy whenever things grow stale, ensuring they're reliably the life of the party as long as they don't wander off in pursuit of the next thrill. Their charisma draws people in like a whirlwind, sparking conversations, impromptu trips, or bold ideas that keep everyone on their toes. Restless and versatile, they thrive on variety: one day sampling exotic cuisines, the next diving into a new hobby or debating philosophy under the stars. Freedom is their oxygen; routines feel like chains.

In numerology's cosmic dance, the 5 vibrates with Mercury's quicksilver influence, blending intellect, adaptability, and a sensual zest for experience. They're the explorers, the rebels who question norms and invent new paths, resourceful problem-solvers who turn obstacles into opportunities. Yet this love of liberty can lead to scattered focus or avoidance of deep commitments, reminding 5s to ground their wings occasionally.

## Lifepath Number 6:

Count on the 6 for wise, reliable guidance. Generous, sympathetic, self-sacrificing, caring, and an excellent counselor, these traits might remind you of someone close. Whether craving fresh-baked brownies or a comforting shoulder to cry on, the 6 often provides exactly what's needed.

Look closely at how the number 6 is shaped, and you'll see its plump little belly, brimming with love. The 6 embodies romantic love, passionate love, motherly love, and tender affection. It governs marriage and domestic bliss, symbolizing the heart's core where love lives, grows, and flourishes. From community projects and animal care to teaching children, the 6 infuses everything with deep compassion.

Known as the "Cosmic Mother," the 6 stands at the family's center as the nurturing hub of the wheel, loving, supportive, and healing (and not always the mom; plenty of dads excel here too). Above all, the 6 cherishes this role, though it can occasionally overwhelm independent types like the 1 with excessive mothering.

Ruled by Venus, the planet of love, the 6 perfectly reflects this influence through its passion for beautiful homes and elegant objects, a true Venusian perspective. Artistic and imaginative, 6s possess a keen color sense and often shine in music and vocals, blessed with captivating voices.

## Lifepath Number 7:

The Lifepath Number 7: Looking to the Inner Self. No other number craves solitude quite like the 7, making it the perfect vibration for those whose work demands deep contemplation and alone time. Whether scholar or tech enthusiast, the 7 relentlessly pursues the truth at the core of any matter and settles for nothing less than the most precise answer.

Most 7s boast sharp intellects, often excelling in science, research, or technology. They thrive with computers or anywhere data demands collection and scrutiny, like a forensic specialist leveraging their meticulous observation skills.

You'll spot 7s as archaeologists, deep-sea explorers, numerologists, detectives, or spiritual seekers, anywhere in-depth investigation or analysis rules. Utterly devoted to their pursuits, they dig for concealed truths. For the 7, knowledge equals power, driving them to specialize and master their chosen investigative fields.

## Lifepath Number 8:

The Lifepath Number 8: Personal Power and Excellence. Following the 7's inward focus, the 8 bursts forth with unstoppable force. Anything tied to generating wealth likely involves the 8's influence this is the number of abundances, riches, excellence, and authority. While the 7 turns inward, the 8 projects outward, conquering and expanding the world. At its peak, the 8 masters' personal power, finance, and business are destined to lead as the ultimate boss.

Spot a military general or CEO in the crowd? Odds are 8 features prominently in their chart. This vibration embodies innate leadership and command, ensuring everything runs with precision and order.

The 8 isn't always a lucky personal number, given its risk of dramatic fortune reversals. Yet its core strength, problem-solving prowess, and unyielding dedication turn challenges into triumphs.

## Lifepath Number 9:

The Lifepath Number 9: Completion and Compassion

We reach the cycle's final and most potent number: the 9. This high-vibration force absorbs the essence of all preceding numbers. The 9 signifies understanding life's true worth, the depth of human experience, and our link to the Divine. Endowed with intuitive, spiritual, and emotional strength, it compassionately embraces humanity's struggles, serving others from profound love for all people. Astrologically aligned with Scorpio, the 9 mirrors intense emotions, profound transformation, and a drive for influence. Containing the energy of every number, the 9 echoes in symbols like the nine steps of ancient pyramids.

It governs life's grander scope, think global affairs and international business. This vibration calls for educating, comforting, and safeguarding humanity while advancing Earth's well-being. 9s often enjoy financial success, drawing wealth and fortune as rewards. When prosperous, they generously support charities, particularly in the arts.

## Lifepath Number 11:

Learning to Surrender to Higher Ideals, Master Numbers demand surrender to elevated principles. The 11/2 must embody truth, uncovered through life's trials. Their greatest fulfillment arises from living, sharing, and teaching these personal truths while inspiring others upward. Intense and often electrifying, 11/2s grapple with nervousness from their amplified vibration. Yet they possess remarkable courage and boundless creativity.

Humanitarianism flows from the 11/2's essence. The underlying 2 grants their rare skill for fostering peace via diplomacy. It's no coincidence that Jimmy Carter, the 39th U.S. President and 2002 Nobel Peace Prize winner, carries an 11/2 in the last name he was born to the peacemaker's path.

The 11/2 journey frequently feels obscured, requiring stumbles until their inner foundation solidifies. Only then do they step outward to impart hard-won wisdom. This number grasps the big picture, envisions possibilities, and nurtures dreams but thrives only by actively engaging in their realization.

## Lifepath Number 22:

This Master Number doubles the qualities of the 2, amplifying sensitivity, intuition, harmony, and relational gifts while incorporating the 4's essence of hard work, discipline, practicality, construction, organization, and materialization.

For the 22/4, true magic emerges from how these vibrations intertwine. Picture twin 2s fueling empathy and balance alongside the 4's grounded builder spirit. The 22/4's core challenge and triumph lie in harmonizing the 2's demands with the 4's rigor. Like other Master Numbers, it carries heightened sensitivity for profound perception but risks health strains when unbalanced.

The 22/4 excels in organization: Master Organizer for the Good of All.

This stems from its poised mind wedded to lofty ideals, applied masterfully to every endeavor. A born leader, the 22/4 channels spiritual wisdom into action.

Drawn to innovative ideas and fields advancing human evolution, 22/4s leverage their gifts to create enduring, inspiring legacies. They shine in ultra-specialized arenas, where their precision forges monumental impact.

## Lifepath Number 33:

The 33 awakens others to its profound insight into blending spiritual truths with practical reality. Equally vital is the 33's angelic link to Guardian Angel Michael, protector of each soul's spiritual destiny. In everyday life, the 33/6 champions the underdog with boundless compassion, love, and empathy. This vibration selflessly offers encouragement and deep understanding to those in need, often sacrificing for others' sake. Yet its tender heart and sensitivity leave 33/6s vulnerable, readily absorbing the world's profound sorrows.

## What is the Birth Date Number?

Your date of birth profoundly influences your personality and Expression, shaping your outward disposition as well. By understanding this effect, you gain deeper insight into yourself and others. Grasping a person's core nature empowers you to accomplish tasks through them effortlessly. Regardless of the specific date, your birth number plays a pivotal role in character formation. Always distinguish it clearly from your destiny number: the Expression number reveals your fundamental, lifelong personality traits, while the birth date number reflects the aspect of your personality that others perceive.

**The world-famous numerologist Pythagoras declared that nothing exists without numbers.**

## Birth Date 1:

Individuals born on the 1st of any month possess sharp intelligence, strong determination, and leadership qualities. They exhibit ambition, courage, creativity, and a love for initiating changes and projects with full independence, free from external constraints or directives; they resist following others. Independent and resolute, they rarely yield, which can create enemies or opposition.

Their speech tends to be direct and forceful, yet they remain genuine without pretense. Relatives and friends should recognize their inherent nature, as these individuals seldom display emotions openly, though they crave love, attachment, and sympathy from others. They often experience mental stress and tension, sometimes leading to blood pressure issues. To succeed, they must learn to channel their energy positively.

## Birth Date 2:

Those born on the 2nd of any month embody traits that contrast yet complement those of number 1 individuals. They possess feminine qualities: selfless, emotional, cooperative, and inherently helpful. They avoid quarrels, struggles, or conflicts, always striving to foster peace through negotiation and clear communication between parties.

Ideal friends and reliable assistants, they follow others' guidance with enthusiasm and zeal. Independent efforts often yield limited success, but they thrive in teams, groups, or when aligning with others' plans. They must guard against instability, disappointment, and dejection, though they rarely lose confidence amid adversity. A joyful environment suits them best, and they excel in fine arts. Nurturing this hobby brings fulfillment. In careers, they shine as statesmen, government employees, actors, poets, or craftsmen.

## Birth Date 3:

People born on the 3rd of any month are magnetic, charming, intelligent, imaginative, sociable, enthusiastic, attentive listeners, and joyful. They pursue diverse interests and master the art of communication. As visionaries, they vividly recount stories or events, delighting and entertaining friends, effortlessly earning them a wide circle of admirers.

They love movies, drama, hotels, restaurants, clubs, and museums. Universally liked across communities, they risk scattering energy by juggling too many subjects. Focusing on just one or two areas ensures lasting success. Careers as writers or newspaper reporters allow them to share ideas effectively. They may also excel as advertisers, lawyers, doctors, musicians, actors, speakers, or influential hosts (Yajaman).

## Birth Date 4:

Individuals born on the 4$^{th}$ of any month are trustworthy, responsible, methodical achievers who are economical, sentimental, intelligent, authoritative, industrious, reliable, hardworking, determined, traditional, and somewhat challenging to manage. They resist frequent changes and stay immersed in their pursuits, completing tasks punctually while upholding truth and justice.

They often overexert themselves, risking their health. Though they avoid quarrels, they attract enemies. As lovers, they prove steadfast and enduring. Prone to disappointment, they overlook promising opportunities, leading to jealousy, short-tempered reactions over minor issues, tension, headaches, and occasional mental distress. They thrive as contractors, architects, managers, auditors, draftsmen, mechanics, or soldiers.

## Birth Date 5:

People born on the 5$^{th}$ of any month are unstable and restless, yet intelligent learners, quick thinkers, and decisive. They crave change, embracing travel and distancing themselves from home. Their love for variety makes them resist restraint and rules.

Eager for quick gains, they gravitate toward shares, speculation, and gambling, sometimes wagering everything, only to face ruin and beggary due to fate's twists. Life brings constant ups and downs, yet they repeat past mistakes without learning. Wise and cunning, they leverage communication to deceive others. Despite this, they appear intelligent, cheerful, witty, and refined, excelling in eloquence for literature, acting, sales, or dealings.

Their vicious streak drives them to exploit others ruthlessly, even neglecting close kin. To succeed, they must curb emotions, think logically, weigh pros and cons carefully, and pause before acting.

## Birth Date 6:

Those born on the 6th of any month are calm and quiet, reliable, fraudulent, and loving. amicable, practical, responsible, dedicated with a humanitarian nature, and beauty lovers. fond of fine arts, negotiations, peace, and communication, and also loyal to their family. community and children. They always like friendship, cooperation, love, and appreciation. Their criticism makes them unhappy. They have a natural love for music. They have a clear, melodious, and effective voice. Therefore, they may work very well as a social worker or actor, musician, etc. Love and beauty are their characteristics. They believe that love can win anything. Therefore, they love all their near and dear ones and want to work as their subordinates. These are romantic types of people and well-versed in the art of love. They decorate their house decently and always entertain their friends and relatives. They implement their schemes meticulously. Therefore, they can make desired progress in their work. They love their children, but do not get the same in return. Mostly, their financial position is good or satisfactory. The women born on this date are very good at cooking and have all the qualities of an ideal housewife as they take utmost care of their husband, children, and the entire family at large.

Normally, they do not get angry. However, whenever they lose their temper, it becomes very difficult to calm down. For people who are not to their liking, they have enmity for a long period. At times, these people become unnecessarily adamant. Therefore, to achieve success in their life, they should try to keep all these evils under check.

**<u>Birth Date 7:</u>**

Those born on the 7th of any month are people of strong personality with a peaceful and solitary nature. They are serious, intelligent, wise, skilled, unique, introverted, independent, creative, imaginative, analytical, original thinkers with a unique character, studious, humble, sensitive, and fault-finders. They analyze everything systematically and can achieve their targets. They do not make a show of their feelings.

Therefore, they are considered to be heartless people by other people. They have a liking for changes. Therefore, the start of their life is not stable, and they experience frequent changes of job or business. Due to this nature, they have their changing relations with the people and go out on frequent small journeys. These people are wise and adept in the art of minting money. But some of them mostly neglect the financial and physical achievements. They work with a feeling of social work and do not enjoy the external side of rituals. For these people, service of humanity is the service of God and the actual religion. They have an aptitude for literature, music, dance, fine arts, and astrology.

**<u>Birth Date 8:</u>**

Individuals born on the 8th of any month are kind, generous, practical, utilitarian, creatively skilled, managerial, ambitious, determined, hardworking, authoritative, progressive, and sympathetic. They possess all the acumen needed for business, handling transactions with utmost care, which propels them to great success in trade and commerce. Life brings them abundant wealth, property, and popularity.

They seek to dominate others, expecting unwavering trust from relatives and family. Intolerant of others' flaws, they show deep sympathy for the socially weak, backward, exploited, downtrodden, and aggrieved, offering every possible aid. In crises, people seek their counsel and support. Though selfishly motivated, they dispense advice freely but rarely tangible help.

They flaunt their wealth ostentatiously, embracing luxury. They adorn homes and furniture, acquire ornaments and gems, and lavish facilities on spouses, children, subordinates, and servants, often just for show. They buy preferred books to own but seldom read or engage with them. Charities and major institutions earn them respect and acclaim, fostering satisfaction and a sense of triumph. Truly fortunate in property, finances, and prestige, they excel as lawyers, executives, accountants, musicians, or village panchayat leaders.

## **Birth Date 9:**

Those born on the 9th of any month are intelligent, strong-willed, resolute, intuitive, generous, sympathetic, emotional, and spiritually empowered yet short-tempered due to their sensitivity. Humanitarian at heart, they embrace service, finding joy despite life's losses. They possess innate talent for music, dance, acting, fine arts, and poetry.

Eager to exercise their powers freely, they suffer deeply from separations or deaths of loved ones. Frequent travel and life away from home define them, exposing them to diverse customs, communities, values, and global issues. This broadens their perspective, amplifying qualities like sympathy, endurance, equality, and universal peace. Far from self-centered living, they derive true pleasure, peace, and fulfillment from serving humanity.

They excel in acting, drama, poetry, writing, eloquence, teaching, music, painting, gardening, and other artistic, literary, or intellectual pursuits as lawyers, speakers, activists, preachers, advertisers, tourists, or those engaging foreigners. Some become renowned spiritual leaders.

## Birth Date 10:

Persons born on the 10th of any month are intelligent, strong, resolute, original, independent, aggressive, creative, impulsive, unconventional, short-tempered, cheerful, ever-ready, amiable, and generous. They resist family constraints, readily aiding others yet rarely receiving help in their own crises.

Undaunted by dire situations or impossible challenges, they devise solutions and progress steadily. Blessed with professional expertise, they shine as organizers and managers in business or careers. Generally healthy, they rebound swiftly from physical or mental setbacks.

## Birth Date 11:

Modern numerologists hail 11 as a master number, blessing those born on the 11th of any month with exceptional luck. Emotionally, excitable, charming, and gifted organizers, managers, and administrators, they think and act with originality, creativity, and precision. They deeply care for and protect those they favor, ensuring their well-being.

Treating everyone like friends, they amass a few enemies. Adept at reading situations, they respond effectively and execute ideas flawlessly, prioritizing action over daydreams. Endowed with divine intuition, they transform inspirations into practical realities. Nervous by nature, they fret over trifles; despite strong willpower, they shift ideas and desires often. Outwardly calm, impressive, and happy, they inwardly battle tension.

In love and emotions, they swing to extremes, demanding a high-quality life from others, too. Success comes from following conscience over logic or mind. Their organizational and administrative skills shine, though wavering thoughts mix with radical creativity. Lucky yet facing recurring challenges, they ultimately embrace spirituality and religion. Humanitarian at core, they take offense easily, prioritizing social status and prestige above all.

## Birth Date 12:

Authoritative and ambitious, they balance open-minded thinking with responsibility as revolutionary reformers and diplomats. Possessing strong character, leadership qualities, and a taste for luxury, their external charm captivates. Endowed with most virtues, they impress through speech and writing. Deeply romantic, excitement, love, and sympathy shape their lives. They express affection via words, gestures, and actions when needed.

Though eloquent, they sometimes turn overly vocal or uncivil. To manage ups and downs, they must temper harshness and rudeness. Strict yet caring parents, they enforce discipline meticulously. Exceptional leaders in any field should avoid scattering energy, focusing intently on chosen plans, which yields results. Unyielding to power but soft toward loved ones, their dual nature blends calm balance with occasional impatience. Cooperative yet stubbornly adamant at times, they crave variety despite mental stability, occasionally growing nervous or tense but mastering emotional control. Success blooms later in life; advancing years and old age bring prosperity and fulfillment. They excel as orators, writers, preachers, advertisers, actors, designers, architects, or lawyers.

## Birth Date 13:

Though often deemed unlucky, 13 proves auspicious for most, far from inauspicious reality drawing combined strength from 1 and 3, symbolizing enthusiasm, power, life force, ambition, and practicality.

Born on the 13th, they are intelligent, generous, enthusiastic, reliable, patient, dedicated, authoritative, emotional, sympathetic, leadership-endowed, skilled administrators and organizers, adamant, ambitious, tirelessly hardworking, simple, and innocent. They meticulously plan every endeavor beforehand, executing with care and vigilance.

**Birth Date 14:**

Combining digits 1 and 4 to reduce to the basic number 5, this date blends traits from 1, 4, and 5. Those born on the 14th are intelligent, creative, legislative-minded, learned, resolute, thoughtful, ambitious, sensitive, wise, hardworking, industrious, efficient, linguistically gifted, eloquent orators, diplomatic, authoritative, conservative, and charming.

They crave changes and variety, thriving on life's sensations and excitement. Blessed with abundant life force, they often fixate on trivial matters, causing disruptions, ups and downs, and wasted potential. They must curb strength misuse, avoiding excess sensual pleasures, rivalries, cold drinks, and frequent snacking. Non-quarrelsome yet enemy-prone, they prove extra-emotional, taking offense at minor slights.

**Birth Date 15:**

People born on the 15th of any month have traits from numbers 1, 5, and 6. They are wise, powerful, smart, strong, brave, determined, honest, quick to decide, kind, giving, gentle, loving, welcoming, bold thinkers, helpful, caring, friendly, and easy to get along with. Sometimes they can be stubborn or bossy. They love their family and make great parents and teachers as strong, independent people. They have youthful energy and sharp observation skills that help them learn a lot. They enjoy fine arts and have a nice voice.

They like music, help others, and care for older family members. They often put others first and may sacrifice for them, though some live luxuriously. They hold grudges and jealousy for a long time against people they dislike. They love learning and gaining knowledge. They work hard for peace, fairness, and financial success in life. They reach their goals and get a good education. They can succeed as lawyers, doctors, teachers, professors, speakers, leaders, government workers, nurses, or in smart jobs, arts, or music.

**Birth Date 16:**

This number mixes 1 and 6, with a root number of 7, so it carries traits from 1, 6, and 7. People born on the 16th of any month are smart, strong, brilliant, brave, self-reliant, firm with sharp focus, inventive, driven, and full of insight. They take a long time to decide and rarely lead big fields. Others get pulled in by their warm, likable charm. They look calm and silent on the outside, but inside, they deal with stress and constant worry. They cut off anyone who opposes them. They move ahead quickly and well, leaving rivals far behind. So, people envy them. They have quick tempers and get upset easily. They should not get mad at odd events or unknown results, and must keep calm. Sometimes, their dreams predict future happenings. They enjoy being guided by those they love.

They are dreamy and perfect romantic partners. They want a pretty, fancy home. They decorate well without any lessons. They support artists and fine arts workers generously. They welcome guests with full kindness. They succeed in business and trade. They love their family deeply and do anything to help them grow. As dreamers, they spot their own flaws, get very down, and feel blue at times. They prefer village life in nature. They should pick jobs in science, writing, teaching, decorating, gardening, painting, acting, mining, metals, business, or trade. They can do well as news reporters or builders. Folks born on this date gain lots of worldly wins and success.

**Birth Date 17:**

This number blends 1 and 7, giving a root number of 8. People born on the 17th of any month are strong, brilliant, goal-driven, self-reliant, brave, emotional, creative, giving, commanding, and always wrapped up in their tasks. They have tons of energy and grit. So, their hard work in one area often leads to the success they want. They are eager to learn new things. With their drawing and charming ways, they pull people toward them. Because they cooperate well, they notice others' emotions and feel kindly toward them. They have mixed traits. Sometimes they spend way too much, and other times they pinch every penny. At times, they seem old-fashioned and careful; at others, they run businesses in fresh, new ways. They stick to old habits and steady work methods with full duty. No one can change them.

They feel proud of their family and work hard for their joy and comfort. They enjoy music that mixes reason and fancy. So, they can shine as writers, poets, actors, directors, guides, and artists. They may also win in business with land, rocks, oil, and farm animals. They can succeed as bank bosses, group starters, managers, deal-makers, helpers in society, book publishers, and library keepers. These folks usually live happy and lucky lives.

**Birth Date 18:**

This number mixes 1 and 8, adding up to the root number 9, so it holds traits of 1, 8, and 9. People born on the 18th of any month are very smart, all-rounded, brilliant, emotional, touchy, cultured, self-reliant, logical, debate-loving, perfection-seeking, power-hungry, a bit unkind to flaws, caring for others, dreamy, and people-focused. They handle any job top-notch and want the same skill from everyone else. So, they get impatient with others. They might point out faults in people. In money matters, they follow old ways. They take on duties to aid the poor and old. They are born creators. They can excel as writers and critics, but hate tips or cautions from others. They love traveling or taking trips. They show strong interest in politics, law, faith, and spiritual matters. They may win in business or factories tied to travel, oil, and home animals. If they don't live smart and sharp, they face many letdowns and losses. They don't get long, joyful marriages. They can do great as cash handlers or trust keepers for groups.

**Birth Date 19:**

This number blends 1 and 9, making root number 1, with traits from both 1 and 9. Double 1 energy makes these people extra strong. All born on the 19th of any month are brave, full of zeal, energetic, mighty, smart, many-sided, brilliant, iron-willed, tricky leaders who are gentle and caring, independent, and kind-hearted toward others. They express themselves perfectly. They stay strict in thoughts, words, feelings, and tasks. They love lots of changes and push for steady growth. They think in bold, new ways. They rarely take others' advice. So, they face many shifts in life. They get both wins and losses. For them, no middle path exists. Life brings constant twists, ups, and downs. Sometimes they feel very tense or worked up, but hold no hate, grudge, or spite against anyone. In marriage, they find true joy, yet even multiple weddings don't end their feelings. With their wide genius, they win in many areas and jobs. They can shine as eye, nose, ear, throat specialists, lawyers, music makers, government workers, and builders. They are mostly lucky, but their too-daring side sometimes brings flops.

**Birth Date 20:**

This number mixes 2 and 0, with root number 2. Zero is seen as quiet and silent in numerology, so this date mainly shows number 2 traits. People born on the 20th of any month are smart, far-seeing, kind, yielding, warm, giving, emotional, loyal, trusty, skilled, people-loving, good-wishers, knowledgeable, caring for the sad, friendly, and always ready to help. They look after their family and those who depend on them well. They avoid big duties. So, instead of leading, they prefer teaming up in small or large groups. They love music and acting, plus time with family in nature or village spots. They succeed only with creative living; a bad path makes them shaky and sad. So, they must use control, smarts, and think of many sides. They handle any task well and in order. They make perfect parents, spouses, partners, and pals. Anyone seeking their aid or tips leaves happy. They give full support, but some misuse their kindness. So, they should not spend money and effort on others' good; it leaves them weak for their own half-done work. They must watch so others don't overuse them. They don't speak well, but write their thoughts sharply. So, they are fine writers. They should avoid being too touchy, emotional, unsure, shaky, or fidgety; else, they face letdowns, gloom, and hard times that hurt body and mind. They can win as thinkers, mind experts, gatherers, actors, prayer leaders, faith teachers, leaders in rule, number readers, music makers, office helpers, shorthand writers, or law guides.

## Birth Date 21:

This number has two parts: 2 and 1, making the root number 3. So, it carries traits of 1, 2, and 3. People born on the 21st of any month are smart, deep-thinking, far-seeing, emotional, creative, team players, guided by gut feelings, mentally tough, curious about many topics, a bit touchy and jumpy, goal-driven, joyful, funny, romantic, and full of charm. They are super popular, care about others, and live with advice and help from people around them. They have loads of friends and known faces. They skip heavy topics. Mostly, they see things lightly, not too seriously. They master drawing people in and hang with like-minded or total opposites. They love music, dance, arts, and books. They join club events, meetings, and fun gatherings, enjoying tunes, plays, laughs, jokes, and imitations with pals. They speak well and paint vivid pictures of what they see and live. They have many skills to help their family, community, and jobs. They gain their wins even while aiding others. They think and work their own way, pushing tasks they like. So, they make some foes. They don't make great spouses due to rush, nerves, and doubt. They must work hard to tame their emotional and edgy sides. They need to guard against high blood pressure and heart issues. They should do the steady corpse pose and meditation. They are fortunate and grab plenty of cash, fame, and respect in life. They can win as teachers, writers, book makers, actors, artists, news writers, and ad creators.

## Birth Date 22:

This number consists of double 2, which makes the basic number 4. Therefore, this number has a combined effect of numbers 2 and 4. According to modern numerology, the number 22 is considered to be a master number and, for that matter, a powerful or outstanding number.

All the great persons of this world were born on this birth date and had accomplished the general welfare of humanity with a missionary zeal. All those born on the 22nd of any month are emotional, strong, courageous, conscious, busy in others' welfare, humanitarian, and practical. They have a fine mixture of idealism and practicality. They chalk out systematic big plans for the general welfare of society and humanity at large and execute them with the fullest dedication. In a way, they are the creators of a new world. Generally, they have only a small bit of material gain. They should maintain their skills and organizational as well as managerial capacity. They should not be too generous, emotional, pessimistic, or lazy. Since they become frequently nervous, they experience the pricks of mental tension. Therefore, as far as possible, they should live in isolation with proper rest and regular meditation, etc. They may be successful as social welfare officers, labor welfare officers, trade union leaders, nursery school teachers, dancers, accountants, lawyers, mechanics, geophysicists, mine engineers, and also in the field of business of export and import.

**Birth Date 23:**

This number blends 2 and 3, making the root number 5. So, it mixes the effects of 2, 3, and 5. People born on the 23rd of any month are very smart, far-seeing, touchy, wise, keen to share thoughts, well-read, great speakers, outgoing, warm, down-to-earth, brave, doubtful, unsure-minded, quirky, and firm. They skip the usual polite rules but share their real feelings. Their charming pull grabs the eyes of like-minded and opposites. They have tons of fans and friends. They should stay away from mind tricks or odd fantasies. They love social fun like weddings, meetings, and hangouts. They gain from folks from other lands. They bend to fit shifting times. They live plain lives without big dreams or wild events. They read and grasp others' thoughts well. They are free, loose, and in charge. So, they hate limits, rules, or curbs. They must watch their health or face acid issues, joint pain, and shaky nerves in later years. They should fix their flip-floppy ways and stick to one job or business.

**Birth Date 24:**

This number mixes 2 and 4, making the root number 6. So, it blends the effects of 2, 4, and 6. People born on the 24th of any month are very smart, busy-working, tireless, watchful doers, team helpers, caring, true, steady, committed, sharp-focused, a bit strict and rough, dutiful, hard to sway, stubborn, inventive, art and beauty fans, and into making things. They love tough tasks. They feel deep love for family and try their best to aid them. They choose real-world and art goals. They like teamwork over going solo and often win that way. They make fine teachers and learn much from pupils, so they are good learners too. They are perfect parents, but must stay real, not dreamy, to succeed. They tend to the old and love decking out home and work with art items. They should drop worry, envy, and nitpicking. They live long lives. Mostly, they speak well and act strongly. They have sweet voices and should aim to sing well. They can win as speakers, writers, artists, music makers, actors, money handlers, business folks, community helpers, teachers, cooks, nurses, or doctors.

**Birth Date 25:**

This number blends 2 and 5, making the root number 7. So, it mixes traits of 2, 5, and 7. People born on the 25th of any month are lively, shining, shaky, too-touchy, thinking deeply, commanding, true, committed, far-seeing, aware, gifted with holy sight and invention, giving, soft, team players, caring, and truth seekers. They crave switches, mix-ups, buzz, thrills, growth, moves, trips, love, and sparks. They hide feelings and true thoughts from others, causing mix-ups and wrong ideas about them. They don't take new stuff fast. But after long thought, they agree. They must not let feelings rule, as it harms the mind and work power. They don't grasp their own skills. They should skip two-faced ways, hopes, letdowns, grumps, and taking on others' mad or judging vibes. They need to build advice skills, steadiness, and grit. Sometimes they turn super calm, grave, and locked-in, so even family and pals can't get them. They should live plain and naturally in village air. Many times, waits and flops hit their life, but patience gets them goals. They can win in fine arts, painting, carving, handicrafts, ad art, rule-making, writing, and detective work.

## Birth Date 26:

This number blends 2 and 6, making the root number 8. So, it mixes traits of 2, 6, and 8. People born on the 26th of any month are tough, smart, driven, grave, giving, team helpers, caring; they see others' struggles, shy-inside, self-thinking, and pros at striking, pulling charm. Mostly, they wed young, so they face love life snags. Still, they hold deep love for home, family, spouse, and kids, and fret over their well-being. They like to flaunt. They have solid learning and values. Skip arts; pick business or trade as top runners and bosses, they manage huge factories and groups well. But drop doing tons at once; it drains and spreads energy thin. They act like always-set fighters in life's fights. Don't take life too seriously; live normally and gladly, or joy slips away. They itch to share tips and know-how. They love hot but can't show it. They watch skills closely, so sometimes trap in tough spots. Drop the over-worry habit. They can win as fine engineers, law pros, rule makers, book makers, teachers, head teachers, number keepers, trip runners, team guides, and music makers.

## Birth Date 27:

This number blends 2 and 7, making root number 9. So, it holds traits of 2, 7, and 9. People born on the 27th of any month are smart, touchy, far-seeing, sharp-analyzing, science-minded, dreamy, perfection-chasers, well-read, many-skilled, inventive, thoughtful, logic-based thinkers, team players, caring, and firm. As lone wolves, they skip group-sharing ideas. They love mix-ups, with wide life know-how. They have leader skills and hate underling roles instead of aiding or helping, they shine as bosses, heads, or planners in groups or factories. They got writing gifts and acting skills. They dig yoga, spirit ways, and hidden knowledge. They make fine lovers, but most wed as kids, and marriages seldom last. They map big, long plans and turn dreams into real shapes. Sometimes they get edgy and grumpy. So, skip long alone time be social, mingle, stay sharp. Stay off booze and drugs. They can win as teachers, head teachers, writers, poets, makers, speakers, news writers, deal-makers, doctors, and lawyers. They may also thrive in trains, moving goods, talk lines, mail wires, and TV.

### Birth Date 28:

This number is a combination of numbers 2 and 8, which makes the basic number 1. Therefore, this number has all the traits of numbers 2, 8, and 1. All those born on the 28th of any month are intelligent, taking initiative in every work, self-dependent, equipped with leadership qualities, creative, strong-willed, ambitious, materialistic, independent, idealistic, generous, working for others' welfare, patient, courageous, enthusiastic, cooperative in nature, and to some extent authoritative for others. They have capacities of good management and administration. They can give a practical shape to their ideas and plans. Since they stand for personal liberty, they do not like any rules, limitations, or restrictions. They try to be independent thinkers and workers. Therefore, they miss the sympathy of their friends and colleagues. In order to achieve success, they should keep away from laziness and an authoritarian attitude. They may achieve success as a teacher, professor, scientist, advisor, advocate, engineer, or architect.

### Birth Date 29:

This number blends 2 and 9, making the basic number 11 (root 2). In modern numerology, 11 is a master or top number, so it mixes traits of 2, 9, and 11. People born on the 29th of any month are wise, smart, big thinkers, dreamers, friendly, warm, team players, caring, spirit-led, gifted with inner knowing, holy sight, sharp analysis, many skills, self-reliant, and born leaders. They join big meetings, hangouts, and club events. Their friendly ways help them grow in reading, writing, and solo study on any topic. They push deep till perfect, never quitting halfway.

They eye many fields, drawing folks to their smarts and know-how. They have endless pals and never lack friends. They dive into others' troubles and give full aid. Feelings don't sway them

They help smartly. They speak kindly to family and kin, aiding as much as possible. Some moments they're super glad, others deeply let down or self-only. Skip extremes; take the middle path in all. As edgy and moody types, they worry nonstop. They should keep busy to stay busy and cut their worry load. They feel world-citizen over one country. Mostly lucky. They win as writers, speakers, teachers, head teachers, business folks, music makers, music guides, and ship, radio, or engineering.

## Birth Date 30:

People born on the 30th carry strong number 3 effects. They are smart, far-seeing, gut-driven, outgoing, warm, loving, sharp, charming, and pulling. In talks, they toss in laughs, jabs, and teases. Many traits sleep inside them. Though life hits hard with troubles, they awaken hidden powers to win tough spots. They must not misuse brains, strength, cash, or charm. Drop selfish, tight minds that work without eyeing gains. They skip steady small jobs or body work. They love and have skill in the fine arts. They dig magic tools, chants, number lore, and hidden sciences. They share ideas and hearts freely. Wise ones, their views and aims stay true. Endless friends and fans surround them. They lead groups to wins. Skip emotional nerves, live creatively and right. They win as writers, teachers, head teachers, bosses, ad makers, and people helpers.

## Birth Date 31:

This number mixes 3 and 1, making the root number 4. So, it holds traits of 1, 3, and 4. People born on the 31st of any month are far-seeing, watchful, inventive, touchy, calm and still, iron-willed, sharp, steady, true, bold-changing, commanding, hard-working, real-world, penny-pinching, and strong-set. They skill their hands and fingers best, so shine as makers, fixers, and artists. They chase clear goals and sometimes turn super stubborn. They cling tight to work ways and old rules, refusing any switch. To win in life, they must heed their inner voice. They put others first and take big hits. So, mind their own business, too. Mostly, they wed young and live long. Drop gloom and letdowns. They can win as healers, body docs, chem-mixers, med sellers, office scribes, shorthand pros, writers, number trackers, and machine builders.

# What is the Expression Number?

The Expression number is a key part of numerology that points directly to the natural talent or special skill deep inside your soul. It's like a built-in gift that you carry with you from birth, guiding how you express yourself in the world. People often call this the Destiny number because it maps out the path your life is meant to take based on your unique strengths. You calculate your Expression number by taking every single letter in your full birth name, the one given to you at birth, including your first, middle, and last names. Each letter has a number value (like A=1, B=2, and so on up to I=9, then it repeats with J=1).

You add them all up and reduce to a single digit (or master number like 11 or 22) to find your Expression number. This makes it personal and tied to how the world named you. What does this number really mean? It symbolizes all the opportunities and possibilities that life puts right in front of you, waiting for you to grab them. It shows what you truly aim to become or achieve in your lifetime, your big dreams and goals. At the same time, it highlights the capabilities and talents you bring to the table, like being a natural leader, a creative artist, or a caring helper. But it's honest too: it also reveals the shortcomings or weaknesses you started life with, such as fears, bad habits, or areas where you need to grow. These aren't punishments; they're challenges to overcome so you can shine brighter.

## Pythagoras Chart For Expression Number:

| Pythagoras Chart | | | | | | | | |
|---|---|---|---|---|---|---|---|---|
| 1 | 2 | 3 | 4 | 5 | 6 | 7 | 8 | 9 |
| A | B | C | D | E | F | G | H | I |
| J | K | L | M | N | O | P | Q | R |
| S | T | U | V | W | X | Y | Z | ----- |

## How to Calculate The Expression Number?

- As we used in Lifepath, take the same 5 readings and keep the Date of Birth after calculation.
- By calculating the Date of Birth, you calculated 2 core numbers: those are Lifepath and Birth Date.
- Now we will learn the 3rd core number, which is the Expression Number.
- Take the same 5 details of the same people and write down their complete name (remember First Name, Middle Name, Last Name, and simplify them).
- Write the number allocated to letters according to Pythagoras' chart and write them carefully, verify the calculation twice, then simplify it to a single digit or Master number (11,22,33,44).
- And then add all the numbers, which we call the Expression Number.

**Expression Example Chart Complete Name: Anvita Hiremat.**

| Expression Number | | | | | | | | | | | | | | |
|---|---|---|---|---|---|---|---|---|---|---|---|---|---|---|
| First Name | | | | | | | | Last Name | | | | | | |
| Vowel | 1 | | | 9 | | 1 | | | 9 | | 5 | | 1 | |
| Name | A | N | V | I | T | A | | H | I | R | E | M | A | T |
| Consonants | | 5 | 4 | | 2 | | | 8 | | 9 | | 4 | | 2 |
| First Name: 22/4 | | | | | | | | Last Name:38/11 | | | | | | |
| 22+11=33/6 | | | | | | | | | | | | | | |

**Expression Number 1:**

Number 1 symbolizes achieving your goals and dreams through bold, decisive action. It stands for fresh starts, forward momentum on your life's journey, and unshakeable self-confidence rooted in personal ego. This number pulses with the energy of leadership and independence, urging you to step into the spotlight and carve your unique path. People influenced by Number 1 are natural trailblazers, think of innovators like inventors or entrepreneurs who turn visions into reality, driven by an inner fire that refuses to settle for less.

Spiritually, Number 1 embodies the Creator and your higher Spiritual Self, the divine spark within. It represents the profound union and balance between the spiritual realm and the material world, dissolving any illusion of separation. In this sacred perspective, there is only The One: a unified whole where everything physical is infused with spirit. No longer do we view the earthly plane as "separate" from the cosmos; every atom, every ambition, vibrates with divine essence. This awareness awakens a sense of oneness, aligning your ego-driven pursuits with universal purpose.

In numerology, Number 1 often links to the Sun in planetary influences, radiating vitality, authority, and creative power. If 1 dominates your core numbers (like Life Path or Destiny), you thrive on autonomy but may face lessons in balancing self-reliance with collaboration. Embrace its energy to manifest dreams, but temper ego with humility to avoid isolation.

**Expression Number 2:**

Expression Number 2 governs relationships with yourself, others, and the world around you. It embodies friendship, love, and peace. This number navigates dualities like negative and positive, male and female, and more. Spiritually, it signifies the descent of Spirit into Matter or the act of Creation itself. It represents the connection between your Higher Self and Lower Self.

**Expression Number 3:**

Expression Number 3 represents self-expression. To share who you truly are, you first need to know yourself deeply. For those who've hidden their real emotions due to reasons like abuse or fear of rejection, Number 3 challenges you to heal, build inner strength, and finally reveal your authentic self. It also signifies the journey of discovering and voicing that true identity. You'll feel a strong pull to create and share peace and beauty in various forms while surrounding yourself with these vibes. Social connections will draw you in endlessly, and your ideals will guide your steps.

On a spiritual plane, Number 3 marks the emergence of three layers of consciousness: body awareness, soul recognition, and the enlightenment of Spirit.

**Expression Number 4:**

Expression Number 4 stands for work, responsibility, and organization. It embodies trust and devotion. Spiritually, it represents the Path of Evolution, Redemption, and Karma, where you harvest the results of your choices. This number depicts the soul confined in physical form, bound by all its restrictions. Liberation demands unwavering trust and devotion to a spiritual path. It also marks the initial initiation on the spiritual plane, paving the way for the soul's reunion with its Creator.

## Expression Number 5:

Expression Number 5 signifies personal freedom and transformation. It fuels experiences, travel, and boundless curiosity. With its influence, you'll advance steadily toward your ambitions. Spiritually, it symbolizes the soul's effort to transcend the material realm. It marks the dawn of the spiritual journey, the awakening that life extends far beyond the physical body and world.

It is known as "The Expansion of Man" and represents the Christ resurrected from matter. It is known as "The Limitation of Man," "The Four Lords of Destiny," or "The Four Elements."

## Expression Number 6:

Expression Number 6: The Harmonizer of Hearts embodies responsibility, power, and selfless service. It governs key decisions, necessary adjustments, nurturing home life, and committed marriage. Those touched by this number often become the family's anchor, balancing duties with love while wielding quiet authority to foster unity.

Spiritually, Number 6 fuses justice with mercy, empowering you to deliver fairness infused with deep compassion and understanding. It creates perfect harmony between spirit and matter, seamlessly aligning Divine Will with your human will. This sacred blend turns everyday challenges into opportunities for growth, reminding you that true power lies in empathetic leadership.

In numerology, Number 6 resonates with Venus, the planet of love, beauty, and relationships, amplifying your natural magnetism and creative flair. If 6 features prominently in your chart (like Life Path or Expression Number), you excel in caregiving roles, such as teachers, healers, or community builders, but watch for over-responsibility leading to burnout. Embrace its energy by prioritizing self-care alongside service.

## Expression Number 7:

Expression Number 7: The Seeker of Inner Divinity signifies the God Self within the Christ consciousness or the flawless expression of your true essence. It channels wisdom, profound knowledge, dedicated study, and meditative depth. This number awakens spiritual self-realization, inviting deep introspection and the blossoming of your intuitive gifts.

Often called the "spiritual number," 7 draws you inward like a quiet sage, urging solitude for revelation. It's the mystic's ally, where analytical minds meet heart-centered knowing, revealing truths beyond the surface.

In numerology, Number 7 aligns with Ketu, the south lunar node, symbolizing detachment, past-life wisdom, and enlightenment. If 7 dominates your core numbers (Life Path, Expression), you're a natural philosopher, researcher, or healer think scientists, poets, or meditators who uncover hidden patterns. Strengths include razor-sharp insight and resilience; challenges may involve isolation or overthinking.

## Expression Number 8:

Expression Number 8: The Architect of Abundance governs the material realm of life, channeling the tangible forces that shape success. It embodies raw power, wealth accumulation, political savvy, survival instincts, and unwavering dependability. Under its influence, you'll sharpen focus on the physical body health, vitality, and disciplined routines become key to sustaining your empire.

Spiritually, Number 8 amplifies your inner voice, or intuition, making it crystal clear. If you're already attuned, this number supercharges it, turning gut feelings into prophetic guidance amid worldly chaos.

Known as the "number of infinity" due to its symbol (∞), 8 teaches karmic balance: what you build in matter echoes in spirit. It links to Saturn, the taskmaster planet of structure, discipline, and long-term rewards, often reflecting past-life efforts.

If 8 features strongly in your chart (Expression Number), you're a born executive, investor, or leader, ambitious builders like real estate moguls or CEOs. Strengths: Strategic genius, resilience under pressure; challenges: Workaholism, materialism, or power struggles.

## Expression Number 9:

Expression Number 9: The Universal Compassionate marks completion and closure, guiding you to wrap up chapters with grace and finality. It empowers letting go of what no longer serves, old habits, toxic ties, or outdated beliefs, making space for renewal. This number sparks a deep willingness to serve humanity and fuels wanderlust for travel, broadening your horizons through diverse cultures.

Spiritually, Number 9 elevates the soul's highest expression: selfless service to others, embracing universal knowledge and boundless love, all sharpened by profound intuition. It's the humanitarian's vibration, where personal endings birth collective good.

In numerology, Number 9 resonates with Mars, the warrior planet of courage and sacrifice, often signaling a culmination of the 1-9 cycle before rebirth into new beginnings. If 9 dominates your profile (Life Path or Expression Number), you're a visionary artist, activist, or healer like global philanthropists or spiritual teachers who live for the greater good. Strengths: Empathy, idealism, creative genius; challenges: Martyrdom, unfinished business, emotional overwhelm.

## Expression Number 11:

Expression Number 11: The Illuminated Messenger is a master number, intensifying its vibration far beyond standard numbers and demanding heightened responsibility whenever it activates in your chart. It radiates pure inspiration, propelling you toward selfless service for humanity's upliftment. This powerhouse embodies sudden revelations, soaring idealism, and razor-sharp intuition, often delivering prophetic insights.

At its core, Number 11 symbolizes the Divine Spirit dwelling within, in flawless balance with the vast Universe, a gateway to oneness where personal light merges with cosmic flow.

As a "spiritual messenger," 11 reduces to 2 (1+1=2), blending duality's harmony with elevated vision, often linked to the Moon's intuitive pull. If 11 appears in key positions (Life Path, Expression Number), you're a channeler, artist, or reformer like inventors or spiritual leaders with hypersensitivity to energies. Strengths: Visionary genius, empathy, transformative ideas; challenges: Anxiety, overwhelm, escapism if ungrounded.

**Expression Number 22:**

Expression Number 22: The Master Builder is the ultimate builder's number, empowering you to manifest monumental projects that benefit all humanity think cathedrals of innovation, global initiatives, or legacy systems. It vibrates with absolute Truth, demanding integrity in every blueprint.

If its immense energies feel overwhelming, 22 reduces to 4 (2+2=4), the realm of disciplined work and earthly limitations. This shift brings tests in practicality, organization, work hurdles, and navigating restrictions lessons in grounding dreams into reality.

At its pinnacle, Number 22 heralds' victory over all limitations, freeing the spirit from physical bonds. It symbolizes the mystic marriage: a sacred union of lower (earthly) nature with higher (divine) self, forging harmony between your spiritual core and material form.

As the "Master Architect," 22 blends Saturn's structure with Uranus's genius (reducing from 2's intuition), often marking reincarnated leaders. Prominent in your chart? You're a transformative force like engineers of empires or social reformers. Strengths: Visionary execution, resilience, universal impact; challenges: Burnout, perfectionism, fear of failure.

## Expression Number 33:

Expression Number 33: The Christer Compassion elevates love into boundless compassion. It manifests as the teacher of teachers, enlightened guides who uplift humanity through profound self-sacrifice. Leadership here is divine service: shouldering immense responsibilities with infinite patience and forbearance, expecting no reward or recognition.

This vibration draws you to nature's embrace and sacred solitude, shielding your sensitivity from crowds and chaos. It infuses tireless energy, unyielding courage, and supernatural power over the physical realm via "right timing" events align perfectly when you surrender to cosmic flow.

As the rarest master number (3+3=6, blending creativity with harmony), 33 echoes Jupiter's benevolence and Neptune's mysticism, often marking ascended masters or avatars. Prominent in your chart? You're a global healer, spiritual revolutionary, or quiet, sage like figures embodying universal love. Strengths: Transcendent empathy, miraculous timing, inspirational purity; challenges: Exhaustion, martyrdom, detachment from self.

# What is the Heart's Desire Number?

The Heart's Desire is also known as the Soul's Urge. It shows our deepest inner longing. To understand these hidden feelings, we look at the vowels in a person's full name. These vowels create the Soul Urge number.

In numerology, your Soul number reveals your secrets, private thoughts, and true wishes. It points to what your heart really wants, what you long for most, and your deepest desires.

This number tells what your soul craves and wants to express in this lifetime. Each life, the soul has specific needs and comes here to learn and grow. The Soul number reveals your heart's true desire, as it confirms what you already feel deep down. You already know your inner truth; this number provides you with words and a clear way to better understand your core self.

Sometimes, the Soul number takes over your energy. It pushes aside other traits, even those from your Life Path or Destiny numbers. When that happens, it draws you to people and places that match your own vibe.

## How to Calculate The Heart's Desire Number?

To calculate your Heart's Desire Number (also known as Soul Urge Number).

- As we used in Expression Number, take the same 5 readings and keep the Date of Birth after the calculation.
- By calculating the Date of Birth, you calculated 2 core numbers: those are Lifepath and Birth Date.
- By the complete Name, we calculated the 3rd core number, which is the Expression Number.

- Now we will learn the 4th core number, which is the Heart's Desire Number.
- Take the same 5 details of the same people and write down their complete name (remember First Name, Middle Name, Last Name, and simplify them).
- And refer to the Pythagoras Chart mentioned for the calculation of Heart's Desire Number.
- Look for the only vowels present in the Complete Name and assign the numbers to the letter, and calculate the Heart's Desire Number.
- For example, Anvita Hiremat's Heart's Desire Number is 8(the detailed calculation is mentioned in the below chat).

This intimate number uncovers your innermost motivations, deepest cravings, and what truly fulfills your soul beneath the surface.

**Note:** To find your Heart Desire number, assign numbers to each vowel in your full birth name using the Pythagorean chart (A=1, E=5, I=9, O=6, U=3).

**<u>Heart's Desire Number Example Chart Complete Name: Anvita Hiremat.</u>**

<table>
<tr><td colspan="15">Heart Desire Number</td></tr>
<tr><td colspan="7">First Name</td><td colspan="8">Last Name</td></tr>
<tr><td>Vowel</td><td>1</td><td></td><td></td><td>9</td><td></td><td>1</td><td></td><td></td><td>9</td><td></td><td>5</td><td></td><td>1</td><td></td></tr>
<tr><td>Name</td><td>A</td><td>N</td><td>V</td><td>I</td><td>T</td><td>A</td><td></td><td>H</td><td>I</td><td>R</td><td>E</td><td>M</td><td>A</td><td>T</td></tr>
<tr><td colspan="7">First Name:11</td><td colspan="8">Last Name:15/6</td></tr>
<tr><td colspan="15">Heart Desire Number: 11+6=17/8</td></tr>
</table>

**Heart's Desire Number 1:**

Those with Heart's Desire Number 1 crave leadership above all, often seeking control over others, too. They resist orders or subordination, showing headstrong, willful, ambitious, and fiercely independent traits. Unsurprisingly, 1 Soul Numbers avoid teams, committees, and anything mediocre.

In romance, passion ignites when partners match their charm, cleverness, and independence, yet they hesitate to reveal vulnerability, sometimes appearing cold or distant as self-protection. 1 soul frequently pursues solo endeavors, preferring to work or be alone rather than tolerate "fools."

**Heart's Desire Number 2:**

At its core, Heart's Desire Number 2 yearns for harmony above everything. Those with this number dread conflict, shunning leadership in favor of peace and support. They uniquely perceive both sides of any issue, excelling as negotiators and arbitrators sensitive to others, boosting their confidence with tactful truth that uplifts rather than deflates. Warm and loving, the 2 Soul Number offers steadfast support alongside any other vibration.

In romance, giving defines the 2 Heart's Desire Number, though they risk over-giving and neglecting themselves. Others' appreciation means everything, while criticism wounds deeply. Always thriving in partnership over solitude, no one matches the 2 Heart's Desire Numbers' devotion as a companion.

**Heart's Desire Number 3:**

The deepest desire of Heart's Desire Number 3 is to spread happiness, spark laughter, ignite enthusiasm, and inspire everyone to chase their highest potential. This soul adores life! People with 3 Soul Numbers brim with creativity for spontaneous romance, think balloon bouquets, monogrammed pajamas, hand-painted invites, and arriving at parties in dazzling colors. That's the essence of 3: pure fun, bold expression, and infectious joy. They channel talents into writing, designing, dancing, decorating, or singing with a full heart.

In romance, the 3 Heart's Desire Number flirts playfully, shifting interests often not fickleness, just a zest for fun. Their enthusiasm might trip them up at times, but rest assured, they'll romance you delightfully.

## Heart's Desire Number 4:

At the core of every Heart's Desire Number 4 lies a deep yearning for structure, an organized approach to life, and practicality in every endeavor. Those with a 4 Heart's Desire Number cherish their planners, agendas, firm boundaries, and clear expectations from everyone involved. They thrive on knowing the roadmap ahead and maintaining control, steering clear of unexpected twists. Yet, this 4 excels as a facilitator, drawing out the strengths in others to foster powerful teamwork that sparks extraordinary results.

In romance, the 4 Heart's Desire Number approaches emotional bonds with the same grounded sensibility, favoring control over chaos. They might not appear overtly romantic, opting instead for thoughtful, useful gifts or meticulously orchestrated dinners, but these efforts often weave genuine magic, crafted to captivate and please.

## Heart's Desire Number 5:

Deep within every Heart's Desire Number 5 beats a fierce craving for freedom from all constraints, paired with an intense love for variety and adventure. Those with a 5 Soul Number despise feeling confined or dulled by monotony. They revel in life's rich tapestry of experiences and excitement.

In love, the 5 Heart's Desire Number dances to the rhythm of three key letters:

-S-E-X-, embodying sensuality, exquisiteness, and extraordinary passion. Naturally rebellious and deeply sensual, this number is driven by the thrill of sexual energy in pursuit of change.

## Heart's Desire Number 6:

The 6 Heart's Desire Number holds beauty, harmony, and home as its top priorities. Incredibly understanding, loyal, devoted, affectionate, and all-in on commitment, these individuals bear no resemblance to the free-spirited 5s. People with 6 Soul Numbers are driven to safeguard, care for, and cherish their families and homes.

In romance, they embody the ultimate idealistic lovers who think of roses, candles, and grand gestures. With a 6 Heart's Desire Number, love runs profound and serious, the "committed" type who's ready for marriage. This number yearns for wedlock, a family, and a beautiful home to perfect. Casual dating? Not an option, it's marriage or nothing.

## Heart's Desire Number 7:

These emotional recluses seldom reveal their inner feelings. Many opt out of marriage altogether, favoring their own thoughts and solitude over sharing life with someone else. A 7 Heart's Desire Number might thrive as a priest, nun, or wilderness guide, drawn to isolation by nature. What truly captivates this soul is the allure of silence, quiet, and inner peace. People with 7 Heart's Desire Numbers genuinely prefer being left alone with a good book!

In romance, if a 7 Heart's Desire Number pairs up, it stays intensely private. Odds are, their partner shares the same 7 Soul Number vibe. Those with 7s guard their thoughts, beliefs, and quirky (even eccentric) lifestyles closely. As deeply sensitive thinkers and analyzers, they often wield psychic abilities and sharp perceptual skills. Don't bother hiding your emotions from a 7; they'll sense them from afar.

## Heart's Desire Number 8:

The 8 Heart's Desire Number craves authority, being the boss, or wielding real power in the world. Those with this number struggle to grasp others' emotions and favor straightforward business over tangled feelings. Deep down, 8 Soul Numbers yearn to feel significant, not just domestically, but in the broader "real world" they value most.

In romance, skip dreams of intimate candlelit dinners tucked in a restaurant nook with an 8 Heart's Desire Number. Expect business calls to derail it, with the 8 stepping away to answer, and the deepest connection might be dissecting the latest deal. This number seeks a robust, competent partner (highly organized, no less) who matches their drive. Rarely, when walls come down, you'll glimpse their warm, affectionate side, but usually, they're too consumed by ambitions for much romance.

## Heart's Desire Number 9:

The 9 Heart's Desire Number embodies pure compassion at its core. It longs to embrace the entire world and everything in it, fueled by lofty ideals and the ability to inspire others toward universal harmony and love. Highly intuitive and generous, those with 9 Heart's Desire Numbers often grapple with their personal emotions and the world's greater demands.

In romance, the 9 Heart's Desire Number shines as loving, idealistic, and deeply romantic. This is likely the number that pioneered the quest for a true soul mate. Their love burns with limitless intensity because it truly knows no bounds.

## Heart's Desire Number 11:

The Master Number 11 soul possesses extraordinary sensitivity, often verging on psychic. Those with 11 Heart's Desire Numbers experience intense emotional waves, little wonder, as they juggle overwhelming psychic insights. Beyond their years in wisdom, they perceive and understand far more than most. At heart, they seek to foster peace across all connections, from partnerships and families to neighboring nations or diverse communities. Their powerful intuitions rarely miss the mark. As old souls, they infuse every pursuit with timeless knowledge and spiritual insight. You might recognize someone who radiates uncanny maturity.

Expect conversations about angels, fairies, wizard lore, or the reality of magic woven into an 11 Heart's Desire Number's unique way of life.

In romance, much like the 2, the 11 offers sweetness and gentleness, always aiming to delight. But beware the dual pull of leadership two 1s, in fact. This soul craves the top role and refuses second place, even while yearning most for harmony.

**Heart's Desire Number 22:**

The defining drive of all Master Number 22 Heart's Desire Numbers is to construct something monumental in life that benefits humanity and endures long after they're gone. These souls are capable of magnificent feats, fueled by profound spiritual understanding channeled through their leadership. This is the Master Number of the futurist, destined to leave Earth having achieved a substantial, lasting impact.

In matters of the heart, this soul proceeds cautiously, seeking a practical partner with clear goals who embodies security. The 22 Heart's Desire Number yearns to find a life companion with whom to realize their grand dreams.

**Heart's Desire Number 33:**

The Master Number 33 Soul Number yearns to give generously to everyone in need. Joyful, loving, and vibrant with energy, it profoundly touches the hearts of those seeking its protection, care, and support. This is the soul that elevates love's vibration to its pinnacle, pure compassion for all.

In romance, with its double 3s, this Soul Number must learn to master its emotions. Bearers of this rare Master Number have chosen to return as advanced souls, volunteering to lift humanity toward a deeper understanding of love's true essence. Note how seldom we encounter this number.

# What is the Personality Number?

Your Personality Number captures the lasting impression you leave after a first meeting. It's the fourth of the five Core Numbers in numerology. This number not only equips you to create the strongest possible impact but also reveals how others truly perceive you.

Calculating it is straightforward: simply sum the numerical values of the consonants in your full birth name. Surprised that people see you as forceful? A 1 Personality Number might explain it. Or if they view you as quiet and introspective, you may carry a 7 Personality.

Remember, this external image isn't always your authentic core that's revealed by the Soul Number. Here, though, we focus squarely on your Personality.

**How to Calculate The Personality Number:**

This captures the consonants that shape how the world sees you.

- As we used in Heart Desire Number, take the same 5 readings and keep the Date of Birth after the calculation.
- By calculating the Date of Birth, you calculated 2 core numbers: those are Lifepath and Birth Date.
- By the complete Name, we calculated the 2 core numbers, which are the Expression Number and Heart Desire Number.
- Now we will learn to calculate the Personality Number.
- Write the complete Name of the person. (First Name, Middle Name, Last Name).
- And refer to the Pythagoras Chart mentioned for the calculation of Heart's Desire Number.

- Look for the only consonants present in the Complete Name and assign the numbers to the letter, and calculate the Personality Number.
- For example, Anvita Hiremat's Personality Number is 8(the detailed calculation is mentioned in the below chat).

**Note:** To find your Personality Number, assign numbers to all the consonants present in your full birth name using the Pythagorean chart (B=2, C=3, ..., J=1, etc.).

**<u>Personality Number Example Chart Complete Name: Anvita Hiremat.</u>**

| Personality Number | | | | | | | | | | | | | | |
|---|---|---|---|---|---|---|---|---|---|---|---|---|---|---|
| First Name | | | | | | | Last Name | | | | | | | |
| Name | A | N | V | I | T | A | | H | I | R | E | M | A | T |
| Consonants | | 5 | 4 | | 2 | | | 8 | | 9 | | 4 | | 2 |
| First Name:11 | | | | | | | Last Name:23/5 | | | | | | | |
| Personality Number: 11+5=16/7 | | | | | | | | | | | | | | |

# What is the Growth Number?

People often call out our first name when talking to us. It's no surprise that this everyday name carries special qualities. Our first name acts like a repeated sound or mantra; it sets an intention every time someone says it. What makes the first name different from our full name? Everyone has a first name. Many have a middle name or initial. Most have a last name. But our first name, or "personal name," is the one used most in daily life to identify us. It's key to how we see ourselves and connect with others. Its energy gets repeated all the time.

In numerology, the first name shows our personal self. It sets us apart from other family members. It also holds our Growth Number.

**<u>How to Calculate The Growth Number:</u>**

Your first name holds the vibrational key to your evolving potential and personal development.

- As we used in Personality Number, take the same 5 readings and keep the Date of Birth after the calculation.
- By calculating the Date of Birth, you calculated 2 core numbers: those are Lifepath and Birth Date.
- By the complete Name, we calculated 3 the numbers, which are the Expression Number, Heart Desire Number, and Personality.
- Now we will learn to calculate the Growth Number.
- Write the complete Name of the person, only the First Name, and refer to the Pythagoras Chart mentioned for the calculation of Growth Number.
- See the chart properly and assign the number to each letter present in the First Name.

- For example, Anvita Hiremat's Growth Number is 7(the detailed calculation is mentioned in the below chat).

**Note:** To find your Growth Number, assign numbers to all the letters present in your first name using the Pythagorean chart (A=1, B=2, ..., I=9, J=1, etc.).

**Growth Number Example Chart First Name: Anvita.**

| Growth Number | | | | | | |
|---|---|---|---|---|---|---|
| First Name | | | | | | |
| Vowel | 1 | | | 9 | | 1 |
| Name | A | N | V | I | T | A |
| Consonants | | 5 | 4 | | 2 | |
| Growth Number:22/4 | | | | | | |

# What is the Maturity Number?

Your Maturity Number: Discovering Your True Self. Finding the number that governs the second half of your life. The Maturity Number, also known as the reality number, realization number, power number, ultimate goal, or true self number, serves as a profound midlife message. It guides you toward living at your best potential by revealing the essence of your authentic, the first step is understanding who that self truly is. This final of the five Core Numbers in numerology compiles the vibrational energies of your full birth name and birth date. In practical terms, you derive it by adding your Destiny Number (from your birth name) to your Life Path Number (from your birth date) and reducing the sum to a single digit or master number (11, 22, or 33).

The Maturity Number offers a roadmap for maturity, typically influencing your life after age 30-40, when the lessons of youth give way to deeper wisdom. It illuminates the opportunities, challenges, and innate gifts that emerge as you integrate your core energies. The Maturity Number combines the vibrations of your birth name and birth date. It reveals what lies ahead in the second half of life and shows how you may experience the merged influences of your Destiny Number and Life Path Number.

**<u>How Calculate The Maturity Number:</u>**

- As we discussed earlier, take 5 readings of the closed one or the desired person's Name and Date of Birth.
- Write the 5 different reading sheets. Initially, try to do it manually to get better clarity.
- Now write each Name and Date of Birth in 5 different sheets.
- By calculating the Date of Birth, you calculated 2 core numbers: those are Lifepath and Birth Date.

- By the complete Name, we calculated the 3 numbers, which are the Expression Number, Heart Desire Number, and Personality.
- And by only First Name, we calculated the Growth Number.
- Now we will learn to calculate the Maturity Number.
- To calculate your Maturity Number, begin by writing down your Life Path Number, derived earlier from reducing your complete birth Date (Date + Month + Year, each to a single digit, then summed).
- Then, followed by noting your Expression Number, obtained from summing all letters in your full birth name via the Pythagorean chart and reducing to a single digit or master number.
- Finally, add the Life Path Number and Expression Number together, then reduce that total by adding its digits until you arrive at a single digit or master number (11/22/33),
- This Maturity Number unveils the wisdom and purpose that blossoms in your later years, typically after age 30.

**Note:** To find out your Maturity Number, add your Life Path Number + Expression Number.

**Maturity Number Example Chart: Complete Name Anvita Hiremat, Date of Birth 10/02/19.**

| Maturity Number | |
|---|---|
| Lifepath:9 | Expression Number:6 |
| 9+6=15/6 | |

## Maturity Number 1: The Independent Leader Emerges.

### Core Vibration: Pioneering Self-Mastery.

When your Maturity Number is 1, the second half of life unfolds as a triumphant awakening to your innate power. You have honed the art of true independence, stepping fully into the role of leader not through force, but through authentic self-reliance and visionary drive. This number marks the culmination of your journey, where the combined energies of your Expression and Lifepath crystallize into unshakeable confidence. In the sacred geometry of numerology, 1 symbolizes the primal spark of creation, the singular point from which all manifestation flows, echoing ancient wisdom from Pythagoras, who viewed it as the "monad," the source of unity and divine will. As you mature, this vibration empowers you to pioneer new paths, free from the need for external validation.

### Key Traits and Gifts:

Unwavering Independence: You've shed dependencies, trusting your inner compass to navigate life's uncertainties. Decisions flow effortlessly from self-knowledge.

Natural Leadership: Others gravitate to your clarity and initiative. You inspire by example, leading projects, communities, or personal revolutions with quiet authority. Innovative Vision: Creativity surges as originality; you birth ideas that reshape realities, whether in business, spirituality, or personal endeavors. Resilience in Solitude: Comfortable alone, you recharge through introspection, emerging stronger to guide those around you. Midlife Message and Potential:

This number signals a phase of bold self-actualization, often after 30, when past lessons forge your leadership mantle. Challenges like isolation or stubbornness may arise, but they teach balance, leading with heart, not just will. Living Your Best Potential Career: Excel in entrepreneurship, executive roles, or trailblazing fields like spiritual coaching or innovative research. Relationships: Attract equals who honor your autonomy; lead by fostering mutual growth. Spiritual Practice: Meditate on oneness affirmations like "I am the source of my power," amplify your vibration.

**Ancient Tie-In**: Like the Egyptian concept of the "ka" (vital self), embrace Number 1 as your eternal leader within. Those with Maturity Number 1 often report midlife reinventions: launching books, businesses, or movements that reflect their soul's command. Yours is a life of firsts, fearlessly original.

Calculate and confirm: Expression + Life Path = 1 (or 10/1, 19/1, etc.).

## Maturity Number 2: The Harmonious Peacemaker Rises.

## Core Vibration: Emotional Mastery Through Tested Grace.

With a Maturity Number 2, your later years bloom into profound emotional equilibrium, forged in the fires of past pain. You have learned to master your emotions not despite hardship, but through it, transforming betrayals and self-inflicted wounds from trusting the wrong people into stepping stones for unbreakable inner peace. This number heralds your evolution into a beacon of diplomacy and empathy, where sensitivity becomes your greatest strength. In numerology's ancient tapestry, 2 embodies duality's sacred union, the lunar yin to 1's solar yang, symbolizing balance, partnership, and the intuitive wisdom of the divine feminine. Pythagorean sages revered it as the number of reconciliations, mirroring the soul's journey from fracture to wholeness.

### Key Traits and Gifts:

Emotional Alchemy: You've transmuted pain into profound empathy, managing feelings with grace rather than reaction. Tactful Diplomacy: Skilled at mediation, you foster harmony in relationships and groups, turning conflicts into connections. Intuitive Nurturing: Your quiet strength supports others, often as a counselor, healer, or behind-the-scenes influencer. Resilient Trust: Past hurts teach discernment; now, you trust wisely, building alliances that endure. Difficulties once overwhelming now reveal your gift for cooperation. Living Your Best Potential Career: Thrive in collaborative roles like therapy, diplomacy, arts, or spiritual guidance, where your insight shines. Relationships: Form deep, soulful bonds; lead by listening, creating spaces of mutual trust. Spiritual Practice: Moon rituals or affirmations like "I balance my heart with wisdom" restore your flow.

**Ancient Tie-In:** Echoing the Taoist yin-yang, Number 2 calls you to harmonize opposites, turning adversity into enlightened partnership. Individuals with Maturity Number 2 often share stories of rebirth: from heartbreak to heartfelt service, authoring works of compassion, or mending communities. Your path? Overcoming through grace, emerging as the ultimate harmonizer.

Calculate and affirm: Expression + Lifepath = 2 (or 11/2, 20/2, etc.).

## Maturity Number 3: The Joyful Creator Awakens.

## Core Vibration: Artistic Independence and Radiant Maturity.

A Maturity Number 3 signals a vibrant midlife renaissance, where you fully embrace leading life on your own terms. Having cultivated deep independence, you now express yourself through boundless creativity and artistic flair. Matured by wisdom's clarity, you navigate existence with joyful self-assurance, your once-scattered energies now channeled into pure, expressive maturity. Numerology hails 3 as the trinity of creation: mind, body, spirit in harmonious expression, rooted in ancient triads like the Pythagorean "triad" of beginning, middle, and end, or the Hindu Trimurti of creation, preservation, transformation. It vibrates with Jupiter's expansive joy, turning life's canvas into a masterpiece of self-realization.

## Key Traits and Gifts:

Independent Self-Leadership: Free from external chains, you chart your course with confidence and playfulness. Artistic Brilliance: Creativity flows effortlessly; writing, music, design, or spiritual storytelling becomes your voice. Clear, Matured Wisdom: Emotional fog lifts; you communicate with clarity, humor, and infectious optimism. Social Magnetism: Your light draws others, inspiring through authentic, heartfelt expression. Midlife Message and Potential: In your later years, Number 3 matures your spirit, transforming youthful exuberance into disciplined artistry. Past lessons in independence sharpen your focus, clearing the path for unbridled joy. Living Your Best Potential Career: Excel in writing, performing, teaching, or creative entrepreneurship, like authoring numerological insights with flair. Relationships: Attract vibrant souls; lead by uplifting, fostering fun and depth. Spiritual Practice: Affirm "I create with joyful clarity" amid art or nature; chant mantras for expansive flow.

Ancient Tie-In: Like the Celtic triple spiral, Number 3 spirals you toward eternal growth art as sacred rite. Those with Maturity Number 3 often reinvent midlife through books, performances, or innovations that blend art and wisdom. Yours is a life of colorful independence, matured into timeless expression.

Calculate and ignite: Expression+ Life Path = 3 (or 12/3, 21/3, etc.).

## Maturity Number 4: The Steadfast Builder of Security.

## Core Vibration: Enduring Foundations of Stability.

With Maturity Number 4, the second half of life becomes a masterful construction of unshakeable security. You have learned to forge rock-solid foundations in every realm, financial, emotional, relational, and spiritual, transforming chaos into order through disciplined effort and practical wisdom. This number crowns your journey with the quiet power of reliability, where hard work yields lasting sanctuary. In numerology's sacred architecture, 4 represents the square of stability, the four elements, directions, and seasons honored by Pythagoras as the number of justice and the material world. It echoes the Egyptian four pillars upholding the sky, symbolizing the soul's triumph over instability.

**Key Traits and Gifts:**

Security Mastery: You create tangible safety nets, from structured finances to nurturing homes. Methodical Discipline: Patience and persistence turn visions into enduring realities. Practical Wisdom: Grounded intuition guides decisions, blending logic with heartfelt purpose. Loyal Reliability: Others lean on your steadfastness, making you the cornerstone of communities. Midlife Message and Potential: Emerging in maturity, Number 4 teaches that true security arises from within, built brick by brick, not wished into being. Past upheavals refine your resolve, aligning Destiny and Life Path into a fortress of self-sufficiency. Living Your Best Potential Career: Thrive in building roles in architecture, management, farming, or systematic spiritual teaching. Relationships: Cultivate deep, loyal bonds; lead by providing unwavering support. Spiritual Practice: Earth rituals or affirmations like "I build eternal security from within" anchor your energy.

**Ancient Tie-In:** Mirroring the Native American four directions, Number 4 centers you in balanced, secure wholeness. People with Maturity Number 4 often manifest midlife legacies: secure estates, family dynasties, or foundational works like enduring numerology texts. Yours is the art of building heaven on earth.

**Calculate and fortify: Expression + Life Path = 4 (or 13/4, 22/4, 31/4, etc.).**

## Maturity Number 5: The Adventurous Seeker of Freedom.

### Core Vibration: Dynamic Liberation and Adaptable Wisdom.

Maturity Number 5 heralds a thrilling midlife odyssey of boundless freedom and exhilarating change. In your later years, you embrace life's adventures with fearless adaptability, having mastered the art of flow amid uncertainty. This number liberates your spirit, blending curiosity, versatility, and sensual vitality into a life of purposeful exploration. Numerology celebrates 5 as the pentagram of humanity, the five senses bridging spirit and matter, evoking Pythagoras's "pentad" of health and harmony. It resonates with Mercury's quicksilver energy and the five elements of ancient Chinese philosophy, symbolizing transformation through motion.

**Key Traits and Gifts:**

Embraced Freedom: You thrive on independence, shedding restrictions to pursue passions unhindered. Adaptable Versatility: Quick shifts become opportunities; you reinvent effortlessly across experiences. Magnetic Curiosity: A thirst for knowledge draws diverse adventures travel, learning, and sensory delights. Charismatic Influence: Your zest inspires others, communicating change with persuasive charm. Midlife Message and Potential Post-40, Number 5 accelerates your evolution, merging Destiny and Life Path into restless growth. Early restlessness matures into wise wanderlust, teaching that true security lies in flexibility. Living Your Best Potential Career: Excel in dynamic fields travel writing, sales, media, or metaphysical exploration. Relationships: Form exciting, egalitarian bonds; lead by embracing spontaneity together. Spiritual Practice: Breathwork or affirmations like "I flow freely in change's embrace" fuel your fire.

**Ancient Tie-In:** Like the Norse five worlds of Yggdrasil, Number 5 connects realms through adaptive journeys. Those with Maturity Number 5 often embark on midlife quests: globetrotting, career pivots, or authoring tales of transformation. Yours is a symphony of senses, free and forever unfolding.

**Calculate and venture: Expression+ Life Path = 5 (or 14/5, 23/5, etc.).**

## Maturity Number 6: The Nurturing Guardian of Harmony

### Core Vibration: Loving Responsibility and Familial Devotion

Maturity Number 6 crowns the second half of life with the profound beauty of selfless love and steadfast guardianship. You step into a role of ultimate nurturer, creating homes filled with warmth, beauty, and justice, prioritizing family, community, and creative service above all. This vibration matures your heart into a sanctuary of compassion and equilibrium. In numerology's cosmic family, 6 is the perfect hexagon, Venus's emblem of balanced love revered by Pythagoras for its marital harmony and the six days of creation leading to sacred rest. It mirrors the Star of David, uniting heaven and earth in protective grace.

### Key Traits and Gifts:

Devoted Nurturing: You heal and harmonize, making others feel deeply cherished. Responsible Leadership: Duty calls you to protect and provide, with fairness and artistry. Creative Beauty: Aesthetics infuse your world, designing spaces, stories, or rituals of love. Empathic Justice: Intuitive discernment upholds truth in relationships and causes. Midlife Message and Potential: Around midlife, Number 6 integrates your core paths into selfless fulfillment, where personal desires yield to the greater good. Past imbalances teach boundaries, birthing wise, loving authority. Living Your Best Potential Career: Shine in caregiving, teaching, counseling, healing arts, or family-oriented enterprises. Relationships: Build soul-deep alliances; lead through unconditional support and beauty. Spiritual Practice: Heart-centered meditation or affirmations like "I nurture with boundless love" amplify your light.

**Ancient Tie-In**: Echoing the Greek Hera's protective hearth, Number 6 sanctifies home as a divine temple. Individuals with Maturity Number 6 often create lasting legacies: tight-knit families, artistic havens, or community pillars. Yours radiates love's eternal homecoming.

**Calculate and embrace: Destiny + Life Path = 6 (or 15/6, 24/6, 33/6, etc.).**

## Maturity Number is 7:The Seeker.

## Core Vibration: Inner Wisdom, Spiritual Insight & Truth-Seeking.

Maturity Number 7 reveals your soul's quest for profound wisdom and inner truth, activating strongly after age 35. This vibration draws you into deep analysis, spiritual exploration, and intellectual mastery, transforming curiosity into universal insights. Unlike more social paths, 7 thrives on solitude, where penetrating perception uncovers life's hidden layers. Your authentic essence embodies the philosopher and mystic, blending sharp intellect with intuitive knowing. A rich inner world fuels endless study, prioritizing perfection over superficiality. Refined reserve in company masks profound depth that fascinates far more than external noise.

## Key Traits and Gifts:

Penetrating Insight: You dissect realities others accept blindly, like a detective unveiling cosmic patterns. Spiritual Depth: Intuition senses truths beyond logic, guiding research into philosophy or metaphysics. Poised Independence: Solitude recharges your analytical power; selective sharing offers rare, valuable wisdom. Lifelong Quest: Every experience becomes a lesson, excelling in invention, teaching, or esoteric fields. Challenges to Master Excessive Withdrawal: Balance reflection with connection to avoid isolation. Over-Analysis: Trust gut feelings when logic loops endlessly. Emotional Guard: Share vulnerabilities to deepen bonds beyond surface intellect. Life Path Guidance

Honor 7 through daily rituals: meditate at dawn, journal revelations, study sacred texts. Align with Neptune for dreams and Ketu for detachment. Echoes of Isaac Newton reflect this archetype; his solitary genius reshaped knowledge.

**Ancient Tie-In**: The Number of Sacred Knowledge, Divine Order & Inner Awakening. Across ancient civilizations, Number 7 was never ordinary; it was revered as the number of mysteries, cosmic law, and higher wisdom. When this vibration appears as a Maturity Number, it echoes an ancient calling: to move beyond the visible world and live from inner truth.

**Calculate and venture: Expression+ Life Path = 7 (or 16/7, 25/7,34/7, etc.).**

## Maturity Number is 8: The Infinite Master of Power.

### Core Vibration: Karmic Authority and Boundless Prosperity.

When Maturity Number 8 defines your later years, you rise as an unstoppable force of achievement, mastering the art of turning vision into tangible empires. Karmic lessons culminate in profound power, financial abundance, influential leadership, and spiritual sovereignty, where you orchestrate success with unyielding determination and cosmic fairness. The figure-eight infinity loop captures 8's essence: endless cycles of effort and reward. Ancient numerologists like Pythagoras linked it to cosmic justice, while in Vedic traditions, it aligns with the eight siddhis (spiritual powers), blending material mastery with enlightened detachment.

### Key Traits and Gifts:

Commanding Ambition: You direct resources and people toward grand outcomes with laser focus. Wealth Magnetism: Business acumen attracts prosperity, often through innovative or high-stakes ventures. Balanced Judgment: Intuitive ethics ensure power serves the greater good, resolving karma gracefully. Legacy Vision: Your influence endures, shaping generations through philanthropy or pioneering work. Midlife Message and Potential: This number activates around 40-50, fusing Destiny and Life Path into a powerhouse of realization. Early struggles build resilience, revealing that true power flows from inner strength. Living Your Best Potential Career: Conquer realms like entrepreneurship, real estate, politics, or metaphysical consulting empires. Relationships: Attract dynamic partners; lead with protective generosity and shared vision. Spiritual Practice: Chakra balancing (root and crown) or mantras like "Power and plenty flow through me now."

**Ancient Tie-In**: Like the octagon in sacred geometry, Number 8 stabilizes chaos into perfected abundance. Celebrated figures with strong 8 energy think Oprah's media dynasty or Elon Musk's innovations exemplify midlife mastery. Your path? Harvesting karma's fruits into a world-changing legacy.

**Calculate yours: Expression+ Life Path = 8 (or 17/8, 26/8, 35/8).**

## Maturity Number is 9: The Compassionate Visionary of Completion.

### Core Vibration: Universal Love and Selfless Fulfillment.

Maturity Number 9 ushers in the grand finale of your soul's earthly cycle, a midlife ascension to universal compassion and enlightened detachment. You embody selfless service, releasing attachments to uplift humanity with wisdom, creativity, and boundless generosity. This pinnacle number marks completion, where personal growth blossoms into global impact. Numerology views 9 as the ennead of perfection, the sum of 1 through 9 symbolizing wholeness and Mars's humanitarian fire. Pythagoras praised it as the "horizon number," encompassing all before renewal, while in Mayan cosmology, it governs collective evolution.

### Key Traits and Gifts:

Universal Compassion: Deep empathy drives you to heal and serve without expectation. Creative Idealism: Visionary ideas inspire art, activism, or spiritual movements. Detached Wisdom: You forgive easily, letting go to embrace life's impermanence. Inspirational Influence: Your presence motivates profound change in others. Midlife Message and Potential: In later years, Number 9 integrates all prior lessons, urging release of ego for humanitarian purposes. Trials forge your lightworker essence. Living Your Best Potential Career: Lead in philanthropy, arts, healing, counseling, or authoring transformative texts. Relationships: Form soul-elevating connections; guide with unconditional love. Spiritual Practice: Forgiveness rituals or affirmations like "I release and radiate universal love."

**Ancient Tie-In:** Echoing the nine muses of Greece, Number 9 channels divine inspiration for the collective. Icons with 9 prominences, like Gandhi's nonviolence or Mother Teresa's devotion, illustrate 9's legacy. Yours closes the circle in selfless radiance.

**Calculate to culminate: Expression + Life Path = 9 (or 18/9, 27/9, etc).**

## Maturity Number is 11:The Master Illuminator.

The Maturity Number 11 arises when your Life Path and Destiny numbers both reduce to 11/2, fusing their intuitive brilliance with heightened spiritual awareness. This exalted master vibration ignites powerfully in midlife, guiding you toward profound enlightenment and inspiration. Unlike common paths, 11 calls you to channel inner light into illuminating truths, awakening others to higher consciousness. You hold masterful insight as the Master Illuminator, capable of unveiling cosmic revelations. Anticipate intensified trials, tests of faith, emotional waves, and perseverance, yet your unshakeable spiritual intuition triumphs over them. Success emerges organically from your dual role as visionary and empath, anchored in divine principles, soul wisdom, and intuitive mastery.

### Key Traits and Gifts:

Intuitive Illumination: You perceive hidden truths like a lighthouse piercing fog, revealing paths others miss.

Inner Power: A radiant, compassionate presence attracts seekers and synchronicities, powered by harmony with universal energies (e.g., unity, inspiration, empathy).

Resilience: Challenges refine your light; what dims others amplifies your inner glow.

## Challenges to Master

Overwhelm: Floods of intuition can scatter focus; ground with daily breathwork or nature walks.

Self-Doubt: The 2's sensitivity heightens rejection fears. Counter by trusting your soul's voice.

Perfectionism: Let go of ideal outcomes to share your light freely.

## Life Path Guidance

Embrace 11 by tuning in daily: journal one insight today, share it tomorrow. Meditate on numbers like 2 (harmony) and 9 (universal love) for equilibrium. Historical echoes include illuminators like Nikola Tesla, whose inventions channeled spiritual genius. Your authentic essence blends the qualities of a visionary and an empath. You possess an inner stability and inner power derived from a deep grounding in universal principles, spiritual truths, and intuitive expertise.

**Calculate to culminate: Expression + Life Path = 11 (or 20/2, 29/11/2, etc).**

## Maturity Number is 22: The Master Builder.

The Maturity Number 22 emerges when your Life Path and Destiny numbers both reduce to 11/2, blending their visionary sensitivity with profound practical genius. This rare master vibration activates strongly in midlife, propelling you toward monumental achievements. Unlike ordinary paths, 22 demands you channel inspiration into tangible reality, turning dreams into enduring structures that benefit humanity. You possess masterful competency as the Master Builder, capable of manifesting large-scale visions. Expect heightened obstacles, tests of patience, doubt, and resilience, but your unshakeable inner stability overcomes them. Success flows naturally from your dual role as manager and leader, rooted in universal principles, spiritual truths, and expert management know-how.

## Key Traits and Gifts:

Visionary Execution: You intuitively grasp big-picture blueprints, like an architect envisioning a city from blueprints, then building it brick by brick. Inner Power: A calm, magnetic authority draws resources and allies, fueled by alignment with cosmic laws (e.g., harmony, service, integrity). Resilience: Barriers sharpen your skills; what crumbles others fortifies your foundation. **Challenges to Master**

Overwhelm: Grand ideas can paralyze if not grounded; prioritize step-by-step action. Self-Doubt: The 2's sensitivity amplifies criticism. Counter it by affirming your spiritual rooting. Perfectionism: Release minor flaws to complete major works.

## Life Path Guidance

Embrace 22 by starting small: sketch one idea today, gather a team tomorrow. Meditate on numbers like 4 (stability) and 11 (intuition) for balance. Historical echoes include builders like Frank Lloyd Wright, whose structures embodied spiritual harmony. Your authentic essence combines the qualities of a manager and a leader. You possess an inner stability and inner power derived from a deep grounding in universal principles, spiritual truths, and management expertise.

**Calculate to culminate: Expression + Life Path = 22 (or 18/9, 27/9, etc).**

## Master Maturity Number 33: The Master Manifesto.

Master Maturity Number 33 shines as the rarest master vibration, formed when your Life Path and Destiny reduce to 11/2 and 22/4, totaling 33/6. This heavenly gift activates in midlife, guiding you toward profound service through unconditional love, creative nurturing, and selfless healing for humanity. Expect decades of responsibility that blossom into pure expressions of affection, joy, and compassionate care. Your mastery lies in sympathetic understanding and problem-solving, uplifting others through heartfelt presence and boundless generosity.

**Key Traits and Gifts:**

Christ Consciousness: You embody limitless love, radiating healing energy that mends emotional wounds effortlessly. Creative Nurturing: Abundant inspiration flows into art, counseling, or community-building that fosters joy and unity. Balanced Service: Intuitive wisdom harmonizes self-care with global giving, knowing when to receive as freely as you offer. Magnetic Healing: Others gravitate to your empathetic aura, finding solace and transformation in your presence.

**Challenges to Master**

Martyrdom Risk: Guard against over-giving; affirm personal boundaries to sustain your light. Emotional Overload: Shield sensitivity from collective pain through daily grounding rituals. Self-Neglect: Honor your needs first, as a depleted vessel cannot pour forth endlessly.

**Life Path Guidance**

Embrace 33 by practicing daily acts of love: mentor one soul, create beauty for the world. Meditate on 6 (harmony) and 9 (universal love) for alignment. Echoes of Mother Teresa reflect this path; her tireless compassion reshapes lives globally. Your true essence pulses from the heart, boundless in devotion to others. Rich creative vitality merges with profound nurturing care for everyone around you, creating extraordinary healing. Maturity Number 33 arrives as a divine blessing. You master the equilibrium between duty and healthy responsibility, self-honor and others' welfare, generosity and acceptance.

**Calculate to culminate: Expression + Life Path = 33 (or 18/9, 27/9, etc).**

# What is the Missing Number?

In Pythagorean numerology, missing numbers (1-9) show gaps in your charts. They appear in two main spots: Full birth name chart: Letters to numbers (A=1, B=2, C=3, etc.). Core birth numbers: From a date like Life Path (reduce full birth date to a single digit). Their role: Hidden signals from past lives. They flag weak areas your soul chose for growth this lifetime. Name gaps: Influence daily habits and interactions with people. Birth gaps: Trigger major destiny challenges. How to find them: List all numbers present. Absences = lessons.

**How to Calculate The Missing Number:**

- As we discussed earlier, take 5 readings of the closed one or the desired person's Name and Date of Birth.
- Write the 5 different reading sheets. Initially, try to do it manually to get better clarity.
- Now write each Name and Date of Birth in 5 different sheets.
- By calculating the Date of Birth, you calculated 2 core numbers: those are Lifepath and Birth Date.
- By the Name, we calculated the 3 core numbers, which are the Expression Number, Heart Desire Number, and Maturity Number
- Now we will learn to calculate the Missing Number.
- To calculate your Missing Number, begin by gathering your entire numerology picture. First, write your complete birth name, letter by letter.
- Next, write your full Date of Birth and list all your core numbers derived from it and your name Life Path Number, Birth Date Number, Expression Number, Heart's Desire (Soul Urge) Number, and Maturity Number.

- Now, carefully look at which digits from 1 to 9 appear across your Name, and the core Numbers.
- If any number between 1 and 9 that is completely absent is your Missing number. Those are the Missing Numbers for you, which reveal qualities and lessons that feel less natural and require conscious development in this lifetime.

**Missing Number Example Chart: Complete Name Anvita Hiremat, Date of Birth 10/02/19.**

<table>
<tr><td colspan="14">Missing Number</td></tr>
<tr><td>1</td><td></td><td></td><td>9</td><td></td><td>1</td><td></td><td></td><td>9</td><td></td><td>5</td><td></td><td>1</td><td></td></tr>
<tr><td>A</td><td>N</td><td>V</td><td>I</td><td>T</td><td>A</td><td></td><td>H</td><td>I</td><td>R</td><td>E</td><td>M</td><td>A</td><td>T</td></tr>
<tr><td></td><td>5</td><td>4</td><td></td><td>2</td><td></td><td></td><td>8</td><td></td><td>9</td><td></td><td>4</td><td></td><td>2</td></tr>
<tr><td colspan="3">Lifepath Number: 9</td><td colspan="3">Expression Number:60/ 6</td><td colspan="3">Heart Desire Number:28/ 8</td><td colspan="3">Maturity Number:15/ 6</td><td colspan="2">Birth Date:10/ 1</td></tr>
<tr><td colspan="14">Missing Number:3,7</td></tr>
</table>

**Missing Number 1: A Missing Spark of Solar Vitality**

In the sacred language of numbers, the number 1 radiates the pure essence of the Sun, symbolizing life force, vitality, leadership, and the pioneering spirit that ignites creation. When your core numerology chart (birth date, name vibrations, or personal cycles) lacks the number 1 entirely, it signals a subtle but significant void: the positive, empowering influence of the Sun is diminished, leaving a noticeable gap in your innate life force.

Without this solar energy, individuals often grapple with a pervasive sense of low vitality, as if their inner fire flickers dimly rather than blazing brightly. Picture a plant starved of sunlight still alive, but struggling to thrive, its growth stunted, and its colors faded. Similarly, those missing the 1 may experience:

Chronic fatigue and lack of drive: A quiet undercurrent of exhaustion, where motivation wanes, and even simple tasks feel like climbing a mountain without oxygen.

**Some of the Key Traits:**

- Hesitancy in leadership: Opportunities to step forward pass by unnoticed, replaced by self-doubt or a preference for the shadows over the spotlight.
- Diminished self-confidence: The bold "I am" assertion of the Sun feels elusive, leading to reliance on others for direction and validation.
- Blocked creativity and initiative: Ideas spark but rarely ignite into action, as the primal urge to create and conquer remains subdued.

This absence doesn't doom one to a joyless life, far from it. The universe, in its wisdom, presents compensatory lessons through life's challenges, urging you to consciously cultivate that missing solar power. Ancient remedies like wearing ruby or sunstone gemstones, chanting solar mantras, or aligning with Sunday rituals can help recharge this energy. Over time, embracing practices that build inner strength, such as leadership roles, sunrise meditations, or bold goal-setting, transforms this lack into a profound strength, turning a dimly lit path into one bathed in self-generated light.

Remember, every number's absence is an invitation to growth. The missing 1 teaches resilience, drawing the Sun's full radiance from within, forging a uniquely empowered soul.

## Missing Number 2: A Void in Romance and Relational Harmony.

The number 2 embodies the gentle, nurturing glow of the Moon, ruler of emotions, partnerships, intuition, and the delicate dance of romance. It vibrates with the energy of connection, empathy, and the sweet pull of "we" over "me." When your numerology profile (from birth date, name, or cycles) completely lacks the number 2, this lunar essence fades, creating a profound challenge: true happiness in relationships feels elusive, starved of its romantic spark.

Without 2's influence, people often wander through partnerships feeling unfulfilled, as if sipping water from a cup with a hidden crack, it quenches momentarily but never satisfies the soul's deeper thirst for emotional intimacy.

### Some of the Key Traits:

- Strained romantic bonds: Relationships start with promise but falter under miscommunications, emotional distance, or a nagging sense that something vital is missing, like love without the poetry of touch or whispered affections.
- Difficulty trusting or opening up: The Moon's intuitive flow is blocked, leading to guarded hearts, over-analysis of feelings, or a subconscious push-pull dynamic that keeps partners at arm's length.
- Loneliness amid company: Even in crowds or committed unions, a quiet ache persists; harmony feels forced, and the joy of mutual understanding slips away.
- Imbalanced give-and-take: One-sided efforts dominate, breeding resentment or a cycle of short-lived connections lacking depth.

This gap isn't a curse but a cosmic call to awaken your inner lunar light. Life presents mirrors, challenging relationships that teach patience, vulnerability, and self-love until you learn to generate 2's energy from within. Simple remedies abound: pearl or moonstone jewelry to amplify emotions, full-moon rituals for heart-opening, or pairing with a strong

2-influenced partner for balance. Practices like couples' meditation, expressive journaling, or fostering empathy through service can reignite romance, turning relational voids into profound unions.

Embrace the lesson: the missing 2 invites you to become your own source of tenderness, magnetizing authentic love that flows effortlessly, like moonlight on still waters.

## Missing Number 3: Imbalance in Guru's Vibrations.

Number 3 vibrates with boundless creativity, joy, self-expression, and optimism powered by Guru, the grand benefactor Jupiter. As the cosmic teacher, Jupiter expands wisdom, abundance, and social charm. But when 3 is scarce or absent in your name chart, this energy tips into shadow: imbalance reigns, unleashing Jupiter's malefic side like overexpansion, indulgence, or stifled inspiration.

### Signs of 3's Absence: Jupiter's Shadow at Play

Without 3's light, life feels muted in areas of growth and glee. Common challenges include:

- Blocked Creativity: Ideas fizzle before takeoff. You might dream big but struggle to articulate or execute, leading to frustration.
- Social and Joy Gaps: Parties feel flat; networking is awkward. Optimism wanes, replaced by cynicism or isolation.
- Abundance Hurdles: Jupiter's wealth-building promise stumbles due to financial leaks via overspending, missed opportunities, or "luck" that slips away.
- Health Echoes: Prone to liver issues, weight fluctuations, or thigh-area discomfort (Jupiter's domains), often tied to excess eating/drinking.
- Real-life snapshot: Imagine a talented artist with no 3s their canvases gather dust, invitations ignored, prosperity elusive. Or a teacher whose lessons drone without spark, students disengaged, mirroring inner stagnation.

## Abundance of 3s: The Bright Side

Flip it: Loads of 3s? You're a charismatic storyteller, a life-of-the-party vibe, a magnet for fortune. Jupiter blesses with mentors, travels, and "right place, right time" magic.

### 3 in Your Life Chart: Jupiter's Call to Expand

Spot 3 in a personal year, month, or pinnacle cycle? Guru activates time to amplify positives and heal lacks. This phase sparks:

- Creative Bursts: Launch that book, song, or venture; expression flows freely.
- Social Expansion: New friends, collaborations, or wisdom-sharing gigs.
- Abundance Alignment: Investments bloom; gratitude practices multiply blessings.

## Remedies to Balance Missing 3s

Reclaim Jupiter's grace proactively:

- Name Tweaks: Add 3-value letters (C, L, U) to signatures or business names.
- Guru Boosters: Chant "Om Gurave Namah" on Thursdays; donate yellow items (bananas, books) to teachers.
- Crystals & Gems: Yellow sapphire (wear after consultation) or citrine for creativity.
- Daily Practice: Affirm: "I express joyfully and attract abundance." Dance, write, or laugh daily to ignite 3's fire.
- Tracking 3's presence unveils Jupiter's role in your cosmic script. Cultivate it, and watch creativity, joy, and prosperity unfold like a lotus under the sun.

## Missing Number 4: Disruptions in Daily Stability.

Number 4 embodies structure, discipline, practicality, and grounded hard work vibrating under Rahu's enigmatic influence. Known as the "builder," it anchors routines, endurance, and tangible progress. But a scarcity or total absence of 4 in your name chart unravels this foundation, spilling chaos into even the simplest day-to-day activities.

**Signs of 4's Absence: Rahu's Restless Ripple**

Without 4's steadying force, life feels like a house on shifting sands. Everyday tasks turn into battles:

- Routine Breakdowns: Cluttered homes, missed deadlines, forgotten errands. Mornings start late; evenings end in disarray.
- Practical Struggles: Tech glitches, vehicle breakdowns, or money mismanagement plague the mundane bills unpaid, groceries spoiled.
- Discipline Drought: Procrastination rules; long-term goals crumble under short-attention whims.
- Health Echoes: Lower back pain, joint issues, or fatigue (Rahu's shadowy zones), often from instability stress.

Real-life example: Picture someone with no 4s juggling a job—emails pile up, meetings botched, coffee spills en route. Commutes drag with flat tires; shopping lists vanish. Small frustrations snowball, eroding confidence in basics.

## Abundance of 4s: The Rock-Solid Counterpoint

Plenty of 4s? You're the reliable organizer, meticulous planner, marathon worker, master of order. Rahu channels into innovative stability. 4 in Your Life Chart: Rahu's Push for Structure. When 4 surfaces in personal cycles, Rahu demands discipline amid illusion. This window offers:

- Routine Rebuilds: Perfect for habit-stacking, decluttering, or skill-building.
- Endurance Tests: Challenges forge resilience; breakthroughs follow persistence.

- Grounded Innovation: Blend Rahu's ingenuity with 4's practicality for lasting wins.

## Remedies to Anchor Missing 4s

Restore Rahu's balance and invite 4's steadiness:

- Name Adjustments: Incorporate 4-value letters (D, M, V) in signatures or nicknames.
- Rahu Rituals: Offer black sesame oil on Saturdays and chant "Om Raam Rahave Namah." Avoid arguments during Rahu kaal.
- Crystals & Tools: Hessonite gemstone or blue sapphire alternatives; use planners obsessively.
- Daily Anchor: Affirm: "I build stability step by step." Start with 4-minute meditations or "one task at a time" lists.
- By addressing missing 4s, you transform daily drudgery into a fortress of flow, Rahu's chaos tamed into cosmic order.

## Missing Number 5: Mercury's Negative Shadows.

Number 5 pulses with Mercury's dynamic energy communication, adaptability, intellect, curiosity, and quicksilver change. Budha (Mercury), the swift messenger planet, fuels learning, trade, and versatility. Yet, when 5 is missing or rare in your name chart, Mercury flips to its malefic mode, stirring mental fog, misfires, and restless imbalance.

### Signs of 5's Absence: Mercury Malefic in Motion

Life's wires cross without 5's clarity. Daily pitfalls emerge as:

Communication Snags: Words tangle arguments that spark from misunderstandings; emails are misread; speeches stumble.

Mental Mercurial Mayhem: Restless thoughts scatter focus; decisions waver; learning feels uphill.

Adaptability Blocks: Change resists your travel delays, job shifts flop, and new ideas fizzle.

Health Hints: Nervous system glitches, skin issues, or respiratory tweaks (Mercury's realms), amplified by anxiety.

Real-life example No 5s: A salesperson garbles pitches, losing deals; a student mishears lectures, grades slip; gadgets betray at crucial moments. Witty banter? Replaced by awkward silences or foot-in-mouth blunders.

## Abundance of 5s: Mercury's Golden Flow

Overflowing 5s? You're the adaptable genius, eloquent networker, fast learner, thriving in flux. Mercury gifts charm and commerce savvy. 5 in Your Life Chart: Mercury's Messenger Mission A 5-cycle activates Budha's positives amid negatives, prime for mental upgrades. Expect:

- Intellect Ignites: Courses, books, debates sharpen your edge.
- Social Sparks: Networking booms; travel beckons with breakthroughs.
- Versatile Wins: Pivot gracefully through shifts for growth.

## Remedies to Harmonize Missing 5s:

- Counter Mercury's mischief and summon its sparkle:
- Name Boost: Slip in 5-value letters (E, N, W, Y) via initials or aliases.
- Budha Boosters: Green offerings Wednesdays; chant "Om Budhaya Namah." Read scriptures aloud.
- Gems & Aids: Emerald (panna, post-consult) or green aventurine; carry a small notebook for thoughts.
- Daily Ritual: Affirm: "My mind communicates clearly and adapts with ease." Practice tongue twisters or short writings.

Tuning into missing 5s rewires Mercury's negatives into neural superpowers, turning static into seamless, sparkling synergy.

## Missing Number 6: Shukra's Negative Grip Laziness and Beyond.

Here's a rewritten and expanded version of your updated statement on the missing number 6. I preserved the core emphasis on Venus/Shukra's negative impact, specifically increased laziness, while integrating it seamlessly into the established style of previous sections. This blends it with relational/emotional challenges, examples, remedies, and growth insights for your numerology book.

Number 6 channels Venus's (Shukra) warm glow of love, beauty, harmony, nurturing, and disciplined grace. But when 6 is absent or rare in your name chart, Shukra turns malefic, dimming motivation and fostering inertia. Laziness becomes a hallmark shadow, sapping drive from daily life while rippling into relationships and self-care.

### Signs of 6's Absence: Venus's Lethargy Takes Hold

Shukra's imbalance manifests as slothful stagnation, compounded by emotional and aesthetic voids:

- Laziness Dominates: Procrastination reigns, chores pile up, goals gather dust, and even simple tasks feel monumental. Venus's pleasure-seeking flips to avoidance.
- Relational Drift: Bonds weaken from neglect; nurturing others (or self) demands effort you sidestep, breeding isolation.
- Beauty and Harmony Lapses: Homes clutter, personal style fades; luxury tempts, but execution lags.
- Health Ties: Sluggish metabolism, indulgent overeating, or lower abdominal discomfort (Venus zones), fueled by inertia.
- Real-life example No 6s: Someone skips gym sessions indefinitely, lets relationships coast on autopilot, and dreams of a cozy home but lives in disarray. Shukra's fire reduced to flickering embers of "later."

## Abundance of 6s: Shukra's Radiant Discipline.

Plenty of 6s? Effort flows naturally, you're the devoted partner, artistic homemaker, balancing indulgence with inspired action.

### 6 in Your Life Chart: Shukra's Wake-Up Call

When 6 activates in cycles, Venus urges shaking off laziness for loving momentum. This period sparks:

- Motivation Revival: Habits stick; small wins build to beauty and bonds.
- Nurturing Flow: Family duties energize rather than drain.
- Creative Discipline: Art or home projects thrive with steady Shukra grace.

## Remedies to Counter Missing 6s and Laziness.

Ignite Venus's positive fire:

Name Shift: Incorporate 6-value letters (F, O, Z) in signatures to amplify energy.

Shukra Rituals: Fridays, donate white flowers or sweets; chant "Om Shukraya Namah" 108 times. Embrace routine with gentle yoga.

Gems & Supports: Opal or clear quartz; six-mukhi Rudraksha for vitality.

Daily Kickstart: Affirm: "I move with love's graceful energy." Begin days with a 6-minute walk or beauty ritual to combat sloth.

Addressing missing 6s transmutes Shukra's laziness into luminous action, restoring harmony, beauty, and purposeful flow to your cosmic dance.

## Missing Number 7: Ketu's Negative Shadows.

Number 7 vibrates with Ketu's mystical energy, spirituality, intuition, inner wisdom, detachment, and profound self-discovery. Ketu, the south lunar node, guides soul evolution and hidden truths. However, when 7 is scarce or absent in your name chart, Ketu's malefic influence dominates, manifesting as delays in marriage, chronic relationship hurdles, and spiritual disconnection.

### Signs of 7's Absence: Ketu's Karmic Delays

Ketu's imbalance blocks relational and inner harmony, creating persistent obstacles:

- Marriage Delays: Unions repeatedly evade ideal partners, timing misaligns, or family obstacles arise.
- Relationship Strains: Bonds fracture from mistrust, emotional distance, or unspoken karmic baggage; solitude feels fated.
- Spiritual Voids: Intuition dulls; meditation wanders; life's purpose feels elusive amid doubt.
- Health Echoes: Nerve disorders, isolation-induced anxiety, or mysterious ailments (Ketu's ethereal domains).

Real-life example No 7s: Weddings cancel at the last minute, dates fizzle into ghosting, deep connections are rare, Ketu's lessons lingering as relational eclipses.

## Abundance of 7s: Ketu's Enlightened Flow

Overflowing 7s You're the intuitive sage, spiritually attuned, magnetically mysterious, drawing soulmate unions effortlessly.

### 7 in Your Life Chart: Ketu's Soul Awakening

Spot 7 in personal cycles? Ketu accelerates karmic clearance for relational breakthroughs.

This phase invites:

- Union Opportunities: Past lessons resolved; compatible partners emerge.
- Inner Clarity: Meditation deepens; intuition guides love choices.
- Karmic Release: Old patterns dissolve, paving spiritual partnerships.

## Remedies to Balance Missing 7s

Pacify Ketu and invite 7's grace:

- Name Adjustment: Add 7-value letters (G, O, Z wait, 7 is G, P, Y) to signatures or nicknames.
- Ketu Rituals: Tuesdays feed dogs; chant "Om Ketave Namah." Visit temples barefoot.
- Gems & Tools: Cat's eye (lehsunia, after consultation); seven-mukhi Rudraksha for intuition.
- Daily Practice: Affirm: "I release delays and embrace soul connections." Meditate 7 minutes daily on the heart chakra.

## Missing Number 8: Saturn's Fog of Uncertainty

Number 8 resonates with Saturn's (Shani) disciplined energy, clarity, ambition, authority, karma, and material mastery. Shani, the stern teacher, forges resilience through structure and long-term vision. When 8 is absent or rare in your name chart, Saturn's malefic side clouds judgment, leaving life direction blurred and achievements elusive.

### Signs of 8's Absence: Shani's Clarity Void

Without 8's anchoring force, decisions drift, and purpose fades:

- Life Direction Fog: Career paths waver; goals shift like sand, clarity on "what next" remains perpetually out of reach.
- Authority Struggles: Leadership roles evade; recognition is delayed, and confidence is undermined by doubt.

- Karmic Confusion: Past lessons repeat without insight; financial or power pursuits stumble aimlessly.
- Health Ties: Chronic fatigue, bone/joint weaknesses, or teeth issues (Saturn's domains), mirroring inner disarray.

Real-life example: No 8s? Job hops without fulfillment, investments falter from poor timing, big dreams dissolve into "someday." Saturn's lessons taught through prolonged haze.

## Abundance of 8s: Shani's Crystal Focus

Plenty of 8s? You're the visionary executivelaser-focused, karmically empowered, building empires with unshakeable resolve.

### 8 in Your Life Chart: Saturn's Clarity Catalyst

When 8 emerges in cycles, Shani sharpens vision amid trials.

This period delivers:

- Purpose Revelation: True calling crystallizes; bold steps align.
- Authority Gains: Promotions or respect are solidified through effort.
- Karmic Breakthroughs: Debts clear; power balances restored.

## Remedies to Ignite Missing 8s

Harness Saturn's discipline:

- Name Tune-Up: Incorporate 8-value letters (H, Q) in signatures.
- Shani Rituals: Saturdays, donate sesame oil or iron; chant "Om Shanaye Namah." Serve the elderly.
- Gems & Anchors: Blue sapphire (neelam, post-consult); eight-mukhi Rudraksha for focus.
- Daily Ritual: Affirm: "Clarity guides my path with Saturn's strength." Track goals in an 8-column journal.

## Missing Number 9: Mars's Shadow of Cruelty and Unhappiness.

Number 9 pulses with Mars's (Mangal) fiery energy, compassion, leadership, humanitarianism, courage, and universal love. Mangal, the warrior planet, inspires selfless service and joyful fulfillment. Yet, when 9 is scarce or absent in your name chart, Mars turns malefic, breeding inner cruelty, chronic discontent, and a life starved of true happiness.

**Signs of 9's Absence: Mangal's Harsh Edge.**

Mars's imbalance twists noble fire into destructive embers, poisoning peace:

- Cruel Tendencies: Harsh words wound others; impatience sparks conflicts; empathy erodes into callousness or rage.
- Persistent Unhappiness: Joy evades grasp success feels hollow, relationships strain, a void lingers despite achievements.
- Leadership Lapses: Humanitarian impulses falter; isolation grows from a self-centered survival mode.
- Health Warnings: Blood pressure spikes, accidents, or inflammatory issues (Mars's domains), fueled by suppressed anger.

Real-life example: No 9s A rising star barks orders cruelly at teams, climbs ladders alone, yet wakes unhappy Mars's generosity eclipsed by a joyless throne.

## Abundance of 9s: Mars's Radiant Compassion

Loads of 9s? You're the selfless hero, inspiring leader, endlessly generous, radiating fulfillment through service.

- 9 in Your Life Chart: Mars's Redemptive Fire
- Spot 9 in personal cycles, Mangal ignites compassion's return and happiness quests.
- This phase unleashes:
- Heart Opening: Kindness flows; old grudges dissolve.

- Joyful Purpose: Humanitarian wins bring deep satisfaction.
- Courageous Bonds: Leadership unites, healing isolation.

**Remedies to Soften Missing 9s.**

Tame Mars and reclaim its light:

- Name Boost: Add 9-value letters (I, R) to signatures or nicknames.
- Mangal Rituals: Tuesdays offer red lentils to warriors; chant "Om Angarakaya Namah." Donate blood.
- Gems & Aids: Red coral (moonga, after consultation); nine-mukhi Rudraksha for mercy.
- Daily Practice: Affirm: "Compassion fills me with Mars's joyful strength." Perform one act of kindness daily.

# Combination of Numbers.

Life Path, Expression, and Heart's Desire numbers create numerology's essential triad, disclosing your genuine character through the vibrant fusion of fate, capabilities, and soul motivation.

True Character Blueprint

This trio reveals your real self beneath outward appearances. Life Path (derived from birthdate) charts your soul's voyage and primary lessons that you're here to master across incarnations. Expression (from full name at birth) reveals natural gifts, outward persona, and how you manifest destiny in the world. Heart's Desire (from name vowels) uncovers secret yearnings, the quiet pulse of what your soul truly seeks, often hidden from casual view.

Together, they illustrate destiny (Life Path) uniting with talent (Expression) via passion (Heart's Desire), shaping your fundamental nature. No single number stands alone; their harmony or tension crafts your unique blueprint. For instance, a pioneering 1 Life Path with artistic 3 Expression and security-driven 4 Heart's Desire becomes a creative trailblazer grounded in structure

**1,2,4:**

Your life pattern, shaped by Life Path 1, Expression Number 2, and Heart's Desire 4 points to a clear path of bold leadership built on steady discipline and teamwork. The pioneering spirit of 1 drives you to take charge, spark new ideas, and stand out as an independent trailblazer. Yet, it thrives best when paired with the cooperative harmony of 2, which draws support from society, partners, and communities who rally behind your vision. Deep down, your Heart's Desire 4 craves solid routines and practical work, giving you the foundation to turn ambitions into real results. Together, these numbers reveal a person meant to lead through structure, not chaos. You must learn leadership by weaving discipline into your daily life, thinking fixed schedules for work, rest, and goals that build momentum step by step. Your Expression 2 ensures you're never alone; friends, mentors, or groups will step up to help you succeed, balancing your 1's solo drive with shared strength. Avoid scattering your energy or skipping routines, as 4 warns that without order, even the strongest leaders falter. Picture this pattern in action: You launch a project (Life Path 1), gather a supportive team (Expression 2), and follow a disciplined plan to finish strong (Heart's Desire 4). Start today with simple habits like a morning checklist or weekly check-ins with allies. Embrace this trio fully, and you'll achieve lasting goals that inspire others, creating a legacy of reliable, influential leadership.

### 2,1,4:

Your Life Path 2, Expression 1, and Heart's Desire 4 blend into one clear life pattern: a calm, steady leader who builds success through teamwork and smart habits. This mix gives you quiet strength. Deep down, number 2 pulls you to work with people who listen well, stay patient, and help groups find peace. At the same time, number 1 pushes you to act boldly, start new ideas, and lead on your own when needed. Number 4 ties it all with a love for order: you shine by making daily plans, working hard, and creating things that last. The Big Picture: Balanced Team Leader You lead best by mixing solo fire with group harmony. Start projects with your inner drive (1), then invite others to join (2), and follow strict steps to win (4). People trust you because you stay calm under stress, see all views, and deliver real results. Careers like manager, teacher, counselor, or planner fit perfect you guide teams without bossing. Strengths That Shine Patient pioneer: Spark change alone, then unite friends for bigger wins. Rock-solid worker: Habits like morning lists and team talks build lasting trust. Wise guide: Your calm eyes spot needs and solve fights with fairness. Key Lessons for Growth: Slow your rush. Use 2's patience to hear others before acting on 1's ideas. Add rules to freedom: 4's routines stop scatter set work times and stick. Open your heart: Share feelings to avoid lone wolf traps or stiff plans.

## 4,1,2:

You are a disciplined trailblazer, a hardworking builder (Life Path 4) who leads boldly on your own (Expression 1) while quietly craving harmony and support (Heart's Desire 2). This rare blend forges a resilient soul who constructs enduring success through grit, innovation, and inner balance, even amid solitude. Unified Character Profile Rooted in Life Path 4's steadfast work ethic, you methodically build solid foundations, turning visions into reality one disciplined step at a time. Expression 1 ignites your pioneering spirit, urging you to take calculated risks, trust your instincts, and seize the lead without waiting for permission. Yet Heart's Desire 2 adds a subtle layer of diplomacy; you yearn for emotional alignment, mutual understanding, and peaceful partnerships that validate your path. Together, these numbers create a self-reliant architect: precise and productive on the surface, yet deeply intuitive and harmony-seeking within. Core Dynamics and Tensions The fusion sparks powerful synergy but also friction. Number 4's love for structure and routine tempers 1's impulsive drive, channeling bold ideas into practical execution. Think of a lone engineer designing bridges that withstand storms. However, 2's soulful need for connection clashes with this independence; you naturally expect others to grasp and back your goals, only to face the stark truth that few truly will. This breeds isolation, testing your risk-averse patterns: will you hide in safety, or step forward alone? Discipline bridges the gap, transforming unmet expectations into empowered autonomy. Everyday Strengths in Action Work and Achievement: Excel in roles demanding persistence, like project management or craftsmanship, where your blended traits deliver reliable results with fresh leadership. Relationships: Offer quiet loyalty and mediation, drawing people in with your calm strength, though you thrive most when balancing solitude with selective bonds. Personal Growth: Overcome hesitation by practicing small, daily risks, affirm your vision, set non-negotiable routines, and release the need for external cheers. Path to Full Mastery Embrace the solo journey as your greatest ally: lead with 1's courage within 4's framework, nurturing 2's harmony through self-validation rather than others' nods. Daily discipline, structured routines, self-trust exercises, and reflective pauses alchemize tension into triumph. Over time, you manifest not just personal wins, but legacies that quietly inspire, proving one determined soul can reshape reality.

## 9,1,2:

You are a visionary humanitarian leader a compassionate world-changer (Life Path 9) who boldly pioneers (Expression 1) while seeking emotional harmony (Heart's Desire 2). This potent blend promises a wonderful life of purpose-driven triumphs, adapting fluidly to situations with solo strength and quiet relational grace. Unified Character Profile Life Path 9 infuses you with universal love, wisdom, and a drive to uplift humanity, often through selfless service or creative giving. Expression 1 fuels your independent leadership, making you quick to seize opportunities, innovate fearlessly, and handle challenges alone without hesitation. Heart's Desire 2 adds intuitive diplomacy and a deep craving for partnership. You thrive on mutual support, emotional bonds, and collaborative peace. Together, they form a magnetic force: adaptable, resilient, and capable of turning chaos into meaningful impact. Core Dynamics and Strengths You live wonderfully because situational awareness lets you pivot effortlessly. 9's big-picture insight meets 1's decisive action, enabling solo mastery in crises, while 2 ensures graceful interactions. Leadership flows naturally; you take charge intuitively, building bridges or blazing trails as needed, often emerging stronger from solitude. Yet that expectation of support from others highlights your relational core: you draw allies with charm, but true magic happens when self-reliance meets selective harmony. Everyday Strengths in Action: Adaptability and Leadership: Excel in dynamic fields like activism, entrepreneurship, or counseling, reading the room to lead boldly yet inclusively. Relationships: Magnetize deep connections through empathy, offering quiet wisdom while inspiring collective good. Personal Fulfillment: Turn ideals into reality via humanitarian projects, where your solo capability shines amid supportive networks.

## 8,9,11

You are a strong, ethical leader, a success-driven builder, Lifepath 8 with kind wisdom Expression 9 and deep inner sight Heart's Desire 11. This mix helps you see life clearly, handle people with feelings, and lead in a good, right way. Main Traits Life Path 8 gives power, hard work, and skill with money and goals. Expression 9 adds care for all people and a big heart. Heart's Desire 11 brings strong gut feelings and a call to guide others to the light. Together, you are clear-minded, kind with emotions, and fair in charge. Key Strengths: You bring clarity to a mess, 8 cuts to the truth, 9 sees the big good, 11 feels what is real. You manage people by heart: read feelings, calm fights, and win trust. You love to lead right: honest, just, for everyone's win, not just for yourself. Daily Wins Lead Teams: Good at boss jobs, helping, or teaching fix problems with smarts and care. See Clear: Make fast, right choices in work or hard times, with kind rules. Touch Lives: Build big wins that help many, earn true friends by real power. Way to Best Self: Grow clarity with quiet think time, set good goals, give to others. Use feeling skills to lead strongly, not hide the soft side. This makes huge success: fair power, changed lives, lasting good name.

## 9,6,8:

Life Path 9, Expression 6, and Heart's Desire 8 combine into a powerful numerology profile: a caring leader who serves humanity with heart, creativity, and a strong drive for success. This blend pushes you to help people on a large scale through selfless acts (from 9), while nurturing others with love, family focus, and artistic skills (from 6). At the same time, your inner drive seeks power, money, and control to make big things happen (from 8). You thrive in roles like charity leader, teacher, healer, counselor, or business owner who helps society turn kind ideas into real-world change that lasts. Key Strengths: Big-picture vision to fix world problems, mixed with warm support for those close by. Natural talent to lead teams, build stable groups, and create beauty in daily life. Smart use of money and authority to grow helpful projects, like starting a nonprofit or community center. Possible Challenges: Risk of burnout from giving too much without rest or saying no. Clash between wanting to help everyone for free (9 and 6) and chasing wealth or status (8). Need to avoid bossing people around, use power with kindness instead. Best Path Forward: Focus on jobs or goals that mix service with success, such as running a healing center, writing helpful books, or leading fair businesses. Practice balance: give generously but set limits, share wealth to help others, and rest to recharge. This way, you build a lasting legacy of positive impact.

## 5,6,7:

The Balanced Path: Freedom, Family, and Wisdom United (Life Path 5, Expression 6, Heart's Desire 7) Imagine a wild river rushing freely through mountains that's your Life Path 5. You thrive on adventure, change, and breaking free from limits. Travel excites you, new faces spark your energy, and routines feel like chains. Your spirit demands variety, urging you to explore the world without looking back. But life adds a warm anchor: your Expression 6. This number gifts you a deep sense of responsibility, especially for family and home. You naturally care for others, cooking meals, solving problems, or holding space during tough times. Loved ones lean on your steady heart, and you step up with love, even when it pulls you from your free-spirited dreams. At your core hums Heart's Desire 7, the quiet seeker of truth. You crave knowledge beyond the surface spiritual secrets, ancient wisdom, or deep self-reflection. Solitude recharges you, like a sage meditating under stars, uncovering life's hidden meanings. The Core Lesson: Blend It All with Courageous Travel. These energies clash at first: freedom versus duty, adventure versus quiet study. Yet your path shines brightest when you unite them. Learn to lead a truly free life while honoring family ties.

Sometimes, this means traveling long distances: a job abroad to support your loved ones, a pilgrimage blending family visits with personal quests, or moving cities to build a stronger home base. Picture this: You journey far for work, but turn it into wisdom-gathering by reading books on the plane, meditating in new lands, and sharing stories that heal your family. Fresh air of change keeps your 5 alive, responsible actions fulfill your 6, and inner insights from 7 grow richer. Avoid the trap of escaping duties or burying your wanderlust. Instead, let travel become your bridge, carrying family love across miles while feeding your soul's hunger. In this balance, you become a modern mystic: free as the wind, rooted in care, wise beyond years. Embrace it, and your life flows like a river reaching the sea full, purposeful, and eternally alive.

## 7,6,1:

The Wise Pioneer: Inner Depth, Loving Service, and Bold Leadership (Life Path 7, Expression 6, Heart's Desire 1) Your Life Path 7 draws you into the world of quiet wisdom and spiritual seeking. Like a lone philosopher or mystic in the mountains, you thrive on solitude, deep study, and uncovering life's hidden truths. Questions pull you. Why are we here? What lies beyond? And you trust intuition over crowds. Knowledge is your treasure, gained through reflection, books, or sacred silence. Yet your Expression 6 shines outward in beautiful contrast. You express your inner world through care and harmony: nurturing family, creating peaceful homes, or helping others heal. Your words comfort, your actions build beauty, whether advising a friend, designing a garden, or leading community efforts with a gentle touch. Service feels natural, turning your wisdom into practical love. At heart burns Desire 1, the fierce drive for independence and originality. You crave to lead, innovate, and stand out to pioneer new paths, start bold projects, or claim your unique power. This inner fire pushes you to be first, not follow, fueling ambition with self-reliance. The Core Lesson: Channel Solitude into Inspired Leadership. These vibrations create a rich tension: 7's retreat versus 6's giving and 1's charge-ahead energy. You might hide in books while longing to lead, or serve others at the cost of your dreams. The mastery? Blend them, use inner wisdom (7) to fuel loving actions (6) and pioneering steps (1). Travel unlocks this flow: solitary journeys for reflection, then return to guide family or start ventures. A quiet retreat sparks ideas; your 1 drive turns them into reality, expressed through 6's caring leadership. Real-Life Flow in Action Daily Harmony: Morning meditation (7) leads to family time or a creative project (6 + 1). Challenges to Watch: Isolation can dim your leadership step out to share wisdom without losing depth. Strengths Unleashed: Your insights make you an innovative caregiver; others follow your unique, heartfelt vision. Spiritual Growth: Affirm, "My quiet knowing leads with love and power," to unite your energies. In this balance, you emerge as the wise pioneer: delving deep within, serving with grace, and blazing trails that inspire all. Your life becomes a beacon, thoughtful, nurturing, triumphantly original.

## 8,7,6:

Your Life Path 8 thrusts you into the arena of power, achievement, and material mastery. Like a builder of empires, you excel in business, leadership, and turning dreams into wealth. Authority comes naturally; you attract big opportunities, manage resources with skill, and thrive on challenges that demand strength and strategy. Success is your measure, but true power lies in ethical use. Your Expression 7 adds a layer of quiet depth. You communicate through insight and analysis: pondering mysteries, sharing profound thoughts, or teaching spiritual truths. Words flow sparingly but wisely like a sage offering a gem from solitude. Research, philosophy, and intuition shape how you connect, preferring depth over small talk. Deep in your soul hums Heart's Desire 6, a gentle pull toward love, family, and harmony. You yearn to nurture, protect, and create beauty, building warm homes, caring for loved ones, or fostering community peace. Responsibility to others softens your drive, reminding you that true wealth includes emotional bonds. The Core Lesson: Power Through Compassionate Wisdom. These forces create dynamic balance: 8's bold ambition risks isolation, 7's introspection can slow momentum, and 6's heart seeks softness amid strength. The path to fulfillment? Merge them wield power (8) with inner knowing (7) and loving service (6). Let wisdom guide your empire-building toward family and community good. Journeys amplify this: business trips become quests for insight, blending deals with time to nurture ties back home. Real-Life Flow in Action: Daily Harmony- Strategic planning (8) with evening reflection (7) and family dinners (6). Challenges to Watch: Avoid workaholism, honor your heart's call for connection to prevent burnout. Strengths Unleashed: Your depth makes you a visionary leader; others trust your caring authority. Spiritual Growth: Affirm, "I build abundance with wisdom and love," to harmonize your core. In this fusion, you rise as the empowered sage: commanding success outwardly, wise within, and deeply loving at heart. Your legacy endures prosperous, insightful, and eternally compassionate.

## 3,6,9:

The Joyful Healer: Creativity, Nurturing, and Universal Love (Life Path 3, Expression 6, Heart's Desire 9) Your Life Path 3 sparkles with creativity, joy, and self-expression. Like an artist painting the world with color or a storyteller captivating crowds, you bring lightness and fun everywhere. Words, art, music, your gifts shine through humor, optimism, and endless ideas. Life calls you to inspire, communicate, and embrace play amid the serious. Your Expression 6 channels this vibrancy into caring action. You speak and act with warmth: comforting friends, creating harmonious homes, or guiding others like a loving mentor. Beauty flows from you through home decor, heartfelt advice, or community service. Responsibility feels joyful, as you blend creativity with a nurturing touch. At your deepest core beats Heart's Desire 9, the compassionate visionary. You long to serve humanity, let go of the past, and uplift the world. Universal love drives you to help strangers, fight injustice, or share wisdom for the greater good. Endings teach you; forgiveness frees you. The Core Lesson: Create, Care, and Give on a

Grand Scale. These energies dance beautifully but need balance: 3's playfulness can scatter focus, 6's duties might stifle fun, and 9's big heart risks overwhelm. Mastery comes in weaving them express joyfully (3) through service (6) for humanity (9). Turn talents into healing forces that touch many lives. Travel fuels this: artistic trips abroad become chances to volunteer, blending fun with global impact. Real-Life Flow in Action Daily Harmony: Morning writing or drawing (3), family caregiving (6), evening charity work (9). Challenges to Watch: Scatter energy, focus creativity on meaningful service to avoid emptiness. Strengths Unleashed: Your charm draws crowds; nurturing wisdom sparks worldwide change. Spiritual Growth: Affirm, "I create joy, nurture hearts, and love all," to align your vibrations. In this radiant blend, you embody the joyful healer: spreading creativity's light, wrapping it in care, and offering it to the world. Your path glows with purpose, playful, devoted, infinitely loving.

Here are a few powerful combinations of numbers you can refer to and try according to your chart.

# NUMEROLOGY CHART ANALYSIS.

## Part -2: Advanced & Predictive Numerology.

In Part 1, we mastered finding your Core Numbers Life Path, Birth Date, Expression (Destiny), Hearts Desire (Soul Urge), Personality, Growth, Maturity, and Missing Number, and learn to calculate each one precisely to uncover deep insights into your character, strengths, motivations, and life purpose.

Now, Part 2 shifts focus to dynamic timing: your Personal Year Number and how it reveals the rhythms of your life's nine-year cycles. Each of the nine numbers represents one year in this complete cycle, delivering its own distinct vibration, theme, opportunities, and demands unfolding alongside your four Pinnacles (major life phases) and their corresponding Challenges (growth tests).

These cycles act like cosmic seasons, guiding when to plant seeds (initiate), nurture growth (build), harvest rewards (achieve), or release and renew (transform). Understanding them empowers you to flow with universal timing rather than resist it.

Each month adds a Personal Month Number for finer monthly guidance, while every day vibrates with its own Personal Day Number for daily decisions. We'll explore those next chapter. But first, let's calculate and decode your Personal Years to map your immediate path ahead.

## The Universal Year.

The Universal Year captures the dominant planetary energy that shapes global events, collective moods, and opportunities for everyone during a calendar year. Imagine it as a cosmic soundtrack playing in the background of our lives, nudging world leaders toward bold moves, sparking cultural trends, or fostering waves of compassion. It influences personal decisions like when to launch a business or nurture relationships while driving societal shifts, economic cycles, and even natural rhythms.

This energy runs from January 1 to December 31, syncing perfectly with our calendar. Calculating your Universal Year is straightforward, empowering you to anticipate the year's flow and align your actions. Here's how, step by step:

**Write out the year: Take any calendar year, like 2026.**

Add the digits: 2 + 0 + 2 + 6 = 10.

Reduce to a single digit: 1 + 0 = 1. So, 2026 is a Universal 1 Year perfect for fresh starts!

Check for master numbers: Sometimes the sum naturally hits 11 (in a potential 2-year period) or 22 (in a potential 4-year period). Keep it intact for its amplified power; don't reduce further unless it feels right intuitively. For example:

2027: 2 + 0 + 2 + 7 = 11 (Universal 11/2: intuition and harmony rule).

2028: 2 + 0 + 2+ 8 = 12/3 (no master; pure power and abundance).

## What is the Personal Year Number?

The Personal Year channels the unique qualities of each number, channeling them as the precise energy required to start, nurture, grow, advance, and ultimately harvest the fruits of life's experiential cycles. These distinct number energies unfold in a natural, organic rhythm that nurtures human potential and evolution. For a deeper dive into each number's essence, revisit Numerology Lesson One.

It follows logically that a 1 Personal Year kicks off the journey, while a 9 wraps it up, carrying the wisdom, empathy, and insights accumulated from completing a full nine-year cycle. After finishing the sequence of nine Personal Years, the cycle restarts anew. The definitions below offer practical guidance on harnessing each number's energy within its Personal Year context.

## How to Calculate The Personal Year Number?

- As we discussed earlier, take 5 readings of the closed one or the desired person's Name and Date of Birth.
- Write the 5 different reading sheets. Initially, try to do it manually to get better clarity.
- Now write each Name and Date of Birth in 5 different sheets.
- To calculate your Personal Year Number, take your Date and Birth Month, plus the Universal Year (like 2026), and reduce each to a single digit before adding them together (like 2+0+2+6=10→ 1+0=1).
- Then, reduce your Birth Date (e.g., 10 → 1+0=1), Birth Month (e.g., February=2), and Universal Year (2026 → 2+0+2+6=10 → 1+0=1). Then sum those results (1+2+1=5) and reduce further if needed to get your Personal Year,
- The Personal Year Number reveals the theme, opportunities, and lessons for that year from birthday to birthday or calendar start. See the example below for further reference.

## Personal Year Number Example Chart Anvita Hiremat's Date of Birth: 10/02/19.

| Personal Year | | | |
|---|---|---|---|
| Birth Day | Birth Month | Universal Year | Personal Year |
| 10(1+0=1) | 02(0+2=2) | 2026(2+0+2+6=10/1) | 1+2+1=4 |
| 10(1+0=1) | 02(0+2=2) | 2027(2+0+2+7=11/1) | 1+2+11=14/5 |
| 10(1+0=1) | 02(0+2=2) | 2028(2+0+2+8=12/3) | 1+2+3=6 |

## Personal year 1:

This is the year to start any project. Begin it now because the energy supports you, and anything you start in a 1 year fits your natural rhythm and gets a boost. It's a time for independence, courage, taking charge, and putting in effort. Unlike last year, 9 years of letting go this year is for fresh starts. Everything you do now shapes your future. You're planting seeds for your entire nine-year cycle.

In the 1 Personal year, focus on yourself. Take self-improvement classes, update your look, and work on your personal goals. More than any other year, get to know your own needs. This plants the seeds for all new beginnings this year. It's time for a new you. If you don't make time for yourself now, you won't get another full year like this for nine years until your next 1 Personal Year. But every year, you'll have chances to catch up on missed opportunities during your 1 Personal Months.

## Personal year 2:

This is the year to step back and regroup. It's time to listen to others and maybe let them lead. Expect waiting and delays. This isn't the year to get things done. But you'll notice details in relationships and others' needs more clearly. Unlike last year, your own needs come second now. People often move every 2 years because it's a time for adapting and finding balance.

In the 2 Personal years, focus on connecting with others. The key lesson is cooperation. Use this year to listen, show sensitivity, and make time for people. More than any other year, compromise and seek harmony in everything. Go slowly, and if you don't take your time now, it will be nine more years before you get a full year like this again.

## Personal year 3:

This year, expand your life and focus. It brings more activity, recognition, and enthusiasm. You'll get busy with extra social interactions. You can plant ideas in the hearts and minds of people around you. If too many options confuse you, choose the one that excites you most. Expression and creativity stand out.

The number 3 is about joy, fun, and socializing. But it can be hard to grasp the pain during this time. In a 3 year, you learn to say what's in your heart, find words for your feelings, and speak your truth to the world. This can be very painful. Once you overcome it, creativity flows easily, and it's time for fun projects and time with friends. If you built relationships last year (the 2-year), you won't need to do the tough emotional work now.

In the 3 Personal year, it's time to express yourself. Write, journal, paint, sing, dance, or have deep talks, anything to share your truth creatively. More than any other year, use your imagination. Play and spend time with others. If you don't express yourself and your emotions now, it'll wait until your next 3 year nine years from now.

## Personal year 4:

This can be a year to manage things, especially your health. It's time to organize, create systems, and build strong foundations for your future. Buy a home, start a family, get insurance; these are key building blocks of life. A 4-year cycle demands a lot of hard work.

Another part of the 4 Personal Year might involve digging into your family roots to fix issues from early childhood drama. This is often called "family of origin" work, and it fits the 4 energies perfectly, getting to the root of problems. That's why this year can feel like hell; it's tough to dig deep and reset the foundations of your adult life.

In the 4 Personal year, it's time to build for the future, lay foundations, or put down roots. Use this year for lasting decisions and to put them into action. More than any other year, focus on security. Build stability and reliability. If you don't build your life now, it'll be nine more years before you get a full year like this again.

## Personal year 5:

This is a year of personal transition, unlike the 9-year period, which focuses on transformation. The 5 brings change in attitude, work, home, or direction. Travel works well this year, and you might do a lot of it. Since the 5th energy is curious, you may dive into metaphysics, take classes, or explore new topics.

In the 5 Personal year, it's time to take risks. Use this year to make big changes in your life. More than any other year, move, switch jobs or careers, or try new, unconventional things. Be curious. If you don't explore what interests you now, it'll be nine more years before you get a full year like this again.

## Personal year 6:

If you have elderly parents, this year is for them. You'll be needed by your family more than in any other year; it's almost uncanny. This year also requires balancing home life with work life. You'll see chances to fix your work balance, even if it means changing jobs.

In 6 Personal year, it's time to focus on family duties and responsibilities. Use this year to nurture and care for loved ones. More than any other year, balance others' needs with your own. Show generosity and sympathy. If you don't give to your family or meet your own needs now, it'll be nine more years before you get a full year like this again.

## Personal year 7:

This is a time to go inside yourself. You'll need alone time and rest to rethink your goals, relationships, and life's direction. In 7 years, people often study spiritual, mystical, or metaphysical topics. You might seek spiritual guidance from a counselor or healer to help your search.

This year is also for purifying your body, so diets, cleansing, or detox programs may interest you. It could be the year to settle insurance claims or handle legal papers. But above all, you'll crave and seek solitude. This is the time to be alone and quiet.

In the 7 Personal year, it's a good time for a sabbatical or vision quest. More than any other year, be quiet and listen to your inner voice. Seek advice from yourself and others, and learn what brings your personal peace. Don't miss this introspective time, you won't get another full 7 years for nine years! But each year, you'll have chances during your 7 Personal Month to catch up on missed opportunities.

### Personal year 8:

This is a year to learn about your own power, handle authority issues, and step up as the boss. People will look to you for leadership or guidance. You'll face challenges to your sense of power, take the lead, stand as an authority, and start empowering others.

In the 8 Personal year, it's time to become a leader, boss, or authority figure and focus on business. Use this year to manage something like family property, a school event, or a company trip. More than any other year, deal with power dynamics. It'll be nine more years before another 8 years, but you can catch missed opportunities in your 8 Personal Month. You might gain recognition in an 8 Personal Year, and money will flow well. It comes to you as long as you work for the good of everyone, not just for personal gain. But it flows out almost as fast as it comes in. Stay focused, and manage your finances wisely. Avoid extravagance or letting emotions take over.

### Personal year 9:

The tide is out for 9 Personal year, but the harvest is in! This is the year of rewards for all your hard work over the past eight years. It's the end and conclusion of your nine-year cycle, so the seeds you planted in your 1 year are now ready to harvest.

When the tide goes out, it signals the end of a cycle. The energy this year is about letting go, finishing up, and dreaming about the next nine years. Revise, dream, and picture how you want your life to go. Let things end, be patient, the new beginning you sense is coming next year. This is also a time for healing and paying attention to dreams, both real and symbolic.

This can be a good money year because selfless giving and love get rewarded. But the opposite is true, too; if you're selfish or need to fix your finances, the 9 Personal years may be tough on money. Don't worry; next year that is a 1Personal year, and fresh starts always go well in a 1.

In a 9 Personal year, it's time to forgive and let go. Use this year to finish things and close chapters on every level. More than any other year, follow your intuition and perfect what you started eight years ago. Tie everything together. If you miss this chance to wrap up now, unfinished business will likely return in nine years.

## What is the Personal Month Number?

Each Personal Month number has a theme that fits into the rhythm of your Personal Year. You find the Personal Month number by adding your Personal Year number to the calendar month number (January=1, February=2, etc.). You get 12 Personal Month numbers, one for each month of the year.

The Personal Year is the most important number overall. Think of it as the main theme for the whole year. The Personal Month number shows that month's special effect within the bigger Personal Year energy. Every Personal Month number brings its own unique energy. This fills the month with special chances and possibilities.

## How Calculate The Personal Month Number?

- As we discussed earlier, take 5 readings of the closed one or the desired person's Name and Date of Birth.
- Write the 5 different reading sheets. Initially, try to do it manually to get better clarity.

- Now write each Name and Date of Birth in 5 different sheets.
- To calculate your Personal Month Number, first determine your Personal Year Number (from Birth Date + Current month + Universal Year). For example, we took Anivta Hiremata's Personal Year Number is 4.
- Then add the current calendar month (January=1, February=2, etc.) to that Personal Year number. Reduce the sum of those two by adding digits until you reach a single digit or master number (11/22/33)
- This Personal Month reveals the specific energies, focus areas, and influences active during that month within your yearly cycle. See the example below for further reference.

**<u>Personal Month Example of Complete Name Anvita Hiremat's Date of Birth: 10/02/19.</u>**

| Personal Month | | | |
|---|---|---|---|
| Birth Day | Current Month | Birth year | Personal Month |
| 10(1+0=1) | 01(0+1=1) | 1986(1+9+8+6=24/6) | 1+1+6=8 |
| 10(1+0=1) | 02(0+2=2) | 1986(1+9+8+6=24/6) | 1+2+6=9 |
| 10(1+0=1) | 03(0+3=3) | 1986(1+9+8+6=24/6) | 1+3+6=10/1 |
| 10(1+0=1) | 04(0+4=4) | 1986(1+9+8+6=24/6) | 1+4+6=11/2 |
| 10(1+0=1) | 05(0+5=5) | 1986(1+9+8+6=24/6) | 1+5+6=12/3 |
| 10(1+0=1) | 06(0+6=6) | 1986(1+9+8+6=24/6) | 1+6+6=13/4 |
| 10(1+0=1) | 07(0+7=7) | 1986(1+9+8+6=24/6) | 1+7+6=14/5 |
| 10(1+0=1) | 08(0+8=8) | 1986(1+9+8+6=24/6) | 1+8+6=15/6 |
| 10(1+0=1) | 09(0+9=9) | 1986(1+9+8+6=24/6) | 1+9+6=16/7 |

| 10(1+0=1) | 10(1+0=1) | 1986(1+9+8+6=24/6) | 1+1+6=8 |
|---|---|---|---|
| 10(1+0=1) | 11(1+1=2) | 1986(1+9+8+6=24/6) | 1+2+6=9 |
| 10(1+0=1) | 12(1+2=3) | 1986(1+9+8+6=24/6) | 1+3+6=1 |

**Personal Month 1:**

A 1 Personal Month is like a chili pepper; it grabs your attention and wakes you up. It's a month for new beginnings, where you start fresh projects, take charge, lead, and get things moving. Use it to set goals and intentions.

This month follows a 9 Personal Month, which was great for wrapping up loose ends and finishing tasks. So naturally, you'll have the time and energy now to launch new projects.

**Personal Month 2:**

A 2 Personal Month needs focus on details. It's time to handle all the small parts of your life. Seeds you planted in the 1 Personal Month start to grow roots now. You'll ask others for help and advice, and work with them on their projects. Cooperation is the key this month. After the "me first" energy of the 1 month, this is a time for relationships and paying attention to others.

**Personal Month 3:**

A 3 Personal Month gets your creative energy flowing. Ideas come in large numbers. This is the month to add creative touches, and you may express yourself through words, emotions, and art.

A 3 Personal Month is playtime for yourself and with others. It's great for shopping, buying gifts, going out to lunch, or treating yourself to that sterling silver pin you've wanted since last Christmas. Play with color and design: redesign your bedroom, add new wallpaper in the bathroom, and do anything that sparks your creativity.

## Personal Month 4:

A 4 Personal Month means being practical, disciplined, and doing hard work. Check that your goals are on track, build for the future, and create a solid base. You'll work hard, but it's to make sure your projects are secure and stable. You may also tackle family issues to ensure your life has a strong foundation with no weak spots.

The 4 Personal Month is also a time for health matters get a check-up, see a therapist, have a massage, buy a juicer, or find the right vitamins and minerals for you and your family. Build a solid health plan, including proper insurance. Do these tasks now, as the 4-month rhythm is about putting down roots, securing things, making plans, and creating stability for the rest of your Personal Year.

## Personal Month 5:

A 5 Personal Month can bring surprises. Things can change fast; your life might head in a new direction, or you may drop something completely. It's a month of transition that supports travel, adventure, and handling uncertainty.

A 5 Personal Month is also good for networking, promoting yourself, or selling. You'll communicate with others using enthusiasm, excitement, and charm. The change in 5-month often comes from finally taking a risk that will shake things up!

## Personal Month 6:

In a 6 Personal Month, you feel a strong sense of duty. You might focus on caring for your mom, grandkids, and family matters, or visiting relatives. You'll likely prefer staying home with family or doing small house projects. This is a perfect time for home tasks like repotting plants, trimming the yard, painting the front door, or just cleaning up to make things nicer. It's ideal for family activities, attending a soccer game, visiting the zoo, or seeing your parents.

## Personal Month 7:

A 7 Personal Month is for rest, plus studying deeper, the hidden parts of your life you haven't thought about before. Plan a retreat this month, you'll crave alone time to reflect on how things are going. In 7 months, it's normal to seek solitude for introspection and to rethink your past and future.

7 months are ideal for heading to the woods, mountains, or ocean to recharge in nature. Curl up with a good book or check out a couple of websites, too. It's the one time of year to focus on your need for alone time to think.

## Personal Month 8:

No messing around in an 8 Personal Month! Grab control of your life and lead with your strong power and authority. You're clear on your path now, so take charge to make sure everything runs right. In an 8 Personal Month, handle all details and you will.

An 8 Personal Month means getting serious about business of all kinds. Talk to neighbors about their noisy dog, call the phone company for a fax line, pay taxes, deal with divorce papers, or invest. This is when you take full control and manage your life. It's also great for sorting finances, closing business deals, and planning growth into new markets. This month focuses on money, power, and management!

## Personal Month 9:

In a 9 Personal Month, you reap what you've sown and harvest the results of your past efforts. You've earned rewards for your hard work, whether money or spiritual growth, and you'll see it was worth it.

A 9 Personal Month is for clearing out, letting go, and releasing. It's the month of endings. Something needs to end now, so you might clean file drawers, closets, or old relationships, or cancel your credit card. This energy pushes you to finish things, release them, and clear space for what's new next month.

**Personal Month 10/1:**

Same as the Personal Month 1.

**Personal Month 11/2:**

Same as the Personal Month 2.

**Personal Month 12/3:**

Same as the Personal Month 3.

# What is the Personal Date Number?

Your personal day number acts like a daily forecast in numerology, hinting at the energy, opportunities, and challenges you'll encounter. It builds directly on your personal month and year cycles, giving a hyper-focused snapshot of *today*. Think of it as the universe's nudge for navigating the next 24 hours whether it's a day for bold action, quiet reflection, or smooth sailing.

Unlike your life path number (fixed from birth), the personal day shifts daily, making it a practical tool for real-time decisions.

Follow these simple steps to crunch your personal day number. You'll need today's date and your birth month/year.

- Reduce the current day to a single digit (unless it's a master number like 11, 22, or 33, which you keep intact). *Example: Today is January 24, 2026 → Day = 24 → 2 + 4 = 6.*
- Add your birth month (reduce if needed). *Example: Born in February → Month = 2.*
- Add your birth year (reduce to a single digit first). *Example: Born in 1986 → 1 + 9 + 8 + 6 = 24→ 2 +4 = 6.*
- Sum them up and reduce to a single digit (again, preserve master numbers).
  *Full example for someone born February 10, 1986, on Jan 24, 2026:*
  Day: 24 → 6
  Birth month: 2
  Birth year: 1986→ 6
  Total: 6 + 2+ 6 = 14 → 1 + 4 = 5
  *Personal day = 5.*

It ties into your personal month (current month + birth day + birth year, reduced) and personal year (current year + birth day + birth month, reduced), amplifying their themes. Why It Depends on Personal Month and Year.

**Numerology views time as layered cycles:**

- Personal year sets the big-picture theme for 12 months (e.g., 5 = adventure).
- Personal month narrows it to monthly flavors (e.g., 9 = closure).
- Personal day zooms in daily, colored by those cycles like a subplot in your life's story.

**How to Calculate The Personal Date Number?**

- As we discussed earlier, take 5 readings of the closed one or the desired person's Name and Date of Birth.
- Write the 5 different reading sheets. Initially, try to do it manually to get better clarity.
- Now write each Name and Date of Birth in 5 different sheets.
- To calculate your Personal Date Number (also called Personal Day Number), combine your Birth Date and Month with the current date, reducing each component to a single digit before summing them all.
- Start by reducing your Current Date (e.g., 1 → 1), Birth month (e.g., February=2), and Birth Year (e.g., 1986→ 1+9+8+6=24 → 2+4=6).
- Then add those three single digits together (1+2+6=9) and reduce further if until single digit
- Personal Date Number reveals the specific energy, opportunities, and influences for that exact day. See the example below for further reference.

**Personal Month Example of Complete Name Anvita Hiremat's Date of Birth: 10/02/19.**

| Personal Date | | | |
|---|---|---|---|
| Current Day | Birth Month | Birth year | Personal Date |
| 1 | 02(0+2=2) | 1986(1+9+8+6=24/6) | 1+2+6=9 |
| 2 | 02(0+2=2) | 1986(1+9+8+6=24/6) | 2+2+6=10/1 |
| 3 | 02(0+2=2) | 1986(1+9+8+6=24/6) | 3+2+6=11/2 |
| 4 | 02(0+2=2) | 1986(1+9+8+6=24/6) | 4+2+6=12/3 |
| 5 | 02(0+2=2) | 1986(1+9+8+6=24/6) | 5+2+6=13/4 |
| 6 | 02(0+2=2) | 1986(1+9+8+6=24/6) | 6+2+6=14/5 |
| 7 | 02(0+2=2) | 1986(1+9+8+6=24/6) | 7+2+6=15/6 |
| 8 | 02(0+2=2) | 1986(1+9+8+6=24/6) | 8+2+6=16/7 |
| 9 | 02(0+2=2) | 1986(1+9+8+6=24/6) | 9+2+6=18/8 |
| 10 | 02(0+2=2) | 1986(1+9+8+6=24/6) | 1+2+6=9 |
| 11 | 02(0+2=2) | 1986(1+9+8+6=24/6) | 11+2+6=10/1 |
| 12 | 02(0+2=2) | 1986(1+9+8+6=24/6) | 3+3+6=11/2 |
| 13 | 02(0+2=2) | 1986(1+9+8+6=24/6) | 4+2+6=12/3 |
| 14 | 02(0+2=2) | 1986(1+9+8+6=24/6) | 5+2+6=13/4 |
| 15 | 02(0+2=2) | 1986(1+9+8+6=24/6) | 6+2+6=14/5 |
| 16 | 02(0+2=2) | 1986(1+9+8+6=24/6) | 7+2+6=15/6 |
| 17 | 02(0+2=2) | 1986(1+9+8+6=24/6) | 8+2+6=16/7 |
| 18 | 02(0+2=2) | 1986(1+9+8+6=24/6) | 9+2+6=18/8 |

| | | | |
|---|---|---|---|
| 19 | 02(0+2=2) | 1986(1+9+8+6=24/6) | 1+2+6=9 |
| 20 | 02(0+2=2) | 1986(1+9+8+6=24/6) | 2+2+6=10/1 |
| 21 | 02(0+2=2) | 1986(1+9+8+6=24/6) | 3+2+6=11/2 |
| 22 | 02(0+2=2) | 1986(1+9+8+6=24/6) | 22+2+6=30/3 |
| 23 | 02(0+2=2) | 1986(1+9+8+6=24/6) | 5+2+6=13/4 |
| 24 | 02(0+2=2) | 1986(1+9+8+6=24/6) | 6+2+6=14/5 |
| 25 | 02(0+2=2) | 1986(1+9+8+6=24/6) | 7+2+6=15/6 |
| 26 | 02(0+2=2) | 1986(1+9+8+6=24/6) | 8+2+6=16/7 |
| 27 | 02(0+2=2) | 1986(1+9+8+6=24/6) | 9+2+6=18/8 |
| 28 | 02(0+2=2) | 1986(1+9+8+6=24/6) | 1+2+6=9 |

**Quick Meanings of Personal Day Numbers.**

- 1: Initiative, leadership, start something new.
- 2: Harmony, partnerships collaborate gently.
- 3: Joy, expression, socialize, and create.
- 4: Stability, work build solid foundations.
- 5: Freedom, change, embrace surprises.
- 6: Nurture, family focus on loved ones.
- 7: Introspection, spirituality, reflect deeply.
- 8: Power, abundance attract success.
- 9: Completion, compassion, let go, and help others.

Master numbers (11, 22, 33) intensify: 11 for intuition, 22 for mastery, 33 for healing.

Use this daily to align your actions, like avoiding big risks on a "4" day, and watch synchronicities unfold.

## Personal Date Chart:

| | | |
|---|---|---|
| 1 | Begin things, focus on self | Channel the pioneering fire of the Sun, start new projects, trust your instincts, and shine as the leader of your own path. This is your cosmic green light for bold first steps without overthinking. |
| 2 | Be patient, attend to details | Embrace the Moon's gentle rhythm: cooperate, listen deeply, and nurture partnerships. Details matter today; harmony blooms from patience, not force. |
| 3 | Be creative, be with friends, communicate | Let Jupiter's joyful spark ignite your words and ideas, socialize, express yourself, and play. Creativity flows freely; share laughs and stories to amplify the fun. |
| 4 | Get organized, attend to your health | Ground yourself with Rahu's steady earth energy: build routines, tackle practical tasks, and care for your body. Stability is your reward for disciplined effort. |
| 5 | Make a change, network, and promote | Ride Mercury's quicksilver winds travel, adapt, and connect widely. Embrace freedom and fresh opportunities; your charisma opens doors today. |
| 6 | Pay attention to work, family, or home | Venus calls you to love and responsibility: harmonize relationships, beautify your space, |

| | | |
|---|---|---|
| | | and serve selflessly. Home and heart take center stage. |
| 7 | Rest and reevaluate; time for quiet solitude and meditation | Ketu invites inner wisdom withdraw, reflect, and seek spiritual truths. Solitude recharges your soul; answers emerge in silence. |
| 8 | Handle money, take charge | Saturn's power surges: master finances, lead decisively, and build abundance. Authority and karma align with integrity for lasting rewards. |
| 9 | Finish up, use your intuition | Mars completes the cycle: release what's done, forgive, and trust your inner compass. Humanitarian vibes peak; endings pave the way for renewal. |

## What is the Pinnacle Number?

The Pinnacle is a key cyclic vibration in numerology. It covers four major life cycles. By focusing on your Pinnacle, you get clear direction and extra insight. This cyclic energy aims to make your life experiences deeper. Each Pinnacle marks a time of growth, and it works accurately during its period. It helps you build fulfillment, destiny, and purpose.

The four Pinnacle Numbers show what you must face to reach the highest point of your Pinnacle. Think of them as doors you pass through to climb the spiral staircase of your personal development

## Age Chart For Pinnacle Number:

| Life path number | Pinnacle 1st | Pinnacle 2nd | Pinnacle 3rd | Pinnacle 4th |
|---|---|---|---|---|
| 1 | (0-35) | (36-44) | (45-53) | (54-on) |
| 2 | (0-34) | (35-43) | (44-52) | (53-on) |
| 3 | (0-33) | (34-42) | (43-51) | (52-on) |
| 4 | (0-32) | (33-41) | (42-50) | (51-on) |
| 5 | (0-31) | (32-40) | (41-49) | (50-on) |
| 6 | (0-30) | (31-39) | (40-48) | (49-on) |
| 7 | (0-29) | (30-38) | (39-47) | (48-on) |
| 8 | (0-28) | (29-37) | (38-46) | (47-on) |
| 9 | (0-27) | (28-36) | (37-45) | (46-on) |

## How To Calculate The Pinnacle Number?

- As we discussed earlier, take 5 readings of the closed one or the desired person's Name and Date of Birth.
- Write the 5 different reading sheets. Initially, try to do it manually to get better clarity.
- Now write each Name and Date of Birth in 5 different sheets.
- As Pinnacle Numbers, here I'm taking Anvita Hiremat's taking Date of Birth, and simplifying.
- To calculate your Pinnacle Numbers, reduce your Birth Date (D), Birth Month (M), and Birth Year (Y) to single digits or master numbers.
- Then apply these formulas:
- 1st Pinnacle = Birth Month + Birth Date (M + D).
- 2nd Pinnacle = Birth Date + Birth Year (D + Y).

- $3^{rd}$ Pinnacle = $1^{st}$ Pinnacle + $2^{nd}$Pinnacle.
- $4^{th}$ Pinnacle = Birth Month + Birth Year (M + Y).

The duration of these life phases depends on your Life Path Number: subtract it from 36 to find the end of the 1st Pinnacle (e.g., Life Path 1 ends at 35 years old), then add 9 years for the $2^{nd}$ (ie,36-44 years old), another 9 for the $3^{rd}$(ie,45-53), with the $4^{th}$(ie,54-on) lasting the rest of life. See the chart above.

**Using Anvita Hiremata's Date of Birth:10/02/1986 as our example:**

| $10^{th}$ | February | 1986 |
|---|---|---|
| 1+0=1 | 0+2=2 | 1+9+8+6=24 |
| 1 | 2 | 2+4=6 |
| 2+1+6=7 Lifepath | | |

**First Pinnacle: (Birth Month + Birth Date=$1^{st}$Pinnacle).**

| 02/2 (Birth Month) + 10/1(Birth Date) |
|---|
| 2 + 1 = 3 (First Pinnacle). |

**Second Pinnacle: (Birth Date + Birth Year =$2^{nd}$ Pinnacle).**

| 10/1(Birth Date) + 1986/24/6(Birth Year) = 7 |
|---|
| 1 + 6 = 7 (Second Pinnacle). |

**Third Pinnacle: ($1^{st}$ Pinnacle – $2^{nd}$ Pinnacle = $3^{rd}$ Pinnacle).**

| 3($1^{st}$ Pinnacle) + 7($2^{nd}$ Pinnacle) = 10/1 |
|---|
| 1 + 0 = 1(Third Pinnacle) |

**Fourth Pinnacle: (Birth Month – Birth Year = 4th Pinnacle).**

| 02 (Birth Month) + 1986/24/6(Birth Year) = 8 |
|---|
| 2 + 6 = 8(Fourth Pinnacle) |

**Pinnacle Number 1:**

A 1 Pinnacle Number means that during this specific time in your life, which could last years, you push hard to build independence, self-reliance, and a strong sense of your own individuality. Standing on your own two feet becomes your top priority. Every challenge, opportunity, and key person who enters your life acts like a teacher, guiding you toward true freedom from depending on others. Real-Life Example: Imagine you're in your First Pinnacle, ages start 0-35.

A 1 here might mean, as a young adult, you leave home, start your first job, or launch a solo project. Bosses or mentors "teach" you by giving tough tasks that force self-reliance.

If the 1 is your Third Pinnacle around ages 45-53? Wait, standard timing varies by birth date, typically First: birth to starts 0-35, Second:36-44, Third:45-53, Fourth:54+, or Fourth Pinnacle later life, 54+, it's even more powerful. You're being shaped into a leader. Your peak success comes from guiding others and living the full leader's life: rock-solid integrity, doing the right things, clear vision, seeing the big picture, real courage facing risks, inner drive, non-stop energy, and fierce determination, never giving up. A business owner in their 50s with a 1 Pinnacle Number with the 4th Pinnacle might expand their company, mentor young staff, and earn respect as the "go-to" visionary boss.

**Pinnacle Number 2:**

If 2 is your Pinnacle Number, your greatest achievement during this cycle, which lasts for years, will be mastering harmonious relationships without sacrificing who you are. You learn balance, giving to others while protecting your own needs. This number vibrates with unions, like marriage or business partners, strong partnerships, patience through ups and downs, and always keeping things fair and equal. Forget going solo here; independence takes a back seat. The real focus is teamwork and "we" over "me." You might spend this time learning key skills: how to cooperate smoothly, share responsibilities and credit, and be truly considerate of others' feelings and views. It's about building bridges, not walls.

The 2 energy shines in connecting facts, seeing how pieces fit, gathering and perfecting tiny details, and sensing what's truly correct or balanced. This makes a 2 Pinnacle perfect for success in jobs needing precision like editing, accounting, counseling, diplomacy, or research. You'll thrive where accuracy rules. Plus, these same skills open endless opportunities to master "the art of relating." Think negotiating deals, mediating arguments, or nurturing friendships, your empathy and detail-focused approach make you a natural peacemaker. A teacher with 2 Pinnacle Numbers might excel at group lessons, spotting each student's needs and creating fair classroom harmony.

## Pinnacle Number 3:

This 3 Pinnacle Number opens the door to personal expression wider than any other Pinnacle cycle. It's a vibrant time focused on your emotions, feeling deeply, imagination, dreaming big, and creative spirit, making art from ideas. Creativity isn't just a hobby here; it's the heartbeat of this phase. Early Life First Pinnacle, (0-35 age): Chase a creative career. Paint, write, perform, design, follow what sparks joy. Middle Life Second/Third, (36-54 age): Dive into emotions. Learn to share what's in your heart honestly, without fear. Heal old hurts through talk or art.

Later Life Fourth, (54+0 age): Embrace friends, pure joy, life's simple pleasures, travel, laughter, hobbies, and free creative expression. A writer in their 40s with a 3 Pinnacle Number might publish a fun novel, host social gatherings, and finally voice long-held feelings in therapy or songs, turning inner chaos into joyful connections.

## Pinnacle Number 4:

The 4 Pinnacle Number is your prime time for building a life with rock-solid, stable foundations that stand forever. No quick fixes, this is about creating what endures. Often, it shows up as constructing a secure home buying property, a steady career climbing the ladder, and a strong family, marriage, and kids. You're laying bricks that won't crumble. Endurance keeps going through tough spots, hard work rolls up sleeves, and patience results take time.

The 4 energy thrives on planning, organizing chaos, building systems like budgets or routines, creating order from a mess, and moving forward step by step. It's hands-on practicality: Take dreams and make them real blueprints to buildings, ideas to businesses. You're carving a reliable spot in the material world. But it's demanding: Expect a need for strict discipline, no slacking, honest recognition of limitations, don't overreach, and a serious attitude play later. In a Second Pinnacle (36-45 age), a 4 Pinnacle Number might mean a parent quits a fun job for stable office work, saves for a house down payment, and sets family schedules, building security amid midlife stress. Kids with 1st Pinnacle born with 4 Pinnacle Numbers often seem serious beyond their years, and mature early. Parents' financial limits, tight budgets, shape them to teach thrift and realism young.

## Pinnacle Number 5:

If you have a 5 Pinnacle Number, buckle up for major change and uncertainty; it's the wild ride of numerology cycles. Ultimately, this period shakes loose old, restricted habits from your past, leading to real freedom and liberation. You break chains, explore new paths, and feel alive. But heads up: 5 is the number of the unexpected. Surprises pop up, and since not everyone loves change, it can feel shaky or unsettling, like the ground shifting underfoot. Expect restlessness, can't sit still, high activity, non-stop motion, and a pull toward public life spotlight, networking. Bonus: It supercharges sales, promotion, and marketing.

Your charisma sells ideas effortlessly. Change is the only constant. Progressive attitudes, bold career pivots, quitting a job for a startup? and forward-thinking business moves thrive under 5's dynamic energy. Forget cozy home vibes, this Pinnacle drags you outward to the big world: travel, events, crowds. In a Third Pinnacle, a corporate worker with a 5th Pinnacle Number might suddenly travel for work, switch to sales, big commissions, or launch a public podcast, have a restless home life, and flip to exciting global adventures.

**Pinnacle Number 6:**

A 6 Pinnacle in any of the four positions turns your life toward love, duty, and responsibility, especially to family. These are the years of stepping up as a caregiver, where priorities shift to nurturing others. Common paths: teaching kids or students, counseling, helping emotionally, or building a marriage partnership.

Core Lesson: Put others' needs first sometimes, but learn balance. Endless giving, handling all loads, and fixing everyone's problems leads to burnout. You'll discover: Love others and yourself. Care for your needs too. The 6 demands home/family harmony restore peace, set fair boundaries.

This Pinnacle screams home, children, and beauty. Fix up your space, decorate, garden, and raise kids with heart. 6 also participates in community service and humanitarian volunteer work, helping neighbors, animals, or local causes. Work here? Think daycare, therapy, and social work. Money flows from service, but expect spending on loved ones, kids' needs, and family trips. Happiness? Huge when you serve joyfully. In a $4^{th}$ Pinnacle, a 6 Pinnacle Number might mean grandparenting full-time, community volunteering, homemaker, or post-retirement bliss in service.

## Pinnacle Number 7:

With a 7 Pinnacle, dive into a phase of study, research, introspection, and soul development. This isn't casual learning, it's a deep, purposeful questing. Education, scientific pursuits, intense study, and specialization aren't optional; they're strongly urged. Expect a strong individualist vibe: loner tendencies, separateness, reclusiveness. Turn inward; explore your inner landscape like a private universe. Ideal Setting: Country living or quiet retreats anywhere for solitude.

Use it to master being alone, self-discovery, niche research, mystical thinking, meditation, spirituality, and "right living" principles, ethics, and philosophy. Outcome? Profound wisdom. Others flock to your insights; you excel at explaining the unexplainable. Specialized tech, writing, healing, and money follow experts who earn well. 2nd Pinnacle, a 7 Pinnacle Number might mean quitting social jobs for online research, writing a philosophy blog, or certifying in astrology, solitude yields bestselling insights.

## Pinnacle Number 8:

This 8 Pinnacle is your boot camp for the business world and authority of all types of bosses, laws, and power structures. Here, you claim personal power and learn its responsible use. It's the peak of authenticity, be real, and master your skills. Core lessons: Money earned, invest wisely, power wield ethically, authority lead fairly.

Essential skills bloom: Organization systems rule, responsibility deliver always, leadership guide teams, financial management budgets profit, efficiency cut waste. Judgment gets tested repeatedly; deals, decisions, and crises sharpen you. Opportunities surge: Manage property business, skyrocket career. Achievement recognition? Abundant promotions, awards for effort. Trade-offs: Home life fades; career success dominates. Not easy shoulder the wheel constantly. Show strength, courage; weakness has no place. Big expenses hit investments, legal, but careful management + hard work = monetary rewards + deep job satisfaction.

Skip luck; vet trusts wisely. Ultimate Lesson: Become your own authority. Grasp true power, use it for the greater good. Forge self-mastery and authenticity. 3rd Pinnacle, an 8 Pinnacle Number means corporate climb, manage a team, buy rental property, navigate lawsuits emerging as CEO, with balanced life lessons.

## Pinnacle Number 9:

With a 9 Pinnacle, step up with tolerance, compassion, and love big time. You're here to inspire and uplift others via your wisdom and deep loving nature. Expect emotional crises: Let go of dead-end ties, jobs, habits, no energy left? Release, despite fear. It's a maturation process of feelings for growth. Not easy: Endings hurt, constant love tolerance exhausts. Skip it? Disappointment looms. Master philosophical attitude: Rooted in global consciousness, universal principles, intuition, humanity love. 9 isn't personal, think BIG, beyond your bubble. Grapple with the human condition, struggles, and joys. Prime successes: Arts, drama express soul, writing share truths, higher-ed, teach wisdom, healing therapy, spirituality yoga gurus, philanthropy donate volunteer, international travel business, global awareness activism. 4th Pinnacle, a 9 Pinnacle Number means retiring to write memoirs on world peace, fund orphanages, travel Asia, and teaching emotional closures lead to legacy.

# What is the Challenge Number?

It's another predictive tool in your Numerology Profile is the Challenge Number. Becoming whole in this life means facing and overcoming our "sticking points." There are four main challenges we meet during our lifetime. Knowing your Challenge Number and what it means can change your life. Instead of hitting your head against the same wall over and over or keep bringing pain into your life, face your Challenge Number. Then, life will flow smoothly in a natural rhythm, not in sudden stops and failures.

**Age Chart For Challenge Number:**

| Life path number | Challenge 1st | Challenge 2nd | Challenge 3rd | Challenge 4th |
|---|---|---|---|---|
| 1 | (0-35) | (36-44) | (45-53) | (54-on) |
| 2 | (0-34) | (35-43) | (44-52) | (53-on) |
| 3 | (0-33) | (34-42) | (43-51) | (52-on) |
| 4 | (0-32) | (33-41) | (42-50) | (51-on) |
| 5 | (0-31) | (32-40) | (41-49) | (50-on) |
| 6 | (0-30) | (31-39) | (40-48) | (49-on) |
| 7 | (0-29) | (30-38) | (39-47) | (48-on) |
| 8 | (0-28) | (29-37) | (38-46) | (47-on) |
| 9 | (0-27) | (28-36) | (37-45) | (46-on) |

## How To Calculate The Challenge Number:

- As we discussed earlier, take 5 readings of the closed one or the desired person's Name and Date of Birth.
- Write the 5 different reading sheets. Initially, try to do it manually to get better clarity.
- Now write each Name and Date of Birth in 5 different sheets.
- As Challenge Numbers, here I'm taking Anvita Hiremat's, taking Date of Birth, and simplifying.
- To calculate your Challenge Numbers, reduce your Birth Date (D), Birth Month (M), and Birth Year (Y) to single digits or master numbers.
- Then apply these formulas:
- 1st Challenge = absolute difference: Birth Month – Birth Date (M – D).
- 2nd Challenge = Birth Date – Birth Year (D – Y).
- 3rd Challenge = 1st Challenge – 2nd Challenge.
- 4th Challenge = Birth Month Birth Year (M – Y).

The timing mirrors your Pinnacle cycles and aligns with your Life Path Number: subtract it from 36 for the end of the 1st Challenge (e.g., Life Path 1 ends at 35 years old, Life Path 5 at 31), add 9 years for the 2nd, another 9 for the 3rd, with the lifelong 4th Challenge thereafter.

## Challenge's Chart.

**Note: Challenge will not include negative digits**

## Using Anvita Hiremata's Date of Birth as our example:

| 10th | February | 1986 |
|---|---|---|
| 1+0=1 | 0+2=2 | 1+9+8+6=24 |
| 1 | 2 | 2+4=6 |

| 2+1+6=7 Lifepath |
|---|

**First Challenge: (Birth Month – Birth Date=1st Challenge).**

| 02/2 (Birth Month) – 10/1(Birth Date) = 1 |
|---|
| 2 – 1 = 1 (First Challenge). |

**Second Challenge: (Birth Date – Birth Year =2nd Challenge).**

| 10/1(Birth Date) – 1986/24/6(Birth Year) = 5 |
|---|
| 1 – 6 = 5 (Second Challenge). |

**Third Challenge: (1st Challenge – 2nd Challenge = 3rd Challenge).**

| 1(1st Challenge) – 5(2nd Challenge) = 4 |
|---|
| 1 – 5 = 4(Third Challenge) |

**Fourth Challenge: (Birth Month – Birth Year = 4th Challenge).**

| 02 (Birth Month) – 1986/24/6(Birth Year) = 4 |
|---|
| 2 – 6 = 4 (Fourth Challenge). |

## Challenge Number 0:

Here's an expanded version with more details on the 0 Challenge Cipher Challenge, real-life examples, how it fits into a full numerology chart, calculation info, and practical tips. I've kept it in basic English, styled like the Pinnacle expansions.

The 0 Challenge Cipher Challenge in Detail. This number, aka Cipher Challenge, screams "all or nothing". Symbol of the circle, endless, complete, it holds everything: full potential and empty void simultaneously. Pure free will reigns: Drift aimlessly or soar to greatness? Your call. Craft a world brimming with love, compassion, integrity, responsibility, vision, and great works, or settle for less. Don't take the 0 Challenge periods lightly. Serious choices demand clarity that aligns with your Destiny/Expression Number and universal laws (karma, ethics). Like the 9 Challenge, nurture a burning desire to better the world. Huge responsibility tags along; wield wisely. Core Theme: Ultimate freedom tests character. Circle closes: What legacy? 2$^{nd}$ Challenge (midlife 27-36 age), a 0 Challenge Number might mean career crossroads, quit drifting job-to-job, or launch an ethical startup? Choice shapes wealth impact.

## Challenge Number 1:

When 1 is your Challenge, it's boot camp for self-assertion. Core lessons: Stand up for yourself (no doormat), stay true to beliefs/ideas (own your truth), self-reliance (handle solo), courage to lead (step forward). Expect test after test, people pressure, doubts attack to prove you stand firm, no compromising your core.

1$^{st}$ Challenge (early life start 0-35 age): Discover "you have a self" and build identity amid family, school influences. Other Positions (2$^{nd}$ Challenge starts 36-44 age, 3$^{rd}$ Challenge starts 44+, Main lifelong): Remain true to that self; cultivate self-confidence. This Challenge forges timid leaders, fades, and bold emerges. 1$^{st}$ Challenge

Number mid-career: Boss steals the credit and claims your idea wins. Speaking up for personal will be lacking.

## Challenge Number 2:

The 2 Challenge Number is one of the most common centers on sensitivity to human relationships. You feel others deeply. Negative side hurts: fear, timidity, and low self-confidence make life painful. Struggles include subordination, people-pleasing, and obsessing over-opinions. The Gift: Heightened awareness of others' feelings, needs, subtleties, without burying your own. True empathy emerges: See them, honor you. Core Dynamic: Constant balance vigilance. 2 symbolizes duality, two opposing forces, self vs. others, give vs. receive. You're the juggler. Find balance point; maintain it. Goal: Balanced, sensitive harmony, peace within and with others.

Office worker with $2^{nd}$ Challenge number (start 36-44 age): Colleague dumps work on you frequently. Old pattern: Say yes, resent silently. Tests repeat, boss asks, "Can you handle more?" Balance choice: "Yes to this task, no to that one." Confidence grows; relationships improve.

## Challenge Number 3:

When 3 is your Challenge Number, you're learning to identify feelings and speak from the heart. Words become your mirror; critical self-talk hurts most. The 3 teaches: Stop harsh words; they shape reality. Common Traps: Hide true feelings behind humor or criticism. Negative 3 traits to conquer: superficiality, surface chats, exaggeration, big fish stories, gossip, tea-spilling, scattered energy, start 10 projects, self-centeredness, me-me-me, moodiness, emotional rollercoaster, empty talk sound, and no substance.

The Invitation: Channel creative energy into a loving, encouraging, positive, joyful spirit. 3 holds pure happiness, don't waste it on drama. Speak truth + uplift = magic. 3rd Challenge (36+ age), a manager snaps at the team, then beats themselves up. Tests repeat: Client complains, family argues. Choice: Critical outburst or heartfelt Growth: Becomes an inspiring leader, and team morale soars.

## Challenge Number 4:

When 4 is your Challenge Number, you're learning the true value of core work ethics, discipline, stick to a plan, organization, order over chaos, thrift, save, don't waste, practicality, realistic choices, and hard work results through effort. Tough Reality: This is a difficult challenge. Restrictions and limitations hit hard, tight budgets, rigid schedules, blocked paths. The test? Work *within* boundaries, not fight them. Bonus lesson: Set boundaries with others.

Impatience, stubbornness, narrow-mindedness, self-righteousness. Main life(lifelong), 4 is the Challenge Number, then the freelancer faces tight client deadlines and low pay. Old reaction: Quit impulsively. Tests repeat budget cuts, slow payments. Growth: Creates schedules, saves emergency fund, negotiates rates politely. Business stabilizes; learns "steady wins."

## Challenge Number 5:

During a 5 Challenge Number, your love for changing rules sparks impatience and restlessness. Freedom calls loud, shake routines! Perfect remedy for rut-living (stuck 4 energy). Loosen up; embrace flux. The Tension: Change scares bring fear, holding back, and confusion. Old limits cling tight. But 5 cheers: Take risks, stay flexible. Free your creative energy from restrictive behaviors. Change rules the game, but timely, positive change wins the Challenge.

Core Lesson: Break chains wisely. Chaos serves growth when directed. 2$^{nd}$ Challenge (start 36-44 age), corporate drone hates 9-5 grind. Tests hit: Job offers risky startups, urges to travel, friends push adventure.

## Challenge Number 6:

When 6 is your Challenge Number, lessons hit hard on responsibility for others and family obligation burdens. You can't escape service mode caregiving calls, loud. Core test: Balance family commitments vs. self-commitments. Give to others, but don't drown. Danger Zones: Idealizing beyond reason unhappiness, family, marriage loss. Stubborn opinions, especially parenting: "My way rules home". Codependency is giving for the wrong reasons, guilt. 6 idealizes loyalty, obedience, and love, which goes too far.

The Shift: Move 6 energy from negative martyr, control to positive warmth, beauty, nurturing, love. Transform home into a haven. 3rd Challenge (36+age), a mom feels trapped, kids' activities, husband's needs consume her. Tests repeat: Skip yoga for one more carpool? Growth: "Family night, yes, spa morning mine." Sets schedule; all thrive. Learns healthy giving.

**Challenge Number 7:**

The 7 Challenge Number, like the tough as 4 Challenge Number cause 7 Challenge to be one of life's most serious periods. Aloneness and isolation hit hard. Turn inward to the rich inner world, meditation, soul development, spiritual awakening, and life meaning contemplation. Your inner self seeks growth experiences. Deep repression or major life trials. Secrecy traps worsen isolation, hiding feelings, holding back, family secrets, and embarrassing events. Challenge: Discern reality from illusions. Be authentic, connect genuinely, listen within for guidance.

Build inner-awareness via intuition-sharpening, philosophy/metaphysics-study, and universal-nature laws understanding. Main Challenge (lifelong), at Challenge Number 7, discovers family secret, Joins meditation group, studies astrology, shares insights vulnerably. Emerges wise counselor.

**Challenge Number 8:**

When 8 is your Challenge Number, you're summoned to step up and achieve. Material tests dominate money struggles, possession battles, and financial peaks/valleys. Chasing cash alone fails. True lesson:

Look beyond dollars to life's meaning. Embody integrity, right living, moral business. Not easy. Power misuse, bullying/dominating, fake authority bluffs big, power addiction, and delayed success.

8 screams: Stop giving away power. Take it back. Learn to empower others, not obey blindly, not crush
underfoot. Balance ambition with ethics. True power serves all.
Second Challenge (starts at 36-44 years old), mid-level manager fears confrontation. The boss dumps work; says yes always. Tests repeat raises denied, colleagues promoted. Growth: Negotiates boundaries, mentors junior staff ethically, and launches a side business. Gets promotion + respect.

## Challenge Number 9:

You cannot get a 9 Challenge in this simple numerology system. Why? Because 9 is the highest number, and all other numbers are subtracted from it. Instead, use the 0 Challenge Number.

# REMEDIES.

## Compatibility Analysis.

In This Chapter

Exploring relationship dynamics through numerology. Assessing compatibility with partners, family, friends, and yourself. Numbers that spark friction when paired closely. Harmonious number combinations for smoother connections. While your Personal Year Number guides you through the year's cycles, relationships deserve their own numerological lens. By now, you likely see how shared numbers between you, your partner, family, or friends reveal a deeper understanding and flow. Decoding Relationship Energies: How you and others interact becomes clear once you read the numbers. Numerology uncovers whether your bond thrives, challenges you, or needs balance. In Part 5: Living by the Numbers, one key factor (often a trio of numbers) carries special weight; use it to strengthen your connections.

Finding Your Ideal Match: Simple formulas reveal top relationship matches by the numbers. For heartfelt bonds, focus on the Soul Number. For reliability, check Life Path and Birthday Numbers. Daily harmony? Examine Personality Numbers. Long-term futures? Maturity Numbers hold the clues. Number-Specific Insights

For loyalty, openness, and appreciation in a new interest, seek 4, 6, or 9 in their Personality or Soul Numbers. Craving compliance, support, and love? A 2 in those positions' shines. Soul-to-Soul Matching: The strongest compatibility arises when Souls align evenly. Sixes and Sevens Dynamics, sharing a Master Number brings intense similarities and shared sensitivity. It creates powerful bonds but may not always feel heaven-sent.

# Complete Chart Interpretation.

This note shows how numerology helps people live better lives and why tools like rudraksha beads, healing crystals, and gemstones can guide them to fulfill their true purpose. Numerology reveals our unique blueprint, our strengths, weaknesses, and life's road. Once we understand these through our numbers, we can set smart goals that match our destiny. This starts after we read the deeper purpose hidden in our birth numbers or name vibrations.

When the road is clear, certain objects become powerful helpers. Rudraksha beads calm the mind and boost inner strength; they link to Shiva's energy for protection and focus. Crystals like clear quartz amplify positive vibes and clear blocks, while gemstones such as ruby or emerald align with planetary forces that match our numbers. These tools bring harmony by balancing energies, reducing stress, and speeding progress toward our goal or destiny.

They lead to complete satisfaction because they work with our natural flow, not against it. We stay happy by wearing or placing them daily: a rudraksha mala for meditation, a crystal grid at home, or a gemstone ring for constant support. This also helps meet the needs of people around us, our calmer, stronger self-nurtures family or teams better. In turn, we create the best place to live: a home buzzing with peace, love, and success.

**<u>These are some of the remedies for the following example, given thought out the book (Anvitha hiremat's)</u>**

| Remedies | |
|---|---|
| Mantra | (Mars) "Om Kram Kreem Kroum Sah Bhaumaya Namah" |
| Suitable Number | 1,9,6,8 |
| Unsuitable Number | 3 & 7 |
| Color | |
| Rudraksha | 6 Mukhi & 7 Mukhi |
| Stone: | Coral/Citrine/Tiger Eye Bracelet |
| Direction: | East |
| Days: | Sunday & Monday |

**Mantra:** In numerology, particularly systems blending Vedic astrology and planetary influences, specific mantras align with numbers 1-9 to amplify their vibrations, aid healing, and support spiritual growth. These are chanted daily (often 108 times using a mala) to harmonize personal energies from birth dates, names, or life charts. Core Number Mantras (1-9):

Use these based on your life path, destiny, or ruling number for balance and manifestation. Number 1 (Sun): "Om Hram Hreem Hroum Sah Suryaya Namah" Boosts leadership, confidence, and vitality. Number 2 (Moon): "Om Som Somaya Namah" Enhances intuition, emotions, and inner peace. Number 3 (Jupiter): "Om Gram Greem Groum Sah Gurave Namah" Promotes wisdom, expansion, and prosperity. Number 4 (Rahu): "Om Bhram Bhreem Bhroum Sah Rahave Namah" Grounds ambition, overcomes obstacles. Number 5 (Mercury): "Om Bram Breem

Broum Sah Budhaya Namah" Sharpens intellect, communication, adaptability. Number 6 (Venus): "Om Dram Dreem Droum Sah Shukraya Namah" Attracts love, harmony, creativity. Number 7 (Ketu): "Om Stram Streem Stroum Sah Ketave Namah" Fosters spirituality, detachment, insight. Number 8 (Saturn): "Om Pram Preem Proum Sah Shanaishcharaya Namah" Builds discipline, karma resolution, and endurance. Number 9 (Mars): "Om Kram Kreem Kroum Sah Bhaumaya Namah" Ignites courage, action, protection.

**Suitable Number/Unsuitable Number:** Planetary Assignments Number 1: The Sun holds the rank of king. Number 2: The Moon serves as queen. Number 3: Jupiter acts as the prime or chief minister. Number 9: Mars commands as the military leader. Number 8: Saturn functions as the judge. Numbers 4 and 7: Rahu and Ketu support Saturn as enforcers or kotwals; they also trigger eclipses of the Sun and Moon. Number 5: Mercury, deemed an impotent planet, takes the role of prince. Number 6: Venus, the guru of demons, collaborates with Prince Mercury and judge Saturn to challenge for the prime minister's position.

**Color:** Colors profoundly link to our mental, emotional, and physical well-being. Studies confirm they impact us both physiologically and psychologically. Yellow boosts blood pressure, respiration, and pulse rates, while Black slows them. Red energizes the brain, and Blue calms it. Clinical psychologist Pink cut violent incidents. To bolster and restore a number's energies, incorporate its color everywhere you wear it, eat matching foods, surround your space with it, and, if feasible, light a room or area with that hue for meditation or focus. This approach shines when tackling traits linked to a number. Suppose you're resisting responsibility and decisions, hallmarks of number 6 (tied to Blue). Blue embodies harmony, willpower, and discipline: it relaxes you into balance, easing stress and confusion, while fortifying the resolve and focus to decide and follow through. Countless studies back these effects. For multiple challenges, blend the relevant colors. Workplace relationship woes? Relationships vibe with number 2 (Orange), work with number 4 (Green), deploy both. One day, you might spot your closet dominated by a single color, or birthday hauls heavy on that shade. Research it: Why now? What strength does it offer? Which issues is it aiding you to heal and evolve? Bringing in lots of Purple and Violet? That's number 7's signature hue.

**Rudraksha;** Rudraksha has captivated people worldwide with its mystical qualities. Remarkably, the seed from a tree-grown fruit has garnered immense attention and global intrigue. Beyond Hindu saints, its devotees span artisans, homemakers, scholars, and entrepreneurs, transcending religious and national divides.

Known and used since ancient times, Rudraksha traces its origins to Lord Shiva, one of Hinduism's divine Trinity. From antiquity, depictions of Shiva show him adorned with these sacred beads.

Mysteries shroud Rudraksha, much like other rare natural treasures such as amber, agar, shwetark, shaligram, or gorochan.

At its core, Rudraksha embodies spirituality. Worn alone or as malas (rosaries), it grants sadhus a sense of special powers and serves as a hallmark for the faithful. Many don it for luck, as a protective talisman, or for vitality, while others wear it simply as jewelry, unaware of its deeper benefits.

I've encountered numerous individuals who shared remarkable benefits from wearing Rudraksha. Publications and Ayurvedic texts also highlight its effectiveness. These range from material achievements and relief from physical ailments to mental tranquility. While some experiences might seem coincidental, the consistent endorsements from many convinced me to pursue further studies and incorporate it into my remedies.

I firmly believe this bead holds far greater value than commonly recognized. It may harbor healing properties against modern human ailments, such as the intense electromagnetic exposure from cell phones, electronic devices, and industrial processes, or shifts in lifestyle like diet, work patterns, and stress. Rudraksha could provide a protective shield for the body. Thus, we must study it with dedication, devotion, confidence, and patience to unlock its full potential.

Rudraksha also serves as an ornament, tying into humanity's timeless tradition of necklaces as premier body adornments. These often feature beads of precious metals, gemstones, bones, shells, and diverse natural or synthetic materials. In my view, among all these pearls, diamonds, gold, and others. As noted earlier, Hindu scriptures link Rudraksha to Lord Shiva, the supreme deity in Hinduism, revered as Mahadev. Legend holds that Rudraksha trees sprang from his tears. In Sanskrit, "Rudra" signifies Lord Shiva, while "aksha" means tears or eyes. Scriptures affirm and many believe that invoking Shiva's blessings unlocks the beads' fullest potential.

From experience, the beads' foremost quality is instilling fearlessness in the wearer. This arises from the union of Shakti, the Goddess of power, with Lord Shiva. The attributes of such divine gifts defy simple scientific explanation.

Several paths reveal Rudraksha's potency, but the most compelling remains its embrace by Lord Shiva himself as an ornament.

**Gemstone/Crystals:** Gems have captivated humanity across civilizations since ancient times, drawing people in with their mesmerizing colors, unparalleled brilliance, and ethereal glow. From the glittering emerald mines of ancient Egypt to the sapphire-adorned crowns of Indian royalty, these treasures transcended mere decoration, symbolizing status, spirituality, and cosmic connection. Beyond their role in jewelry, gems hold profound divine power rooted in mystical traditions. In Vedic astrology and numerology fields, intertwined with planetary influences, specific gems act as conduits for celestial energies. For instance, a ruby channels the fiery vitality of the Sun, enhancing leadership and vitality, while a blue sapphire aligns with Saturn's disciplined force, promoting clarity and protection. Ancient sages believed these stones vibrated at frequencies matching human chakras and life path numbers, amplifying personal energies for harmony and growth.

Gems also shine in healing practices, blending ancient wisdom with modern wellness. Their therapeutic potential stems from piezoelectric properties, where pressure generates electric charges combined with mineral compositions that interact with the body's biofield. Emeralds soothe heart ailments and emotional stress, amethysts ease migraines and insomnia, and pearls balance hormonal imbalances. Archaeological evidence from Indus Valley sites and Ayurvedic texts like the Charaka Samhita documents their use in treating everything from digestive disorders to mental fog, a legacy validated today by crystal healing therapies and gem elixirs.

This timeless fascination endures because gems bridge the material and metaphysical, offering not just beauty but tools for self-transformation. Whether worn as talismans or placed in meditation spaces, they remind us of the universe's hidden rhythms, much like numbers in numerology reveal life's blueprint. There has been a fascination with gems all over the world since ancient times. People have cherished them for their enchanting colors, radiant brilliance, and almost magical allure that seems to capture light from the stars themselves. From the deep greens of emeralds in Cleopatra's crown to the fiery reds of rubies in royal Indian headdresses, gems have adorned the elite and inspired poets across cultures.

Yet, gems are far more than ornaments for jewelry they possess divine power, acting as bridges between the earthly and the cosmic. In ancient traditions like Vedic astrology and numerology, each gem resonates with specific planets and numbers, channeling their energies to influence personality, destiny, and well-being. A diamond, linked to Venus and the number 6, fosters love and creativity; a yellow sapphire, tied to Jupiter and number 3, boosts wisdom and prosperity. Sages from Egypt,

Greece, and India prescribed them as talismans to balance life path vibrations and ward off negative planetary influences.

Equally remarkable is their role in healing diseases, a practice documented since antiquity. Gems' unique mineral compositions and vibrational frequencies interact with the human body to restore harmony. Ayurvedic texts praise coral for vitality and blood purification (number 9 energy), while modern studies explore how tourmaline's negative ions combat stress and inflammation. Healers place them on chakras or infuse water with their essence to cure ailments from joint pain to anxiety, blending science with spirituality in ways that continue to intrigue researchers today.

This enduring topic, woven through history's tapestry, highlights gems as gifts from the Earth, beautiful, powerful, and profoundly useful for those seeking health, fortune, and enlightenment.

# Name Analysis.

Adopting a new name can unlock fresh opportunities and even a unique destiny, serving as a powerful tool to amplify your innate strengths and awareness. However, proceed with caution, as altering your name shifts your personal energy. Choose wisely to ensure it aligns with your essence.

## Things to Consider When Changing Your Name

- Several factors deserve attention when selecting a new name. For instance, dispel the myth that it guarantees a completely new existence. Remember, post-change, you'll operate under two concurrent numerical vibrations. The primary one stems from your birth name, an enduring cosmic blueprint and energy signature. The secondary comes from the new name's vibration, which, if chosen thoughtfully, can harmoniously boost your original energies.
- Select a name that resonates deeply, not one that's trendy, whimsical, or chosen to please family or friends. By "resonates deeply," we mean trusting your intuition. Does it feel good to use now and a decade from now? Does your energy lift when you say or hear it? Let your inner wisdom steer the decision.
- Pick a name that draws positive experiences, avoiding extra trials, karmic hurdles, or frustrations. Achieve this by calculating its numerological meaning with the methods from Chapters 10 through 12, particularly if altering multiple names. Understand its vibrations and the energy it introduces. Check the Soul, Destiny, and Personality Numbers carefully. Dedicate time to this vital choice, you'll thank yourself later.
- Steer clear of a name totaling one of your Challenge Numbers or Karmic Lessons, unless you've already overcome them. The same applies to Master Numbers; ensure you're ready for their heightened demands.

- For optimal results, choose a name matching your birth name's Soul and Destiny Numbers, keeping your core drive and life direction aligned with your original blueprint.
- A new name opens doors to fresh possibilities, but full integration takes about five years. Remember, 5 governs change.

all, imagine being saddled with "Romeo Montague" as Shakespeare noted, "A rose by any other name might not smell as sweet."

Harmonize the new name with your Life Path Number (from your birth date). A powerful Life Path deserves a supportive name vibration, not a weaker one that undermines your destined success. Ensure the vowels sum to a number compatible with your Life Path, and verify the full name (vowels plus consonants) aligns too.

## Naming Your Baby

Selecting a baby's name is a profound responsibility. You're setting the vibrational blueprint for another soul's earthly journey. Approach this with utmost care. Many numerologists avoid guiding baby naming. A child's life purpose and destiny shouldn't rest in the hands of an outsider. Parents alone bear this sacred duty. Ideally, the name emerges as parental inspiration. Parents are seen as chosen vessels for the child's arrival on Earth. By quieting the mind, tuning into inner guidance, and heeding intuition, they'll intuitively select the perfect name.

This unfolds as part of creation's divine mystery, reserved for the souls involved: the newborn and parents. We advise against engineering "ideal" numbers for your unborn child; the name's resulting vibration is precisely what that soul requires. Wait until you're in the baby's presence to finalize the choice. In stillness, silencing inner noise, the incoming spirit will reveal the right name.

For parents retaining separate last names, calculate each family name's vibration using the Family Name Numbers chart and meanings from earlier in this chapter. If blending both appeals, consider hyphenating the baby's surname.

# Conclusion

This book has reached you at the perfect moment, signaling your readiness to take the next step in awakening to the divine essence within you. Armed with this knowledge, you now grasp your numbers and the challenges they represent, empowering you to navigate your journey toward wholeness with greater wisdom. You'll make more informed choices for your healing and spiritual growth.

Revisit your name and life chart from time to time to gain clarity on your current circumstances. During periods of intense stress or profound joy, check the energies at play; they'll guide you in making decisions that ease life's events and obstacles.

Your name interpretation and life chart remain constant, based on your birth name and date, which never change. Yearly forecasts, however, will evolve.

Name changes introduce new vibrations to your name and life chart. In cases like marriage or adoption, combine your birth name with the new one to reflect the fresh energies you're engaging with now.

It's my deepest wish that this book equips you to heal and evolve yourself and others into the divine beings you truly are.

# Volume 2

Volume 2 will deliver comprehensive details on Rudraksha, gemstones, and crystals, presented with authentic references, scientific evidence, and direct collaboration with Himalaya Rudraksha Anusandhan Kendra in Haridwar.

**Rudraksha Coverage:**

(Expect in-depth exploration of Rudraksha types 1-21 Mukhi, and their planetary vibrational).

**Gemstones and Crystals:**

(Detailed profiles cover key gemstones, ruby, emerald, blue sapphire, and crystals, amethyst, quartz, etc., with planetary correspondences.)

**Switch words:**

(Switch words are powerful one-word chants that focus the subconscious mind to make things happen. They often connect to numerology numbers like 1-9 or master numbers such as 11/2 and so on.)

**Tarot and Number Relation:**

(Tarot readings access the subconscious via archetypal symbols, acting as a reflective mirror for concealed thoughts. Numbers, colors, and elements enable this decoding, linking seamlessly to numerology for profound personality and life path revelations.)

# About The Author

I am Sowmya Anil, born and raised with a deep curiosity for numbers that shaped my life from childhood. This hobby grew stronger over time. My Graduation degree in Mathematics and Statistics is perfect fuel for my passion.

Through numerology, I've turned these roots into a simple system to understand myself, the people around me, and life's situations, helping make the right decisions every day.

This book shares those tools: decode your Life Path from birth date for core traits, like a bold 1 or nurturing 6; blend with name numbers to see relationship fits; track yearly cycles for timely choices, such as 2026's fresh starts. Whether easing family talks or timing career moves, these numbers light your path to wiser steps and deeper connections. Dive in, calculate yours, and transform curiosity into clarity.